"Gunter's book makes a significant contribution to the resurgence of scholarship on Jacob Arminius. No longer having to rely on an archaic translation of a translation, English readers are now one step closer to the historical Arminius with this definitive translation of and commentary on his most important treatise."

—KEITH STANGLIN, Professor,
Austin Graduate School of Theology

"The theological depth of Arminius' response to the restrictive dogmatism of some early seventeenth-century Calvinists has inspired others to conceptions that often range far from Arminius' own ideas. Stephen Gunter's careful translation of the *Declaration of Sentiments* once again places Arminius in the midst of contemporary theological discussion. Not merely an antiquarian artifact, Arminius' *Declaration of Sentiments* can once again contribute its inspiration to new conceptions."

—JEREMY BANGS, author of *Strangers and Pilgrims, Travellers and Sojourners: Leiden and the Foundations of Plymouth Plantation*

Portrait of Arminius in his study (based on an engraving). Circa 1705 by Christoffel Lubienietzki (1659–1749). Oil on canvas, 98.5 × 81 cm. In Arminius' right hand is a scroll inscribed with his motto: A clear conscience is paradise. On the shelf are, among others, a book by Augustine as well as Erasmus' Biblia Sacra.
Used by permission, Museum Catharijneconvent, Utrecht, The Netherlands.

Arminius and His
Declaration of Sentiments

An Annotated Translation
with Introduction and
Theological Commentary

W. Stephen Gunter

BAYLOR UNIVERSITY PRESS

© 2012 by Baylor University Press
Waco, Texas 76798

All Rights Reserved. No part of this publication may be reproduced, stored in a retrieval system, or transmitted, in any form or by any means, electronic, mechanical, photocopying, recording or otherwise, without the prior permission in writing of Baylor University Press.

Cover design by Dean Bornstein
Cover image: Portrait of Arminius in his study (based on an engraving). Circa 1705 by Christoffel Lubienietzki (1659–1749). Oil on canvas, 98.5 × 81 cm. Courtesy of Museum Catharijneconvent, Utrecht, The Netherlands.

The Library of Congress has catalogued the hardcover edition as follows:

Arminius, Jacobus, 1560–1609.
 [Verklaring. English]
 Arminius and his Declaration of sentiments : an annotated translation with introduction and theological commentary / W. Stephen Gunter.
   226 p. cm.
  Includes bibliographical references (p. 195) and indexes.
  ISBN 978-1-60258-567-6 (hardcover. : alk. paper)
 1. Theology. 2. Arminius, Jacobus, 1560–1609. Verklaring. I. Gunter, W. Stephen, 1947– II. Title.
  BX6195.A6813 2012
  230'.49—dc23
                          2012003690

The ISBN for the 2017 paperback edition is 978-1-60258-568-3.

Printed in the United States of America on acid-free paper.

CONTENTS

Standard Abbreviations		vii
Preface		xi
Introduction		1

Part I
The Life and Times of Arminius

1	Early Years	11
2	Student Years, 1576–1587	21
3	Amsterdam Pastor (1587–1603) and the "First Arminian Controversy"	43
4	The Leiden Years: A Prelude to the *Declaration*	65

Part II
Declaration of Sentiments

§1	A Personal History	90
§2	The Theological Declaration	103
§3	The Call for a National Synod	149

Part III
A Theological Postscript

5	The Evangelical, Practical Theology of Jacob Arminius	161
Conclusion		185

Selected Bibliography	195
Scripture Index	205
Index of Authors	206
Index of Subjects and Names	208

STANDARD ABBREVIATIONS

Acta
    Rutgers, Frederick L., ed. *Acta van de Nederlandsche synoden der Zestiende Eeuw.* 's Gravenhage: M. Nijhoff, 1899. Reprint, Dordrecht: J. P. van den Tol, 1980. Page references are to the 1980 edition.

Amsterdam
    Evenhuis, R. D. *Ook dat was Amsterdam.* 2 vols. Amsterdam: W. ten Have, 1965–1967.

APPS
    Reitsma, J., and S. D. van Veen, eds. *Acta der Provinciale en Particuliere Synoden.* 8 vols. Groningen: J. B. Walters, 1892–1899.

Bangs
    Bangs, Carl. *Arminius: A Study in the Dutch Reformation.* Nashville: Abingdon, 1971.

BLGNP
    Biografisch Lexicon voor de Geschiedenis van het Nederlandse-Prostestantisme. 6 vols. Kampen: Kok, 1978–2006.

Brandt, *History*
    Brandt, Gerard. *The History of the Reformation and Other Ecclesiastical Traditions in and about the Low Countries.* London: T. Wood, 1720–1723. Originally published as *Historie der Reformatie en andre Kerkelyke Geschiedenissen, in en Ontrent de Nederlanden.* 4 vols. Amsterdam: Jan Rieuwertsz., Hendrik & Dirk Boom, 1671–1704.

Brandt, *Life*
    Brandt, Caspar. *The Life of Arminius, D.D.* Translated by John Guthrie with introduction by T. O. Summers. Nashville: E. Stevenson and F. A. Owen, 1857.

BWNG

    Glasius, V. B., ed. *Godgeleerd Nederland: Biographisch Woordenboek van Nederlandsche Godgeleerden*. 3 vols. 's Hertogenbosch: 1852–1856.

BWPGN

    Biographisch Woordenboek van Protestantsche Godgeleerden in Nederland. 's Gravenhage: Martinus Nijhoff, [ca. 1925]–1949.

Clarke

    Clarke, F. Stuart. *The Ground of Election: Jacobus Arminius' Doctrine of the Work and Person of Christ*. Milton Keynes, UK: Paternoster, 2006.

den Boer

    Boer, William den. "Jacobus Arminius: Theologian of God's Twofold Love." In Leeuwen, Stanglin, and Tolsma, *Arminius, Arminianism and Europe*. Leiden: Brill, 2009, 25–50.

Duplex amor Dei

    Boer, William den. *Duplex amor Dei: Contextuele karakteristiek van de theologie van Jacobus Arminius (1559–1609)*. Apeldoorn: Instituut voor Reformatieonderzoek, 2008. Translated by Albert Gootjes as *God's Twofold Love*. Göttingen: Vandenhoek & Ruprecht, 2010.

Ep. Ecc.

    Limborch, Philip van, and Christian Hartsoeker, eds. *Praestantium ac eruditorum virorum epistolae ecclesiasticae et theologicae*. 3rd ed. Amsterdam: Franciscus Halma, 1704.

Gootjes, *Confession*

    Gootjes, Nicolaas H. *The Belgic Confession: Its History and Sources*. Grand Rapids: Baker, 2007.

Hoenderdaal

    Hoenderdaal, G. J. *Verklaring van Jacobus Arminius*. Lochem: De Tijdstroom, 1960.

Israel, *Dutch Republic*

    Israel, Jonathan I. *The Dutch Republic: Its Rise, Greatness, and Fall, 1477–1806*. Oxford: Clarendon, 1995.

Maronier

    Maronier, Jan Hendrik. *Jacobus Arminius: Een Biographie*. Amsterdam: Y. Rogge, 1905.

Muller

    Muller, Richard A. *God, Creation and Providence in the Thought of Jacob Arminius*. Grand Rapids: Baker, 1991.

NAKG
 Nederlands Archief voor Kerkgeschiedenis/Dutch Review of Church History/Church History and Religious Culture.
NNBW
 Molhuysen, P. C., P. J. Blok, and K. H. Kossman, eds. *Nieuw Nederlandsch Biographisch Woordenboek.* 10 vols. Leiden: Sijthoff, 1911–1937.
NTT
 Nederlands Theologisch Tijdschrift.
Protocollen
 Protocollen der Kerkeraad Amsterdam. Stadsarchief Amsterdam, The Netherlands. (Manuscript Minutes of the Consistory of the Reformed Church of Amsterdam.)
Rijker dan Midas
 Dekker, E. *Rijker dan Midas: Vrijheid, genade en predestinatie in de theologie van Jacobus Arminius (1559–1609).* Zoetermeer: Boekencentrum, 1993.
Stanglin
 Stanglin, Keith D. *Arminius on the Assurance of Salvation: The Context, Roots, and Shape of the Leiden Debate, 1603–1609.* Leiden: Brill, 2007.
Triglandius, *Geschiedenissen*
 Triglandius, Jacobus. *Kerckelycke Geschiedenissen.* Leiden: Adriaen Wyngaerten, 1651.
Uytenbogaert, *Historie*
 Uytenbogaert, Johannes. *De Kerckelicke Historie*, 2nd ed. Rotterdam: Bastian Wagens, 1647. (Bound with *Leven, Kerckelicke bedieninghe ende Zedige Verantwoordinghe.*)
Uytenbogaert, *Leven*
 Uytenbogaert, Johannes. *Leven, Kerckelijcke bedieninghe ende Zedige Verantwoordinghe.* Rotterdam: Bastian Wagens, 1647. (Bound with the 2nd edn. *De Kerckelicke Historie*)
Works
 Arminius, Jacobus. *The Works of James Arminius: The London Edition.* Translated by J. Nichols and W. Nichols. Introduction by Carl Bangs. 3 vols. Kansas City: Beacon Hill, 1986. First published in London, 1825–1875. (The pagination in vol. 1 of the original London edition, pp. 257–706, becomes 351–770 in the 1986 reprint.)

PREFACE

Translation projects are by their very nature the byproduct of a network of people beyond the translator—in this case a combination of people, institutions, and organizations. Gratitude has been conveyed privately to each of these, but I take this opportunity to express my thanks publicly to those without whose direct and indirect support this project simply would not have come to fruition. The Netherlands Organization for Scientific Research (NWO) provided a generous grant for travel and residence expenses in The Netherlands, but even this good fortune was due to colleagues at the VU University Amsterdam. Dr. Annette Mosher made the suggestion that I apply, and she subsequently facilitated the paperwork. Prof. dr. Kees van der Kooi wrote a letter of formal support to assure faculty and administrative support through the office of Prof. dr. Wim Janse, Dean of the Faculty of Theology at the VU. In what veterans of grant-seeking might describe as a miraculous turnaround time, the NWO processed and approved the application. Dean Richard Hays of Duke Divinity School did not hesitate to give me an extended time away from administrative duties as associate dean. Beginning with Carole Baker, who did a significant amount of bibliographic research and compilation of entries from Dutch dictionaries of biography, other Duke divinity and doctoral students have been keen research assistants—most recently Scott Himmel, Brett McCarty, and Bobby Rackley, who compiled the indices and assisted with final proofreading.

During previous shorter visits to The Netherlands in connection with this work, Kees and Margriet van der Kooi extended warmhearted hospitality to me, and this was repeated and amplified when Ruth Ann and I arrived in Holland for the research leave. They had previously introduced me to Prof. dr. Martien Brinkman, and it turned out that his research leave from the VU University Amsterdam overlapped with mine. So Martien and Hannie Brinkman lived in our home in North Carolina, and we lived in their home near Utrecht. As much as this simplified transition and housing, the greatest boon above and beyond a wonderful place to live turned out to be their neighbor, Grace Swart. Grace is a special collections librarian at the University of Utrecht, and she volunteered to be my own personal librarian. She gave me very specific but simple instructions: "You tell me what you need, and I will get it for you." Books that could be checked out of the library were delivered to my door, and special collections items were called and held in reserve for me in the Special Collections Reading Room. Even after returning home to realize that I still needed to verify or locate a citation, she has only been an e-mail away. Words are simply inadequate to express my gratitude to Grace.

Archivists at the City Library of Rotterdam and the University of Leiden respectively provided digital files of Arminius' manuscript and the 1610 edition of his *Verclaringhe*, but even these would not have been possible without the assistance of Dr. Jeremy Bangs. In both libraries the resident librarians had difficulty locating these rare documents, and Jeremy Bangs, an experienced archivist himself in addition to being a superb historian, made trips to those libraries and made sure the documents were located and photographed. My visits and attempts to get this done had been to no avail. Once again the connection of a friend and colleague was crucial in facilitating the research. I count Jeremy as an "inside reader," along with Dr. Keith Stanglin. Jeremy and Keith's knowledge of Arminius and all things Arminian has saved me from embarrassing blunders large and small. Both have been generous with their time and expertise, and the result is a much better piece of work than would have otherwise appeared. The same must also be said for the "outside readers" assigned by Baylor University Press, whose positive comments and constructive suggestions moved the project along. To point out the obvious, books require publishers. From my very first mention about the possibility of this book, Baylor University Press Director, Dr. Carey C. Newman, has been enthusiastically supportive. It is quite natural for a scholar to feel that the current project is really important, but publication requires a knowledgeable professional affirming that it will likely be purchased (and perhaps even read!) beyond the coterie of a precious few.

In biblical metaphor one might say that the value of a loving and supporting spouse is "far above rubies," or in more recent times, gold bullion. Time and again Ruth Ann has made personal sacrifices that were entirely in service to the advancement of my career. When doors opened almost twenty years ago to leave a really fine church-related liberal arts college and move "back East" to a Methodist-related research institution to teach seminary students, Ruth Ann left her post at a Fortune 500 company. When I expressed concern about asking her to do this, she replied: "I have a job; you have a calling. I can get another job, but you don't get a different calling." She consistently lives into those statements in ways that defy description—this time letting complete strangers (who have become good friends!) move into and occupy her home. Although our two sons (Kirk and Jeremy) are adults, we still have a four-legged Bichon-Poodle dependent that controls our daily lives in ways that only dog owners understand. Here again, a true friend came up with the solution to the conundrum. Ruth Ann's best friend, Annette Martin, simply adopted Sadie while we were away. Problem solved. It is a true friend who takes in your dependent and gives up her independence.

We make it through life with the help of others, and scholars write books the same way.

W. Stephen Gunter
Thanksgiving, 2011
Durham, North Carolina

INTRODUCTION

Jacob Arminius' *Declaration of Sentiments* was delivered orally in Dutch before the States of Holland in October, 1608. An English translation of the manuscript from which he delivered his address has not previously been available to the English-speaking world. The translation in all the editions of Arminius' *Works* is based on a Latin translation of the Dutch,[1] but that translation was probably not done by Arminius. In its final form, it was published after his demise. Two English translations were done based on the Latin text,[2] but for the modern reader both of these suffer from the same problem—archaic and stilted prose that is difficult to interpret unless you already know what the author is saying. Scholars can sort this out, but what we have not been able to sort out until now are the places where the Latin text was not faithful to the original Dutch. This, of course, means that the previous English translations misrepresent Arminius in several places. The additional advantage of this new translation is that a more polished prose will make Arminius accessible to the non-specialist. The goal is to provide a dynamic equivalent that adheres as closely as possible to Arminius' original words. Decisions along these lines were greatly assisted by Jeremy Bangs' close reading of the final translation. Arminius' syntax provides a great challenge, because entire paragraphs are often comprised of a single sentence. Lines of thought initiated in the first line or two are completed several lines later, even a half-page later in the text. I have worked basically from the critical text by G. J. Hoenderdaal,[3]

---

[1] *Declaratio sententiae de predestinatione.*

[2] In addition to the version published in Arminius' *Works*, one can find online at Early English Books Online (EEBO) the translation by Tobias Conyers, *The Just Man's Defence; or, The Declaration of the Judgement of James Arminius* (London: Henry Eversden, 1657).

[3] G. J. Hoenderdaal, *Verklaring van Jacobus Arminius—Afgelegd in de Vergadering van de*

but I also consulted Arminius' manuscript as well as the 1610 publication of his *Verclaringhe*. Hoenderdaal worked basically from the 1610 edition in comparison with the manuscript. My footnote apparatus is much more detailed than Hoenderdaal because my audience is different, and I have not always agreed with his notations.

This book's title, *Sentiments*, is chosen as, at the very least, a double entendre. Even though it has always been translated in English as part of the title for his formal declaration before the High Council in The Hague in 1608, the word does not actually appear in the Dutch lead title. The first translators of Arminius' *Verklaring* recognized that what Arminius declared to his peers and governing overseers was a combination of opinions on theological issues as well as his personal feelings about the state of affairs that had *required* him to declare himself. The larger context of the *Declaration* helps us understand its content better—the "feelings" as well as the stated "opinions."

The idea to make this new translation has a history that goes back more than forty years. In the decade that Carl Bangs' magisterial biography on Arminius appeared,[4] during the course of my doctoral studies at Leiden, I came across G. J. Hoenderdaal's critical edition—intended to help Dutch-reading Christians understand Arminius better. Carl Bangs was in The Netherlands on sabbatical leave at that time, and I suggested to him that English-reading scholarship would greatly benefit by having an annotated critical edition of Arminius' *Declaration*. Of course, I was suggesting that he should undertake such a translation, but his twinkle-eyed rejoinder, rather typically deadpan in tone, was: "After you finish your doctoral work, maybe you should do it."[5] With this admonition stored in my random memory, the more

---

Staten van Holland op 30 Oktober, 1608 (Lochem: De Tijdstroom, 1960). My dependence on Hoenderdaal is significant, especially his references to the original manuscript. References to page numbers of the manuscript are based on my digital file copy. The *VERCLARINGHE IACOBI ARMINII. Saliger ghedachten, In zijn leven Professor Theologiae binnen Leyden* (Leiden: Thomas Basson, 1610) contains marginal annotations to Scripture references, secondary sources, Latin phrases, and paragraph or section headings. These are not in Arminius' manuscript. I have followed the scriptural references by placing them in brackets in the text, and I have added additional references, also in brackets. Since all of these are editorial additions, I have not noted where my annotations are added. Also, my division of the *Declaration* into three sections is not in the 1610 edition or in Hoenderdaal.

[4] Carl Bangs, *Arminius: A Study in the Dutch Reformation* (Nashville: Abingdon, 1971).
[5] Bangs did take some steps in the direction of a translation, and his annotations

recent opinion of Stuart Clarke proved to be an added encouragement: "The work is one which . . . all theologians should study."[6] The final thumb in my back was a conversation with Keith Stanglin at the Leiden Symposium honoring Arminius in 2009: "A fresh translation from Arminius's original Dutch *Verklaring* would be most welcome."[7]

Prior to our conversation in Leiden, Arminius' most famous biographer had already published his opinion that the Dutch theologian was misinterpreted and misrepresented from every side, even by those who claimed to be his theological heirs. Bangs had previously set this out in six points of misinformation commonly encountered.[8] Bangs underscores that these errors are common to almost all scholarship produced for an English-reading public. However, these errors and a few more may be found in Dutch scholarship as well, only there they are compounded by the consistent practice of viewing Arminius and his teachings through the Synod of Dort (1618–1619), at which his teachings and his immediate followers were condemned, removed from their clergy posts, and driven out of the country. This compounding of error often results in quite unfortunate caricatures of Arminius' teachings in his native land.[9] We must agree with Roger Olson's lament that a half-century after Bangs' scholarship and two decades after Muller's seminal work (both of which should have taught us otherwise),[10] Arminius is still largely misrepresented and consistently misunderstood.[11] The path to correction, however, must not be paved

---

on Hoenderdaal's edition (supplied to me by Jeremy Bangs) have been a tremendous service—especially in comparing the Dutch and Latin versions.

[6] F. Stuart Clarke, *The Ground of Election: Jacobus Arminius' Doctrine of the Work and Person of Christ* (Milton Keynes, UK: Paternoster, 2006), 174.

[7] Keith Stanglin, "Arminius and Arminianism: An Overview of Current Research," in *Arminius, Arminianism and Europe: Jacobus Arminius (1559/60–1609)*, ed. Th. Marius van Leeuwen, Keith Stanglin, and Marijke Tolsma (Leiden: Brill, 2009), 22.

[8] Carl Bangs, "Arminius and the Reformation," *Church History* 30 (1961): 155–56.

[9] Cf. W. Verboom, *De Belijdenis van een gebroken kerk* (Zoetemeer: Boekencentrum, 2005), esp. the charts on pp. 61–62, where Verboom oversimplifies Arminius to the point of being simplistic.

[10] Richard Muller, *God, Creation and Providence in the Thought of Jacob Arminius* (Grand Rapids: Baker, 1991), ix: "Arminius is one of the most neglected of the major Protestant theologians."

[11] Roger E. Olson, *Arminian Theology: Myths and Realities* (Downers Grove: IVP Academic, 2006). This book is Olson's attempt to redress the situation he previously noted: "Arminius is one of the most unfairly neglected and grossly misunderstood

simply with lament; we need additional resources and markers to proceed in the right direction.

It has always been something of a puzzle to me that Bangs did not undertake an aggressive publishing program to redress the situation that he recognized and pointed out. Perhaps part of his not doing this lies in the fact that as a historian he had done a truly significant piece of work in his biography of Arminius, and he had added to this several complementary articles in scholarly journals. Anyone who cared enough to bother could access this information, but no one seems to have cared enough to do so in any sustained way. The result, clearly not Bangs' fault, has been that for all practical purposes Arminius became a relic assigned to the dust bin of arcane personalities. Beyond a coterie of historians and historians of doctrine, few people cared a great deal about sorting out the *ordo salutis* (order of salvation) and his theory of predestination.

Over the past decade this has changed on the English-speaking scene in North America, but not because the heirs of Arminius have suddenly rediscovered his teachings—*au contraire*. Ironically, Arminius is important again because the misrepresentations of his teachings are the favorite whipping boy of an aggressive New Calvinism. And at times the Neo-Calvinism is wed to a Neo-Fundamentalism that provides absolute certainty to its adherents by ascribing to God the responsibility for every single event in the created order without any place or space for contingency or the risk of freedom. God has the blueprint, and it is designed in every detail. In its most simplistic (and perverse) forms, this line of reasoning veers off into a "new determinism." This set of interrelated issues has reentered the seminary classroom because students preparing for parish ministry are confronted almost daily by this New Calvinism.[12] It is discussed on the religious blogs, in the popular press, and proclaimed by television preachers as well as local ministers.

For almost twenty years, it has been my privilege as a professor of evangelism trained in systematic and historical theology to teach in areas related to setting out theological foundations for evangelism.

---

theologians in the story of Christian theology." Cf. Roger E. Olson, *The Story of Christian Theology: Twenty Centuries of Tradition and Reform* (Downers Grove, Ill.: InterVarsity, 1999), 455.

[12] Cf. Roger E. Olson, *Against Calvinism* (Grand Rapids: Zondervan, 2011), esp. 26–27.

Both with regard to history of doctrine as well as interpreting the Scriptures to set out these parameters, one cannot delve into the *ordo salutis* and avoid topics like election and predestination. Teaching in venues rooted in the Wesleyan tradition (we used to say Wesley-Arminian theology!), the responses I got were rather ho-hum: "Are there people out there who really believe in this narrow type of predestination?" Of late, the responses are more like the student who came to me after a lecture exclaiming: "This stuff is everywhere! How do I respond? These people are really aggressive." Unfortunately, for a few, "fight or switch" is the mantra. Colleagues at professional meetings have related to me that seminary faculties have been "purged" of persons with Arminian sympathies. Surely it is more complicated than a theological purge, but one cannot help but be reminded of the aftermath of the Synod of Dort, all in the name of preserving Christian truth. My response to students and colleagues alike who come to me with these stories: "Don't argue or fight about it. Develop a constructive response." This book is a step in that direction. After four hundred years, the English-reading church will have at its disposal Arminius' most mature theological reflection on these issues.

It was my original design to footnote every variance among the multiple translations, but it quickly became evident that these incidental comments would so clutter the footnotes that the critical annotations important to the textual content would be lost. In the course of translating the *Verclaringhe*, it became clear that not even an audience of historical theologians would have an awareness of the Arminian era in and around Amsterdam to comprehend fully all that Arminius sets out. So, in addition to critical annotations to the text itself (many silently appropriated from Hoenderdaal), introductory chapters precede the translation project to facilitate a better informed reading. Taken together, these chapters are intended to provide a tightly focused theological biography in which the events surrounding and influencing his thought are described.[13] The social and political connections are quite often more important than the doctrinal issues per se. The reader who misses those can easily miss the important subtleties of the presenting issue.

---

[13] These biographical chapters are not a substitute for Bangs' comprehensive biography. My intent is much more modest—namely, to provide the historical context for an informed reading of the *Declaration of Sentiments*.

Fortunately, this publication is not the only contribution to a constructive rediscovery of Arminius. Twenty years ago, Eef Dekker wrote a fine dissertation on Arminius,[14] and although his thesis has not been translated into English, more recent dissertations have gleaned very important insights from Dekker. At about the same time, W. G. Witt produced a mammoth thesis on Arminius that catalogs a huge amount of historical detail.[15] From this earlier period of Arminius studies, pride of place and importance must be accorded to Richard Muller's *God, Creation, and Providence in the Thought of Jacob Arminius*.[16] Comprehensive in scope and impressive in depth, Muller goes to great lengths to help us understand and appreciate Arminius—at times to demonstrate that Arminius was, in his opinion, wrong on some points. On the other side of the spectrum, more succinct and precise in its theological focus on the "ground of election," is the monograph by F. Stuart Clarke—intent at times on demonstrating that Arminius got it quite right.[17] As we shall note later, Clarke and Muller agree that Arminius is less than consequential in his doctrine of the "absolute Trinity," and his strict subordinationist Christology is less than adequate.

Most recently two monographs based on doctoral dissertations have appeared that reflect historically situated doctrinal analysis. Keith Stanglin asserts that a proper understanding of Arminius requires that we recognize the "practical" side of his theology and its concern for assurance of salvation.[18] In my final chapter on Arminius' evangelical, practical theology, Stanglin's insights are crucial. The more recent monograph, now translated into English, is from the pen of William den Boer.[19] When his dissertation first appeared in print

---

[14] E. Dekker, *Rijker dan Midas: Vrijheid, genade en predestinatie in de theologie van Jacobus Arminius (1559–1609)* (Zoetermeer: Boekencentrum, 1993).

[15] W. G. Witt, "Creation, Redemption, and Grace in the Theology of Jacobus Arminius," 2 vols. (PhD diss., University of Notre Dame, 1993).

[16] Richard Muller, *God, Creation and Providence in the Thought of Jacob Arminius*. (Grand Rapids: Baker, 1991).

[17] F. Stuart Clarke: "Whatever disagreements I myself have with Arminius on other subjects, on the subject of predestination, I consider his objections to the opposing doctrine almost entirely correct and his criticisms of them well-deserved" (166).

[18] Keith Stanglin, *Arminius on the Assurance of Salvation: The Context, Roots, and Shape of the Leiden Debate, 1603–1609* (Leiden: Brill, 2007).

[19] William den Boer, *God's Twofold Love: The Theology of Jacob Arminius (1559–1609)* (Göttingen: Vandenhoeck & Ruprecht, 2010), based on his dissertation, *Duplex amor Dei* (2008).

in The Netherlands, the byline of a Christian newspaper announced that den Boer dared to "rehabilitate the heretic Arminius." Den Boer's interpretive point is that Arminius' theology is rooted in twofold divine love: love of justice and love for humanity. Here we might speak of Arminius' dialectical theology of love. As we shall see, there are multiple dialectics at work in Arminius, and the typical tendency is to dissolve the dialectic in one direction or the other. Arminius consistently holds these dialectics in a constructive tension. One cannot possibly understand the *Declaration of Sentiments* without fully appreciating his dialectic of twofold love. Even though attention is given in my final chapter to a certain amount of analysis and interpretation of Arminius' theology, the temptation to go very far in that direction has been resisted. That would be a much larger project than this book allows, so my intention is to provide the information and analysis needed for the reader to understand the primary source document.

Regarding our brief survey of literature, two other items merit note. One has appeared and the other is forthcoming. Keith Stanglin is currently working on an interpretive monograph of Arminius' theology that is scheduled to appear from a major university press, and he has already released an important Arminius collection: *The Missing Public Disputations of Jacobus Arminius*.[20] Published in Latin with annotations in English, these public disputations cry out for a translation that will make Arminius' thought accessible to the Latin-deprived.

Forty years ago when Carl Bangs challenged me to do this work, that possibility was a twinkle in his eye but not in mine. The time now seems right. I do not set out to prove Arminius right, but rather to provide a resource that others might read him aright. Recently at Duke Divinity School, the renowned missiologist Andrew Walls assessed the demographics of Christianity in the 60/40 window and concluded that this rising tide of conversions to Christianity in the southern hemisphere will allow this generation to witness "the second coming of world Christianity." He may be right. It is already clear that multiplied millions will struggle afresh with biblical doctrines and themes, and among the interpretive grids for the *ordo salutis* that gives

---

[20] Keith Stanglin, *The Missing Public Disputations of Jacobus Arminius: Introduction, Text and Notes* (Leiden: Brill, 2010). Scheduled for publication in 2012, Keith D. Stanglin and Thomas H. McCall, *Jacob Arminius: Theologian of Grace* (New York: Oxford University Press).

structure to the biblical message of salvation in Christ, a proper assessment of Arminius' understanding of the disposition of God to save sinful humanity deserves to be among the viable alternatives. Friend and foe alike will be surprised by the pages that follow. Arminius was much more "Calvinian" than either side has typically been willing to allow. Perhaps Arminius was not even an Arminian.

PART I
THE LIFE AND TIMES OF ARMINIUS

1

EARLY YEARS

There lived in Holland a man whom they who did not know could not sufficiently esteem, whom they who did not esteem had never sufficiently known. These words, with which Carl Bangs chose to end a chapter in his magisterial biography of Arminius,[1] come near the end of the "Funeral Oration" by Arminius' lifelong friend, Petrus Bertius.[2] As fitting as these words are to punctuate a man's life and to end a chapter about his life, they may be at this point in time just as appropriate to renew a conversation about Arminius' life, influence, and theology. It was a perilous world into which Arminius was born, as the entire Lowlands (lit: "Netherlands") were locked with Spain in a struggle for political and economic survival.[3] Wars during this period, however, were not only about political control and economic leverage; religion was often at the center of contention. In the case of the Lowlands, a rising tide of Protestant sympathies struggled against an established Roman Catholicism. The gradual breakdown of the Habsburg Regime resulted from battles that were fought city by city over an extended period of time.[4] Jonathan

---

[1] Bangs, 331. This epitaph (in Latin) for Arminius in the Pieterskerk, Leiden, was added at the commemoration of his birth in 1960.

[2] Petrus Bertius, "Bertius' Funeral Oration on Arminius," *Works*, 1:13–47.

[3] Prior to the nineteenth century, the land area that largely comprises what we know today as *The* Netherlands (or Holland) was referred to as the Netherlands, Low Countries, the Lowlands, or (for governmental purposes) as the United Provinces. Since this book refers to that earlier period, the country will be called the Netherlands, Low Countries, or Lowlands when reference is made to the country prior to 1800. It should further be noted that in this period, Holland was the designation for what are now the provinces of North and South Holland—not to the entire country of The Netherlands as in modern times.

[4] See Jonathan I. Israel, *The Dutch Republic: Its Rise, Greatness and Fall, 1477–1806* (Oxford: Clarendon, 1995), esp. 129–54. Carl Bangs has pointed out that it is not as simple as the Catholics leaving and the Calvinists arriving: "The earliest Dutch

Israel has noted, "As the grip of the Habsburg government loosened during the early 1560s, and Protestant preaching and other activity could come out into the open. . . , it was predictable that Calvinism would play the dominant role."[5] This being the case, it does not mitigate the harsh reality of the scenes played out during the process of the lessening Habsburg grip on the Netherlands. The family of Arminius was victimized in the process.[6]

Tradition has it that Arminius was born October 10, 1560, but Bangs places the date of Arminius' father's death "no later than 1558" and concludes that Arminius was born in 1559.[7] Apart from the tradition handed down regarding Arminius' day of birth,[8] we have no corroborating historical record, but we do know that he died in Leiden on October 19, 1609. We also know that his given name was Jacobus Harmenszoon, and that he was born to Harmen Jacobszoon and that his mother, traditionally identified as Engeltje (Angelica) Harmensdochter, was from the city of Dordrecht.[9] From the Oudewater registry we know that his mother's given name was actually Elborch—a given name that was seldom used after the rise of Protestantism. In the registry for 1558, Bangs found a listing for "Elborch Harmen Jacobszoon wed^e," or "Elborch the widow of Harmen Jacobszoon."[10]

Reformers don't seem to be Calvinists at all. They rise out of the soil . . . nurtured by the old Dutch biblical piety, not seized by dogmatic insights but steadily pressing toward a purified life according to the Scripture" (Bangs, 21). Bangs was not alone in holding this opinion. Contrary to perception, the move to Protestantism in the Netherlands was very gradual, with the majority of the population remaining sympathetic to Roman Catholicism during Arminius' lifetime and beyond. Even by the time of the Synod of Dort in 1618–1619, barely one-third of the total population was estimated to be Protestant. Cf. Alastair Duke, "The Ambivalent Face of Calvinism in the Netherlands, 1561–1618," in *International Calvinism, 1541–1715*, ed. Menna Prestwich (Oxford: Clarendon, 1985), 109.

[5] Israel, *Dutch Republic*, 104.

[6] Beyond Carl Bangs, the most reliable biographical sources on Arminius are: Caspar Brandt, *The Life of Arminius, D.D.* (Nashville: Stevenson & Owen, 1857); J. H. Maronier, *Jacobus Arminius. Een Biographie* (Amsterdam: Y. Rogge, 1905); and G. J. Hoenderdaal, "Arminius, Jacobus (Hermansz.)," in *BLGNP*, 2:33–37.

[7] Bangs, 26.

[8] See Bertius' "Funeral Oration," in *Works*, 1:13ff.; and Brandt, *Life*.

[9] The traditional practice of naming in those days was patronymic shortening. Harmensdr. is the abbreviation of Harmensdochter, Herman's daughter, and Jacobszn. is the customary abbreviation of Jacobszoon, Jacob's son.

[10] Bangs, 26.

Knowing the family names of both parents gives the modern reader pause with regard to the name by which we know their son, Jacob Arminius. It was not unusual for a man entering university to choose a Latinized name in honor of an inspiring figure. The common practice was simply to Latinize the father's name, so Arminius could have simply been known as Hermanni. His choice to use "Arminius" was an explicitly polemical act. The original Arminius had been a first century Germanic chieftain who valiantly resisted the Romans—certainly an inspiring persona for a young student whose family had been massacred by the soldiers of "Rome."[11]

When Arminius was born in Oudewater (a town on the river Ijssel in Holland about twelve miles from Utrecht in the direction of Rotterdam), it was still under Spanish control and of Roman Catholic faith. The town did not officially declare itself Protestant until 1574. The stirrings of independence and Protestant sympathy were evidently visible during Arminius' early life, and the town incurred the wrath of the Spanish military after its Protestant declaration. As noted, Arminius' father had died in 1558, and when the Spanish besieged Oudewater, Arminius' mother and all the siblings were murdered in "the massacre of Oudewater" in 1575. Arminius was spared because, since the death of his father, he had been cared for by others and was no longer a resident. With regard to Oudewater itself, one cannot help but wonder why a small town with origins in the thirteenth century, comprised of only 500 structures, 352 houses occupied by owners, and 60 houses occupied by renters—along with a few dozen barns and other uninhabitable structures—would have been interesting to the Spanish conquerors.[12] It is more its topography and less its history and citizenship that made it symbolically and strategically important to the Spanish. Oudewater was built on an oblong dike and walled high ground at the bend of the Ijssel, rising as it were above the depressed fields like a fortified island. Located in what we now know as South Holland, in earlier historical times it was politically connected to the Bishopric of

---

[11] The editor of the *Works* adds the following: Arminius was "the name of the famous deliverer of Germany who defeated Quintilius Varus, Germanicus, and other Roman generals" (16n).

[12] This and other information about Oudewater is from A. C. van Aelst, *Schets der Maatschappenlijken Toestand der Staatkundige en Kerkelijke Geschiedenis en van den Stad Oudewater* (Gouda: Edauw & Johanissen, 1893), 185ff.

Utrecht. When it later became a part of the lands of the Counts of Holland, it was something of a border post. Across the years it had been the scene of politically centered violence more than once. This was again the case when Arminius was orphaned as a teenager.

After the death of his father, Arminius was taken in and cared for by a local priest named Theodorus Aemilius. The only historical account we have for this caring priest is from the memory of Arminius' close friend, Petrus Bertius, who likely recalled what Arminius had personally related to him. No doubt an admixture of fact and pious fiction worthy of a dear friend's eulogy, we read,

> His name was Theodore Aemilius, and, on account of his singular erudition and holiness, his memory is to this day cherished by the living with the greatest veneration.... Finding young Arminius without a father, this excellent clergyman charged himself with his education; and as soon as his tender age was thought capable of receiving the elements of learning, he had him carefully instructed in the rudiments of Latin and Greek languages, and his mind imbued with the principles of religion and virtue.[13]

Bertius implies that Aemilius lived in Oudewater at the time of the death of Arminius' father, and we may assume that he was active as a priest because he is identified as the *pastoor* (Dutch for Roman Catholic priest) there in 1566.[14] In his funeral oration Bertius does provide some additional insight into these early years: "After he [Arminius] had thus, for some years, in a most exemplary manner, advanced in his studies and in personal piety, and had resided at Utrecht, in the house of Aemilius, his opening prospects were suddenly beclouded by an unexpected calamity in the death of that excellent and religious old clergyman, his patron."[15] The death of Aemilius may be calculated in relation to other known events as 1574 or 1575, but we do not know exactly when he brought Arminius to Utrecht. It is almost certain that Arminius spent those years in Utrecht up to the time of his initial matriculation at university, and he most likely studied at St. Jerome School, Hieronymusschool.

---

[13] Bertius, "Funeral Oration," *Works*, 1:17. Bangs relates that Aemilius' given name was Dirk Amelgerszoon, and he was actually a cousin of Arminius' mother. *Works*, 1:ix.

[14] Martinus Soermans, *Kerkelijk Register van de Plaatsen en Namen der Predikanten . . . van Zuyd-Holland* (Haarlem: Wilhelmus van Kessel, 1702), 66.

[15] Bertius, "Funeral Oration," *Works*, 1:18.

It is remarkable that a financially destitute child growing up in a war-torn society would receive the education requisite to a university education. That this is the case for the young Arminius must be credited not only to Arminius' acumen, but more especially to the extended family on his mother's side who generously accepted the role *in loco parentis*. There was more than one! As the first of these "parents," Aemilius provided Arminius with the best classical education at his disposal.[16] The Hieronymusschool was quite likely among the many humanistic schools (rooted in *ad fontes*, "return to the textual sources") characterized by Biblical piety that were founded in the Lowlands under the influence of the Brethren of the Common Life—founded purposely for the instruction of boys from "leading families." The two patron saints of the Brethren were Jerome and Gregory, resulting in those being the two most common names for the schools. The curricula for these schools were established and mandated by "statutes," and from those formalized in 1565, we learn that the students at the Hieronymusschool were instructed in mathematics, rhetoric, dialectic, and physics—as well as grounded in the composition of Latin prose and poetry and in oral expression. In addition, Greek studies included Plato's *Dialogues* and the *Oeconomica* of Xenophon. The names Cicero, Aristotle, Homer, and Plutarch are prominent. To this full curriculum were added a full complement of biblical and Christian sources: Hebrew, reading the Gospels in both Greek and Latin—as well as readings in Chrysostom, Basil the Great, and the Athanasian Creed.[17]

As a schoolboy Arminius was not yet acquainted with Petrus Bertius, but he may have gained acquaintance in Utrecht at Hieronymusschool with another youngster who would become a close friend, ally, and confidant throughout the rest of his life—Johannes Uytenbogaert.[18] Arminius and Uytenbogaert were close contemporaries in age, the latter born in Utrecht on February 11, 1557—the son of Augustijn Pieterszoon Uytenbogaert and Helena (Heylwich) Hamel, from Heusden. Both families were of some substance and renown

---

[16] Cf. Bangs, 34–44.

[17] A. Ekker, *Berigt omtrent de Latijnsche Scholen te Utrecht* (Utrecht, 1864), 57–58.

[18] Cf. Duke, "Ambivalent Face of Calvinism," 119, who notes that Uytenbogaert says they also read moderate Reformed divines like Melanchthon and Bullinger at the school he and Arminius attended. We do not have direct historical confirmation that Arminius knew Uytenbogaert in Utrecht, although their matriculation overlapped several years.

historically,[19] but at the time of his birth, Uytenbogaert's immediate family was financially impoverished. Yet somehow they managed to place their son at the age of ten at the Hieronymusschool (about 1566), and it seems his matriculation continued for some eight years. Regarding his teacher, Lauerman—who was *Rector* (principal) of the school from 1554 to 1573—Uytenbogaert later recalled, "I still remember that the teacher often said to me and to my fellow students that the root of study is very bitter to bite into but that the fruit is very sweet."[20] For both Arminius and Uytenbogaert the appropriation, application, and implications of their acquired theological knowledge would prove to be bittersweet as well. Even if they were not close at the Hieronymusschool, they did become fast friends as theology students later in Geneva, and they remained lifelong allies and confidants amid the ensuing ecclesial conflicts. But once again, we are ahead of ourselves in the narrative, so we return to the story line of Arminius' early life. His study in Utrecht ended with the death of Aemilius in late 1574 or early 1575.

The next period of Arminius' life is not corroborated by any historical accounts other than the funeral oration of Bertius,[21] who relates that the death of Aemilius left Arminius more or less stranded in Utrecht. The details are lost with regard to how they met, but somehow Arminius came to the attention of another distant relative from Oudewater, Rudolphus Snellius van Roijen (Rudolf Snel), who became the second man to provide generously *in loco parentis*.[22] Aemilius had rescued Arminius from danger and certain poverty, and Snellius introduced the young orphan to the university world of which he was himself a part. Only a dozen years senior to Arminius, Snellius was born in Oudewater to a rather prominent and well-to-do family on October 5, 1547.[23] Family wealth and position granted Snellius great academic advantage. He studied at Heidelberg as well as Cologne, where it is reported that he taught Aristotelian logic for some three years. He next

---

[19] Cf. H. C. Rogge, *Johannes Wtenbogaert* [Uytenbogaert] *en Zijn Tijd*, 3 vols. (Amsterdam: Y. Rogge, 1874–1876).

[20] Rogge, *Johannes Wtenbogaert (Uytenbogaert)*, 1:10.

[21] Bertius, "Funeral Oration," *Works*, 1:19–20.

[22] Bangs relates that Snellius was also related to Arminius on his mother's side. *Works*, 1:ix.

[23] For biographical information on Snellius, see van Aelst, *Schets der Maatschappelijken Toestand*, 548–50.

went to Marburg, where he became enamored with the logic of Petrus Ramus (Pierre de la Ramée), leaving behind his former attachment to Aristotelianism. For our story this is notable because Arminius was also, as we shall see, attached to Ramism and even instructed others in its logic. Snellius also traveled to Italy (as did Arminius in his student days), but after living in Pisa from 1575 to 1578, Snellius returned to Oudewater and married a survivor of the massacre of Oudewater, Machteld Cornelisdochter, in the summer of 1578. At about this time Snellius was called to be professor of Hebrew and mathematics at the University of Leiden, where he taught until his death in 1613. This young university (founded in 1575) was not large, and Arminius would have known his "parent" in Leiden—first as his student and then as a colleague after he went there to teach in 1603.[24]

We know that Snellius' care for Arminius began rather soon after the death of Aemilius, and that he took the boy with him to Marburg in 1575, Arminius being about sixteen years of age. This would have been in early summer, and they could have hardly been settled when news of the Oudewater massacre reached them. As natives of the town, this tragedy struck them both hard—the young Arminius being emotionally distraught at the report of the death of his mother and all his siblings. After two weeks of "weeping and lamentation, almost without intermission," Arminius purposed to return to Holland, a distance of some 250 miles that he traversed entirely on foot. It was his goal to "look once more upon his native town, though in ruins, or to meet [his own] death in the attempt."[25] Encountering the aftermath of death and destruction, Arminius stayed only a few days and then began the long walk back to Marburg. Interesting to note is that Oudewater had only become officially Protestant in 1574, was massacred in 1575 and occupied by the Spanish, and then was liberated in 1576 by a "Sea Beggar" unit under the command of a Leiden nobleman, Adriaen van Swieten.[26]

---

[24] Biographical information related to people connected with the University of Leiden may be found in Johannes Meursius, *Athenae Batavae* (Leiden, 1625). For Snellius, see also Bertius, "Funeral Oration," *Works*, 1:55; and Brandt, *Life*, 40.

[25] Bertius, "Funeral Oration," *Works*, 1:19.

[26] Cf. van Aelst, *Schets der Maatschappelijken Toestand*, 162ff. Van Aelst follows the account of J. Walvis, *Bescrijving van Gouda* (Gouda, n.d.). For a more detailed account of these events, see A. W. den Boer and Johan Schouten, *Oud-Oudewater* (Oudewater: Stichting Waagebouw, [1966]).

We noted previously that during the late middle ages and after the rise of Protestantism, wars were often waged with religion at the center. The same may be said for the founding of universities. Arminius' first university exposure was at Marburg, founded in 1527 by Philip of Hesse in order to promote Protestantism in his territories. Martin Luther's successor, Philip Melanchthon, was the guiding intellect in its founding, but we do not know that he was actually a professor there. Two years after its founding, the famous Marburg Colloquy was held there.[27] The leading Protestant Reformers attended the event convened by Philip I of Hessen, who realized that he needed religious harmony in order to unite the Protestant states in his realm. Later in our narrative we encounter this same rationale for convening ecclesial leaders in the Netherlands. The facts about the early days of Marburg itself are well known, but we have no account of Arminius' time there, so we do not know whether Melanchthon's influence on the university was noticed by him. We will note later that Arminius' sentiments in connection with predestination bear some similarities to Melanchthon's, but all that Bertius tells us about this period is that Arminius was there with Snecanus for a brief period of time.[28]

Rather soon after his return from visiting the devastation in Oudewater, Arminius heard that a new Dutch university had been founded in Leiden by decree of William I, the Prince of Orange—a fitting commemorative to Leiden's successful stand against Spanish besiegers that ended on October 4, 1574. Founders' day was February 8, 1575, and lectures were commencing with a theological faculty at the heart of the university, *primus inter pares*. Arminius would be the twelfth student enrolled in the theological faculty, along with Petrus Bertius (only twelve years of age!).[29] The name in the university registry is "Jacobus Arminius," probably the first official use of the Latinized form of his

---

[27] The Marburg Colloquy, October 1–4, 1529, attempted to solve a dispute between Martin Luther and Huldrych Zingli about the "real presence" in the Eucharist.

[28] Bertius, "Funeral Oration," *Works*, 1:18–19.

[29] "Arminius, Jacobus," *BWPGN*, 1:209, col. 1, which cites *Album Studiosorum Academiae Lugduno Batavae* (The Hague, 1875). Bangs, 47, follows this source to assert the twelfth, but G. J. Hoenderdaal, "Arminius, Jacobus (Hermansz.)," *BLGNP*, 2:33, col. 1, asserts that Arminius was the thirteenth student enrolled. Hoenderdaal has misread the *Album Studiosorum*.

name, appropriately marking his transition to university studies at the age of sixteen. Bertius records:

> We were therefore sent off in company to Leyden: and from the moment when, together, we first entered within the walls of this University, the greatest unanimity existed among us, and we were most intimately connected.... But the only one of our order who meritoriously distinguished himself above the rest of his companions was Arminius.... I well recollect the time when Doctor Lambert Danaeus,[30] our learned Professor, paid him a public compliment and eulogized him for the endowments of his genius, and his proficiency in learning and virtue; he also urged us who were Divinity students to imitate the example of Arminius by the same cheerful and diligent attention to the study of sacred Theology.[31]

---

[30] Lambertus Danaeus (ca. 1530–1595) was born in Beaugency-sur-Loire, France, to a rather well-to-do and influential family. Brought up by his uncle Antoine Brachet, he initially studied law. Studying under Calvin in Geneva cemented his commitment to Protestantism. Cf. *NNBW*, 1:685–88.

[31] Bertius, "Funeral Oration," *Works*, 1:21.

2

STUDENT YEARS,
1576–1587

Arminius' student years stretch over more than a decade, and they include several universities in different European cities: Leiden, Geneva and Basel, and Padua (Italy). As we shall see, he was in Geneva on two separate occasions, with a university matriculation between in Basel.[1] Leiden was Holland's first university, and its founding was richly wrapped in sentiment and symbolism—a national event imbued by the new sense of nationhood—even if the rather hasty nature of the founding did lead to a less than perfectly orchestrated set of plans. Although the theological faculty was declared *primus inter pares*, when the Leiden Reformed minister, Caspar Janszoon Coolhaes (Koolhaes)[2] gave the dedicatory address on February 6, 1575 (two days prior to the formal founding ceremony), no theological faculty members were in attendance.[3] It was a rapid-fire set of events that had led to this

---

[1] *Rijker dan Midas*, 24, provides a time line for Arminius' student years after Leiden, although the exact dates are impossible to reconstruct for each location: (1) Geneva—seven months (January–July 1582); (2) Basel—as few as fifteen or as many as twenty-three months, most likely twenty-one months (between August 1582 and April 1584); (3) Geneva—two to two-and-a-half years (May 1584 to August 1586); (4) During a six-month trip to Italy, approximately four months at Padua (fall 1586 and/or spring 1587); (5) A final few months in Geneva (summer 1587).

[2] Coolhaes (January 24, 1536–January 15 [?], 1615) joined the Protestants in 1560. Cf. "Coolhaes (Caspar Jansz.)," in NNBW, 1:cols. 631–36. For complete information, see H. C. Rogge, *Caspar Janszoon Coolhaes, de Voorlooper van Arminius en de Remonstranten*, 2 vols. (Amsterdam: Y. Rogge, 1865). Regarding the latter part of the book's title, E. Dekker, *Rijker dan Midas*, 264n54, refers to an earlier detailed research on Coolhaes that there is little to indicate a connection between the "later Remonstrants and Coolhaes, so that the latter half of the title might just as well be scrapped." I would counter that it can also be said that there is little similarity between Arminius himself and the "later Remonstrants."

[3] For a more complete description of the opening days, see Bangs, 46–48, and J. J. Woltjer, "Introduction," in *Leiden University in the Seventeenth Century: An Exchange of*

inauspicious beginning. On October 4, 1574, Leiden was liberated after a lengthy siege. William of Orange (William the Silent/Willem de Zwijger) entered the city, and rather quickly the idea was born to found a Dutch university. On December 28, William addressed a letter to the States of Holland and West Friesland that called for the founding of "a university where the youth can be educated both in the right knowledge of God and in other good and honorable sciences."[4] The letter was read to the States of Holland in Delft on January 2, 1575, and the agreement was struck the next day to form the university. University curators (three in number) were appointed on January 6, and the university charter was signed. Coolhaes preached the dedicatory address on February 6, and the dedication occurred on February 8, 1575. It is not actually the case that the theological faculty failed to attend, for the faculty had not yet even been appointed. Such was the haste with which the university was founded. The four faculty divisions were theology,[5] law, medicine, and arts—although these bore little resemblance to modern definitions of university faculties by the same name.[6]

The Pieterskerk where Coolhaes and others regularly preached is perhaps only 250 meters from the *Academiegebouw* of the university (a late medieval former cloister on the Rapenburg that is still the university center), but the church and academy were far removed in governing assumptions. Coolhaes had only very recently arrived in Leiden as Protestant pastor, and he was immediately caught in a controversy almost exactly parallel in its driving assumptions to that which would later embroil Arminius. The issues were rooted in Erastianism—the form of governing that places ecclesial as well as civil issues under the oversight of public magistrates and officials. When we read in Arminius' *Sentiments* about the intrigue surrounding these issues, it is important to remember that these conflicts had a much longer history than Arminius' story. The crucial role these conflicts played in Dutch

---

Learning, ed. Th. H. Lunsingh Scheurleer and G. H. M. Posthumus Meyjes (Leiden: Brill, 1975), esp. 1–19.

[4] Rogge, *Coolhaes*, 1:45. West Friesland was originally connected to Friesland; however, successive floods in 1282 and 1287 broke open the North Sea dunes and separated the land masses, forming the Zuider Zee between them. In the sixteenth century it was known as West Friesland, but it was politically part of Holland.

[5] As this book is being researched in 2010–2011, there is no longer a Faculty of Christian Theology at the University of Leiden.

[6] Cf. Woltjer, "Introduction," 1–2.

history also belies the tendency by some interpreters of a later generation to conclude rather simplistically that Arminius' difficulties were comprehensively a matter of theological differences over predestination. Those theological differences were real and really important, but, as is so often the case in church history, power issues related to politics and economics were equally important factors. One might even say that the theological position chosen as the "the correct one" was to an extent dictated by politics and power.

H. C. Rogge asserts that there were two basic issues at the heart of the ongoing controversy within the Dutch Protestant Church—a controversy that was carried on with greater and lesser intensity from Arminius' student years through at least the Synod of Dort in 1618–1619. Even though his name gets unfairly attached to them in posterity, it may be said that Arminius got caught in a decades-long struggle over two main issues: the relationship between church and state, and the relationship between God's foreordination to salvation and human freedom.[7] Some resolution to both of these was required in order to unite and maintain governmental and economic stability in the United Netherlands. Holland's ability to repay the huge debt to Britain from war loans was threatened until the two basic points of contention were resolved. This was not just about theological niceties! At the risk of oversimplification, I would venture that it boiled down to the recurring question, "Who has the right to make final and authoritative ecclesial decisions?" During Arminius' student days, Coolhaes was embroiled in these issues in Leiden, and although Arminius was not directly involved, he would have known the issues. When he personally got caught in them later in Amsterdam and Leiden, it was not the first time that he had thought about them. As an impressionable student, Arminius would have attended worship and heard Coolhaes preach often. So, what would he have heard?

Coolhaes converted to Protestantism in 1588 after a brief span as a Carthusian monk in Coblenz (Koblenz), Germany.[8] He first came to the Lowlands as a pastor in Deventer, where the moderating influence

---

[7] Rogge, *Coolhaes*, 1:3. Jeremy Dupertuis Bangs, *Strangers and Pilgrims, Travellers and Sojourners: Leiden and the Foundations of Plymouth Plantation* (Plymouth, Mass.: General Society of Mayflower Descendants, 2009), 151, adds a third point of contention: the limitation of theological debate.

[8] Cf. "Koolhaes, Caspar," in *BWPGN*, 5:172–205; "Coolhaes," in *NNBW*, 1:632–36.

of the Brethren of the Common Life had shaped the assumptions of incipient Protestantism in Holland. The heated theological controversies among Lutherans, Mennonites, and Calvinists were evidently not front-and-center in that region of the country. When riotous anti-Catholic protests began in other places and threatened the relative tranquility of Deventer as well, the magistrates exercised their Erastian power to take matters in hand to control conflicts between Catholics and those who had declared themselves Protestant. In steps that even today would seem incredibly ecumenical, the magistrates in Deventer assigned the former Catholic church, the Lieve-Vrouwenkerk, to the Protestants, but with a three-fold stipulation: (1) The reformers would not damage the church or its contents in any way; (2) The Reformed congregation would not call a pastor without the approval of the magistrates; and (3) They would allow the Catholics to continue celebrating Mass in the church. These measures were designed to prevent the congregation's falling into the hands of over-zealous reformers, and it must be concluded that the Deventer magistrates were largely successful in their design.[9]

Coolhaes was the first minister to pastor under these conditions, and by all accounts he had a lively and thriving ministry in Deventer. It suited him perfectly, until the Spanish occupation forced him to flee to Germany. When he returned to Holland, the Leiden burgomasters invited him in 1574 to serve the Reformed congregation there. This is where the story gets interesting for our narrative. At the Synod of Emden in 1571, an anti-Erastian declaration had been passed placing pastoral calls in the hands of local church consistories—following the pattern of Calvin's Geneva. When the Leiden burgomasters issued the call to Coolhaes, they were asserting their authority over against the synodal declaration that some referred to as a "Genevan Inquisition." Coolhaes' experience with Erastian structures in Deventer, combined with his ecumenical experience in that setting, resulted in his being something of a "mild Protestant"—which is to say, not inclined to engage needlessly in controversy.

If Coolhaes thought that Leiden could be another Deventer for him, he was severely disappointed. He definitely had the support of the Leiden burgomasters, but there was a strong contingency of more radical reformers in Leiden who reflected a decided proclivity for the

---

[9] Cf. Bangs, 51–55.

Genevan polity that placed control in the hands of the church consistory. Exacerbating the situation considerably was the fact that his fellow minister, Pieter Corneliszoon,[10] was neither theologically mild nor Erastian in his inclinations. In Deventer the Roman Catholics had been allowed to celebrate Mass in the church, but in Leiden Corneliszoon asserted that even the saying of evening prayers through the week and preaching funeral sermons and celebrating Christian festivals on days other than Sunday (even Christmas!) was Romish practice. To say the least, Coolhaes found these opinions unnecessarily radical and confrontational. The magistrates sided with Coolhaes, but the church consistory sided with Corneliszoon. Bangs is insightful in this connection: "The Coolhaes affair was no tempest in a teapot. It was an expression of fundamental cleavage in the Dutch Reformed Church made at the vital university center of Dutch life. Arminius could not have gone from Leiden to Geneva without being made aware of this unresolved antinomy in Dutch Reformed theology and polity."[11]

Although we know that Arminius was quite likely a financially challenged student who, like other students and professors, was entitled to an annual allotment of tax-free wine and beer,[12] we do not have much detailed information about his Leiden student years. Arminius would have been the "Iacobus Hermannus Oudewater" listed as sharing rooms with other students in the home of his Hebrew professor, Hermannus Reynecherus.[13] It was customary for professors to augment their income by renting rooms to students, and we know that Reynecherus taught at Leiden until 1578.[14]

---

[10] Cf. *NNBW*, 2:333–34.

[11] Bangs, 55. The "Arbitral Accord" ending the schism in the Leiden church was signed on October 29, 1580. In addition to ending the public dispute, the Arbitral Accord established guidelines for Leiden's ecclesiastical governance. Cf. Christine Kooi, *Liberty and Religion: Church and State in Leiden, 1572–1620* (Leiden: Brill, 2000), esp. 86–87.

[12] On November 22, 1577, the Leiden City Council drew up a list of persons eligible for the alcohol allotment. It is actually the earliest extant roll of university members. Cf. H. J. Witkam, "Een lijst van Lidmaten der Leidse Universiteit op 22 November 1577," *Jaarboekje voor Geschiedenis en Oudheidkunde van Leiden en Omstreken* 61 (1970): 101–5.

[13] Bangs, 49.

[14] *NNBW*, 4:1138. On Reynecharus and other Leiden faculty members, see Martinus Soermans, *Academisch Register . . . der Universiteyt tot Leyden* (Leiden: Hendrik Teering, 1704). Volume bound with the *Kerkelijk Register van de Plaatsen en Namen der Predikanten . . . van Zuyd Holland* (Haarlem: Wilhelmus van Kessel, 1702).

Until the regular faculty members were named, it seems that Coolhaes lectured in theology, despite his not having university rank. Bangs says, "The names of other teachers are known, and much can be inferred from that about Arminius' education" at Leiden between 1576 and 1581.[15] For various reasons there was much coming and going among faculty posts in the university's early decades. Issues of Protestant versus Roman Catholic identity were at play, and narrow definitions of predestination lurked in the shadows between "precisionists" (*preciezen*) and "latitudinarians" (*rekkelijken*)—the rough equivalent of conservatives versus liberals. Amid these recognized tensions, the university curators studiously avoided extremes: "The extent of moderate, conciliatory, and essentially anti-extremist attitude in the early years of the University was exemplified in the appointment of [Justus] Lipsius."[16] Indeed, so compelling was the influence and fame of this "great humanist" that Lipsius grew to be regarded as the spirit of Leiden University in its early days. The Leiden burgomasters wrote to him on July 2, 1591, forecasting "utter academic ruin" were he to depart.[17] The predicted ruin did not occur, but Lipsius did leave Leiden as well as Protestantism, returning to the Roman Catholic Church. Leiden's first appointed theologian was Guilhelmus Feuguereus (Guillaume Feugueray), from April 1575 to May 1579.[18] For the brief period of approximately four months in the winter of 1577–1578, he had Johannes Bollius as a colleague.[19] They were followed by Hubertus Sturmius, lecturer in theology from November 30, 1579, to May 1584,[20] and Professor Lambertus Danaeus—March 17, 1581, to May 1582.[21] Rather soon after Arminius' departure to Geneva, two other theologians arrived: Johannes Holmannus in 1582,[22] and Adrian Saravia in 1584.[23]

The multiple transitions in faculty tell us more about the theological faculty in general than about Arminius' education in particular;

---

[15] Bangs, 50.

[16] Woltjer, "Introduction," 2.

[17] P. C. Molhuysen, *Bronnen tot de geschiedenis der Leidsche Universiteit* ('s Gravenhage: M. Nijhoff, 1913), 1:179, art. 161.

[18] *NNBW*, 3:398.

[19] *NNBW*, 2:198.

[20] *NNBW*, 10:989.

[21] *NNBW*, 1:685.

[22] *NNBW*, 8:798.

[23] *NNBW*, 9:934.

however, two figures stand out in connection with Arminius and the concerns of this essay.[24] Feuguereus, born in Rouen,[25] was strongly influenced by the Protestant pastor there, Augustin Marlorat. Feuguereus was the Protestant pastor in Longueville at the time of the St. Bartholomew's Day Massacre in 1572.[26] Avoiding the onslaught, Feuguereus fled to London where he encountered in the immigrant Huguenot community the impoverished widow and children of his former pastor, Marlorat. This led to his editing and publishing Marlorat's *Scripture Thesaurus* (London, 1574), an eight-hundred-page topical arrangement of both the Old and New Testaments. It was this publication that led to Feuguerus' appointment in Leiden. Through one Adriaan van der Mijle,[27] William of Orange learned of this exceptional publication, and the Leiden connection was made. The connecting link to van der Mijle was a Huguenot pastor exiled in London, Petrus Lozelerius Villerius, a moderate Calvinist who is approvingly mentioned later by the Remonstrant historian Gerard Brandt.[28] It did not harm Feuguereus' case with Orange that he had previously dedicated a book to the Dutch leader with the admonition to cultivate religion, "not by such methods as are destructive both to the country and to religion itself," for "men in that case may be led, but not driven."[29] Clearly, when he arrived in Leiden, Feuguereus would have received welcoming responses to his milder form of Reformed orthodoxy.[30]

[24] Cf. Bangs, 50–55.

[25] Cf. Christian Sepp, *Het Godgeleerd Onderwijs in Nederland Gedeurende de 16ᵉ en 17ᵉ Eeuw*, 2 vols. in 1 (Leiden: de Breuk en Smits, 1873/1874), 1:34–35.

[26] The massacre began on August 23, 1572 (the eve of the feast of Bartholomew the apostle), in the context of the attempted assassination two days prior of Admiral Gaspard de Coligny, the leader of French Calvinist Protestants known as Huguenots. On order of the Roman Catholic French monarch, with at least tacit approval from Rome, the Huguenots were targeted for death. The violence erupted into the widespread murder of Protestants at the hands of Roman Catholics. Informed estimates of the death tolls are notoriously varied—from 1,000 to 3,000 in Paris alone, and up to 30,000 in the French countryside.

[27] *NNBW*, 8:1190–91.

[28] Brandt, *History*, 1:376.

[29] Brandt, *History*, 1:312–13; see also Uytenbogaert, *Historie*, pt. 3, p. 22. [Note: There were multiple editions of Uytenbogaert's *Historie* published in 1647. The 2nd edn., bound with his *Leven, Kerckelijcke bedieninghe ende Zedige Verantwoordinghe*, begins pagination anew with each part. Other 1647 editions of the *Historie* have sequential pagination throughout. Unless noted otherwise, all citations are to the 2nd edn. bound with his *Leven*.]

[30] Bangs' description of Feuguereus as representing a "mild Reformed orthodoxy"

The other theological mentor to Arminius, Danaeus,[31] represents the stricter form of Calvinism as well as an anti-Erastian attitude toward church polity. In 1560 he had gone to Geneva to study under Calvin, and he served from 1561 to 1572 as pastor at Gien, near Orleans in France. The St. Bartholomew's Day Massacre drove him from his home with all his possessions (including his library), and he returned to Geneva where he served as pastor of two churches and as professor at the Academy. Calvin was deceased (1564), but Danaeus became a close friend of Calvin's successor, and it was Theodore Beza who helped open the doors for him to come to Leiden. Having studied with Calvin and served as a colleague of Beza, he was strongly inclined to the congregational polity in Geneva. It is not an overstatement to assert that the Leiden theological faculty, indeed the university, was caught in an uproar. This led to the resignation and departure of Danaeus in May 1582. The Erastian side had won out in this early skirmish.

So Arminius was mentored in Leiden by theologians who represented the two sides of the polity issue. Representing the milder Calvinism and Erastian polity is Feuguereus, as well as pastor Coolhaes. From among the stricter Calvinists, Arminius heard from Danaeus. When he went to Geneva to study, Arminius was not ignorant of the fault lines. Bangs notes appropriately that the Leiden setting provides a "glimpse into the development of Arminius' theological sympathies, for in later years he cites Coolhaes as one of the early, non-Genevan Dutch Reformers in whose tradition he saw himself standing."[32] This being the case, it is appropriate that H. C. Rogge's unequalled study of Coolhaes describes him as the "forerunner of Arminius."[33] When Arminius later accepted the Leiden appointment as professor of theology, one cannot help but wonder whether he hoped to find a safe haven for his milder Calvinism and Erastian sentiments. After all, during his student days in Leiden, the university had forced out the more strident and Geneva-inclined Danaeus! It is to Arminius' years in Geneva that we now turn our attention.

---

(51) is not shared by Dekker, *Rijker dan Midas*, 263. Dekker asserts that we simply do not know enough about Feuguereus to draw this conclusion. This perspective is reflected in the dictionary article on Feuguereus, *BWGPN*, 3:49–51, which also "corrects" a few historical inaccuracies from Brandt, *History*. See also, *NNBW*, 3:398.

[31] Cf. Sepp, *Godgeleerd Onderwijs*, 1:57–58; *NNBW*, 1:685; and *BWPGN*, 2:379–83.
[32] Bangs, 52.
[33] Rogge, *Caspar Janszoon Coolhaes, de Voorloper* ["forerunner"] *van Arminius*.

Despite its being a journey of several days from Amsterdam, Calvin's Academy in Geneva was extremely successful in attracting Dutch students from the very beginning of its founding in 1559. Approximately fifteen students from the Lowlands had matriculated by 1565, and by 1570 the number stood at thirty-two. Between 1570 and 1580 the number was no less than sixty-four matriculants from Holland, and counting Arminius, seventy-nine Dutch students entered the Academy between 1581 and 1585.[34] We know that Arminius signed the registry on January 1, 1582.[35]

We mentioned earlier that Arminius struggled financially during his Leiden student days, so the question comes to mind how Arminius could possibly afford to spend several years studying in southern Europe. Although we do not know how the young Arminius came to their attention, we do know that it was the Amsterdam "Merchants' Guild" (*Kramersgilde*) that was his benefactor. The financial support came to him on something of a schedule, but since funds could only be "transferred" by personal courier, it was not unusual during his time in Switzerland for Arminius to run short on money. The Merchants' Guild of Amsterdam was among the most influential of its day in northern Europe, so they could afford to be generous. On September 13, 1581, there was an available sum of one hundred guilders allotted to Arminius. This was not so much a scholarship as it was a fellowship with attendant requirements. In return for this (and contingent continued) financial support, Arminius agreed to return to Amsterdam as a pastor upon the completion of his studies, after three or four years.[36] It actually turned out to be at least six years.

Since we do not have anything similar to a journal from the hand of Arminius, we are left to inference and indirect sources as to what he heard and was taught at Geneva.[37] We know that Calvin died in

---

[34] Bangs, 66, citing Herman de Vries [de Heekelingen], *Genève: Pépinière du Calvinisme Hollandaise*, vol. 1, *Les Etudiants des Pays-Bas à Genève au Temps de Théodore de Bèze* (Fribourg: Fragnière Frères, 1918), 1:44ff. These numbers are approximations since the registry for Geneva does not give dates in every instance.

[35] Bangs, 66, citing de Vries, *Genève*, 1:108.

[36] Cf. " 't Kerck'lijk Amsterdam," in *Bronnen tot de Geschiedenis van het Bedrijfsleven en het Gildewezen van Amsterdam, 1512–1611*, ed. J. G. van Dillen (The Hague: M. Nijhoff, 1929), 1:789.

[37] A treatise "On the Lord's Supper" from the hand of Arminius during this period has survived in an extremely rare book. Jeremy Bangs related to me that it had been his father's intention to revise the materials on the Geneva period of Arminius' life in

1564, so that by 1582 his successor, Theodore Beza, was well established as the leading theological voice in Geneva. Indeed, Calvin had placed Beza at the head of the Academy in 1559. Because of Calvin's close association for more than twenty years with William Farel (1489–1565), Beza's naming was in some ways unanticipated. Heiko Oberman has noted, however, a sudden rupture occurred in September 1558, in the correspondence between Calvin and Farel.[38] Since Calvin subsequently named Beza as head of the Genevan Academy, it is important for us to discern in brief the nature of Beza's theological inclination. These would not only determine to a large extent what Arminius heard in Geneva, but, as we shall see, Beza's opinions and his influence were deeply felt in Holland for several decades—if not permanently in some quarters as the authentic interpretation of Calvinism, if not Calvin himself.

The term "Calvinism" seems to have been introduced by Calvin's Protestant opponents in Bern in 1548, intended as an uncomplimentary epithet that lumped Calvin and Farel together.[39] It is a commonplace assertion that Beza took this emerging Calvinism, especially predestination, and rationalized it into a schematized structure. With regard to Beza as an interpreter of Calvin and a theologian in his own right, Mallinson has observed, "Theodore Beza is significant because he successfully conserved and disseminated Calvin's ideas on an international level. . . . Three decades after Calvin's death, Beza still was lecturing in that celebrated city [Geneva]."[40] Beza bridged the gap between the Reformation itself and the era of Protestant orthodoxy

---

the updated edition of his biography, but this was more extensive than the publishers allowed. Arminius's essay is in *Theses Theologicae in Schola Geneuensi ab aliquot sacrarum literarium studiosis . . . sub D. D. Theodoro Beza et Antonio Fayo . . . propositas disputatiae. . . .* (E. Vignon: Geneuae, 1586). English translation: *Propositions and Principles of Diuinitie propounded and disputed in the Vniuer[s]itie of Geneua, by certain students of Diuinitie there, vnder M. Theod. Beza and M. Anthonie Faius. . . . Translated ovt of Latine into English . . . . At Edinbvrgh.* Printed by Robert Waldegrave, printer to the King's Maiestie, Anno Dom. 1591 Cum Privilegio Regali. A second edition appeared in 1595, "newlie corrected with sundrie additions." Arminius' contribution is on pages 273–79, 1595 edn.

[38] Cf. Heiko Oberman, "Calvin and Farel," in *John Calvin and the Reformation of the Refugees* (Geneva: Droz, 2009), 195–222.

[39] Oberman, *John Calvin and the Reformation of the Refugees*, 198.

[40] Jeffrey Mallinson, *Faith, Reason, and Revelation in Theodore Beza, 1519–1605* (Oxford: Oxford University Press, 2003), 3.

that emerged, even shaping it in a distinctive way.[41] Issues related to this assumption will likely be argued in perpetuity among Reformation specialists, but the resolution of this issue is not crucial for our narrative. More pertinent is a discernment regarding what Arminius learned from Beza; and in this regard, a controversy in which both Calvin and Beza were participants is highly instructive.

In the same decade that the Academy was founded, in 1551, Jerome Hermes Bolsec began openly and persistently to challenge Calvin's teaching on predestination. Theodore Beza, at that time in Lausanne,[42] exchanged a series of letters with Calvin and Heinrich Bullinger, the acknowledged leader among Swiss pastors and the successor to Zwingli in the Swiss Reformation—letters setting out Beza's defense of Calvin's position on predestination.[43] For his part the inflammatory Bolsec was permanently banned from Geneva; he later returned to France and eventually reclaimed the Roman Catholic faith prior to his death in 1584.[44] Beyond question Bolsec was a disruptive and perhaps even a socially destructive personality; however, his incisive challenges identified the most awkward aspects of

---

[41] Cf. Jeremy Bangs, *Strangers and Pilgrims*, 472–73, esp. notes 21 and 22. The adoption of rigid Calvinian views of "orthodoxy" were formally proclaimed at the Synod of Dort in 1618–1619, so Bangs asserts: "Any description of the disputes before 1618 that without qualification applies the word 'orthodox' to describe the anti-Arminian ... position is consequently anachronistic."

[42] For biographical information on Beza, see H. M. Baird, *Theodore Beza: The Counsellor of the French Reformation* (New York: G. P. Putnam, 1899); P. F. Geisendorf, *Théodore de Bèze* (Genève: Julien, 1967; 1st edn. 1949); and J. Raitt, "Theodore Beza 1519–1605," in *Shapers of Religious Traditions in Germany, Switzerland, and Poland, 1560–1600*, ed. J. Raitt (New Haven: Yale University Press, 1981).

[43] The material content of these letters, as well as a succinct analysis, are to be found in G. Michael Thomas, "Constructing and Clarifying the Doctrine of Predestination: Theodore Beza's Letters During, and in the Wake of the Bolsec Controversy (1551–1555)," *Reformation and Renaissance Review* 4 (2000): 7–28.

[44] A comprehensive study of the Bolsec controversy is P. C. Hohrop, *The Bolsec Controversy on Predestination, from 1551–1555: The Statements of Jerome Bolsec, and the Responses of John Calvin, Theodore Beza, and other Reformed Theologians* (Lewiston, New York: Edwin Mellen, 1993). The manuscript records of the controversy, including letter correspondence among the congregations, are in R. M. Kingdon and J. F. Bergier, eds., *Registres de la Compagnie des Pasteurs de Genève au Temps de Calvin* (Genève: Droz, 1962, 1964), 1:80–131. English translations for the years 1542–1544 are by Wallace McDonald, *Registers of the Consistory of Geneva in the Time of Calvin* (Grand Rapids: Eerdmans, 2000). I find no record of an English version for the years 1551–1555.

Calvin's doctrine of predestination. Calvin was forced to defend his position publicly, and, as Thomas notes, "The correspondence with other Reformed Churches [in Switzerland] reveals a considerable gap between Geneva and most of the others, who showed a lack of enthusiasm for Calvin's persecution of Bolsec and his [Calvin's] insistence on spelling out the doctrine of double predestination in a stark and logical manner."[45] The correspondence exchanged between Heinrich Bullinger and Calvin is especially reflective of this hesitation.[46] Reflective of the tone in much of the correspondence are Bullinger's words cited by Schaff: "Believe me, many are displeased with what you say in your *Institutes* about predestination, and draw the same conclusions from it as Bolsec has drawn from Zwinglis's book on Providence."[47] Schaff goes on to note that when Bullinger wrote the Second Helvetic Confession in 1562, he included the article on predestination affirming divine election but included no mention of reprobation. Calvin was the acknowledged leader of Reformed Christianity in Geneva, and the Zurich church was certainly not inclined to side with Bolsec; however, neither were they in warmhearted agreement with Calvin (or Beza after him) insofar as their teachings implied a stark double predestination—later identified as "supralapsarianism."

In that Beza was Arminius' teacher in Geneva, it is his theological constructions on predestination that interest us most, and Beza's correspondence provides us important insights. The theological logic that we encounter in his correspondence was also worked out in chart form by Beza. In a letter to Bullinger (October 29, 1551), Beza sets out his foundational assumptions regarding the election of believers and the damnation of non-believers:

---

[45] G. Michael Thomas, "Constructing and Clarifying the Doctrine of Predestination," 9.

[46] Written from Zurich, Bullinger's letter of November 27, 1551, admonishes the church in Geneva for not demonstrating moderation and for engaging in unnecessary contention. It then goes on to reprove them for the harshness in tone of the correspondence received from them in Zurich. Cf. Kingdon and Bergier, *Registres*, 1:124–25. Regarding the correspondence between Calvin and Bullinger, see C. P. Venema, "Heinrich Bullinger's Correspondence on Calvin's Doctrine of Predestination," *Sixteenth Century Journal* 17, no. 4 (1986): 435–50.

[47] Philip Schaff, *History of the Christian Church*, 3rd edn. (New York: Charles Scribner's Sons, 1910), 8:618.

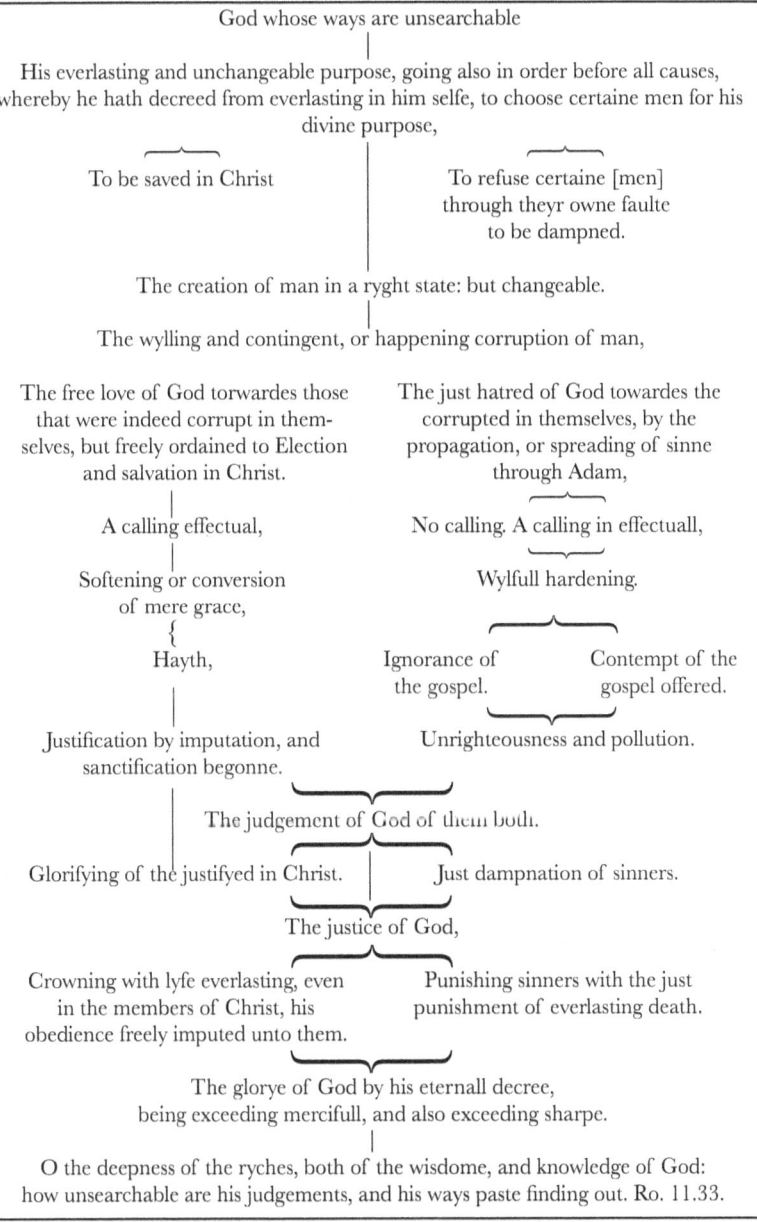

Beza's chart on predestination adapted from Theodore Beza, *The Treasure of Trueth, Touching the ground worke of man, his salvation and chiefest pointes of Christian Religion* (London, 1576), also reproduced in Philip Benedict, *Christian Churches Purely Reformed* (New Haven: Yale University Press, 2002), 106.

If God reprobates someone, he does it because he has foreknown at the same time that he would reject the grace offered to him, which he could have embraced. But, of course, if the Lord reprobates because he foresees unbelief, he also elects because he foresees faith. . . . We say, therefore, that he who abolishes reprobation cannot maintain election. . . . Finally, we say that, as far as the reprobate are concerned, three stages must be distinguished in this ordering of things: reprobation, unbelief (ignorance of God) and eternal death. The same number of stages corresponds to these as far as the elect are concerned: gratuitous election; faith; eternal life.[48]

In the correspondence we encounter references by Beza to Swiss pastoral leaders who find that his delineation of two classes of humanity (elect and non-elect), without reference to the actual act of creation and the subsequent sinful disobedience of humanity, to be an unnecessary and dubious assertion. For those who deem this to be less than reasonable, his response is unequivocal: "If any human mind tries to give some counter argument, I do not listen, and once for all conclude as follows: 'This is the will of God; this is the plan of God, the causes of which, of course, are uncertain and unknown to me. . . . I leave anyone who has learned differently to take his dispute to God.'"[49]

For Beza, and for Calvin as well according to Beza, there is a concern to spell out a doctrine of election with regard to explaining the conversion of specific individual persons. And this must always be explained in terms of divine choice rather than human response to divine overtures—even if that human response is rooted in a grace-enabled ability. Furthermore, the shadow side of the election equation, reprobation, is rooted in divine choice. In Bolsec's onslaught on Calvin's teaching, the issue of God's decision to reprobate specific persons is foundational. Bolsec points out the parallelism between reprobation (damnation of specific individuals) and election (salvation of specific individuals) in Calvin's thought. Bolsec follows a long line

---

[48] Letter from Beza to Bullinger, lines 11–14, 22–26, in Thomas, "Constructing and Clarifying the Doctrine of Predestination," 11, and in Hohrop, *Bolsec Controversy*, 1:725. The corpus of the most pertinent letters are in Hohrop, 1:721–43; and they are partially reproduced in Thomas, "Constructing and Clarifying the Doctrine of Predestination," 11–22.

[49] Letter from Beza to Bullinger, January 12, 1552, lines 50–52, 62–63, in Thomas, "Constructing and Clarifying the Doctrine of Predestination," 13, and in Hohrop, *Bolsec Controversy*, 1:729.

of theologians before and after him who regarded it beneath divine dignity to assert that God should reprobate people with absolutely no consideration of actual sin.[50] It is important to note that in his defense of Calvin's position, Beza does not assert that Bolsec *misrepresented* Calvin by asserting a pure parallelism between reprobation and election. Beza assumes the parallelism to be accurate, and he proceeds under the assumption that if the divine decision to reprobate is conceded, then election to salvation of specific individuals falls also. In other words, if reprobation falls then election falls with it.[51]

Beza is well aware that many of his Reformed colleagues, perhaps even a majority outside the walls of Geneva, are more inclined to an infralapsarianism that takes into account the fall and actual sin on the part of humanity. This might, however, open the door to contingency in the doctrine of election, a door Beza chose to keep closed and locked at all costs. Salvation is purely by divine grace, and that purity is preserved only by conceptualizing election and reprobation as having occurred in the mind of God prior to both creation and the fall:

> Faith is the gift of God. It is necessary for us to be drawn, regenerated and taught. Since these things happen to only a very few, who can deny that particular grace is given to certain men? If it is particular grace, tell me, to whom is it particular? It is to those chosen by God before the foundations of the world were laid, according to his own good plan, that they should be holy, and not because they were going to be holy. Now truly, if they were chosen from eternity, . . . others are reprobated from eternity.[52]

Beza's fundamental theological frame of reference is explicit in this correspondence defending Calvin, actually making explicit some logical implications of Calvin's thought that are at most highly implicit in

---

[50] Cf. Donald W. Sinnema, "The Issue of Reprobation at the Synod of Dort (1618–19) in Light of the History of the Doctrine" (PhD diss., University of St. Michael's College [Toronto School of Theology], 1985).

[51] Cf. Hohrop and Thomas, especially the Letters to Bullinger (October 29, 1551, and January 12, 1552); as well as the Letter to Calvin (January 21, 1552).

[52] Beza to Bullinger (January 12, 1552), lines 18–24, in Thomas, "Constructing and Clarifying the Doctrine of Predestination," 12, and in Hohrop, *Bolsec Controversy*, 1:728. Hohrop's translation of the last line reads: "But now, if they are elected from eternity, then even Jerome, I presume, will affirm that some are reprobated from eternity. If faith is the consequence of election, then unbelief must also find its place after reprobation."

his teachings. It is noteworthy that Calvin did not seem to be inclined to "correct" Beza in his postulations, even though it is generally agreed by scholars that Beza lifted the doctrine of double predestination to a prominence not to be found in Calvin. Indeed, in Beza's hands, double predestination becomes logically an end in itself, worked out rationally in an "order of decrees" preceding the decree of creation. Beza is answering the question whether anything falls outside God's determination, and his answer is an unqualified no. In *Christian Questions*, number 195, Beza asserts,

> Predestination . . . is God's everlasting and unchangeable ordinance, going in order before all the causes of salvation and damnation, whereby God has determined to be glorified, in some by saving them of his own mere grace in Christ, and others by damning them through his rightful justice in Adam and in themselves. And after the custom of scripture we call the former the vessels of glory and the elect or chosen, that is to say, those appointed to salvation from before all worlds through mercy; and the other sort we call reprobates and castaways, and vessels of wrath, that is to say, appointed likewise to rightful damnation from everlasting: both of which God has known severally from time without beginning.[53]

What we encounter here is an incipient hyper-Calvinism, a stark supralapsarianism. Calvin, at least, speaks of predestination with two voices, keeping a constructive dialectic at play in the mystery of salvation. Adam, "by free will had the power, if he so willed, to attain eternal life. . . . Adam could have stood if he wished, seeing that he fell solely by his own will."[54] And yet, "Nor ought it to seem absurd when I say, that God not only foresaw the fall of the first man, and in him the ruin of his posterity; but also at his own pleasure arranged it. For as it belongs to his wisdom to foreknow all future events, so it belongs to his power to rule and govern them by his hand."[55] Consonant with this

---

[53] Theodore Beza, *A Booke of Christian Questions and Answers*, trans. Arthur Golding (London: William How, 1574), 76. See also the modern edition, translated by Kirk Summers, *A Little Book of Christian Questions and Responses* (Allison Park, Penn.: Pickwick Publications, 1986), 84.

[54] John Calvin, *Institutes of the Christian Religion*, trans. Henry Beveridge (Grand Rapids: Eerdmans, 1975), 1.15.8.

[55] Calvin, *Institutes*, 3.23.7. Calvin cites Augustine in support of this stronger statement; however, it should be observed that Augustine's words are strictly speaking

assertion but in contrast to Calvin's nuance, Beza consistently dissolves Calvin's dialectic and speaks in terms of a singular unified scheme. Since God has decreed a priori the salvation of some and the damnation of others, it is then necessary that

> Man should be so created good that notwithstanding he should be mutable and fall from this degree and that by his own good fault. For if sin had not so entered the world, God had not found such cause to magnify his mercy in saving those which he has ordained to salvation, nor matter to declare his justice in condemning those which he has ordained to his wrath to the end that he may punish them for their demerits.[56]

With individual specificity, God decided before all time those who would be damned as well as who would believe (irrespective also of divine foreknowledge, although certainly known by God!), and whoever has a problem with this divine scheme should take it up with God. There is little doubt that this is the predestinarian theology at play in Geneva under Beza's oversight when Arminius studied there, and as Bangs says, "It was the insistence on the details of his system as essential to Reformed orthodoxy which had a great deal to do with the precipitation of the so-called Arminian controversy."[57]

Arminius interrupted his studies in Geneva to go to Basel for a time, but it is not known to us whether his decision to take a break from Geneva was rooted in the theology he was taught. What he heard in Geneva was certainly a "stricter" version of Reformed theology than he had been taught at Leiden by Feuguereus and Coolhaes. What we do know is that already in Geneva, and then with focused attention in Basel, Arminius studied and taught the logic of Peter Ramus—a logic inclined more toward practical reason than abstract constructions—a form of reasoning not held in high esteem in Geneva. Bangs relates that Arminius' propagation of Ramist logic incurred the displeasure not so much of Beza as the staunch Aristotelian, Petrus

---

about foreknowledge, not about the predetermination of specific events. Arminius would quickly affirm the words cited from Augustine.

[56] Theodore Beza, *A Briefe and Pithie Summe of the Christian Faith*, trans. R. F. (London: Roger Ward, 1589), 7. Various editions are accessible on EEBO, and the pagination differs. This citation comes under Trinity, The Third Point, "Of Jesus Christ," no. 8: "It was *necessary* that man should fall from his puritie" (emphasis added).

[57] Bangs, 68.

Galesius (Pierre Galez). As a result, Arminius probably left Geneva for Basel in the summer of 1583.[58]

Peter Ramus (Pierre de la Ramée, 1515–1572) was by the age of twenty-one rather famous for his critique of strict Aristotelian logic. A fable perhaps, but quite well known, is the story that his Master's thesis in 1536 was rooted in a single proposition: "All that Aristotle said is false." Since the panel of judges were all Aristotelians, they would have been guilty of the Aristotelian fallacy of "begging the question" if they used Aristotelian logic to refute Ramus. Hence, as the story goes, Ramus not only passed his thesis defense but at the same time made for himself quite a name. The modern reader will readily recognize that Ramus was quite Aristotelian in many respects, but, as Bangs notes, his intemperate attacks on Aristotle's logic took place "in an age of violent academic partisanship, and any modification of Aristotle at all could be expected to take an extreme form."[59] The consequence for such attacks could be most grave—as is reflected in the fact that Ramus died tragically (most likely murdered) in 1572.[60]

Ramus advocated a move away from the strict practice of Aristotelian logic. With regard to formal logic, he reduced the number of allowed valid syllogisms in an attempt to make logic a more "practical" discipline. Ramus advocated starting with a broad general statement before proceeding to less general and finally to particular assertions. The syllogistic approach is certainly Aristotelian,[61] but the goal for Ramus is not simply a rationally deduced conclusion. It is rather a series of logical moves from the general practical statement to some practical end. In this vein Arminius' appropriation of Ramus is in the spirit of a *sapida scientia* ("savory knowledge"), assuming that the best knowledge could be "felt and applied." Indeed, it had been this move that was foundational to the intellectual environment that produced

---

[58] Bangs, 71. Note that Dekker, *Rijker dan Midas*, 266–67, argues against this conclusion by Bangs on the evidence that Galesius may not have been lecturing at that time in Geneva.

[59] Bangs, 57, following the scholarship of F. P. Graves, *Peter Ramus and the Educational Reform of the Sixteenth Century* (New York: Macmillan, 1912), 365.

[60] Charles Waddington, *Ramus, sa Vie, ses Ecrits et ses Opinions* (Paris: Librairie de Ch. Meyruels et Cᵉ, Editeurs, 1855), 258ff.

[61] See the Ramist charts in Bangs, 58.

the Protestant Reformation.[62] The influence of *sapida scientia* as a governing frame of reference was mediated in the Lowlands through the Brethren of the Common Life and most especially through Erasmus of Rotterdam. Genuine theological knowledge (harkening back to St. Augustine) was a *habitus*, a way of thinking that could not be separated from a way of living. It touched the heart, enlightened the mind, and made one charitable.[63] Arminius' fondness for the practical bent of Ramist logic moved him increasingly in the direction of theological reasoning inclined toward "savory knowledge." Arminius understood well that doctrine (*doctrina*) had connotational roots in the history of the church as religious teaching that enables one to be a good Christian. Following Augustine's *De doctrina Christiana*, true doctrine was to be taught in a manner both faithful to Scripture and "efficacious" in the lives of the faithful.[64] He knew as well that the scholastics had moved doctrine in the direction of *scientia*, a science characterized by logical disputation. To be sure, Arminius was a full participant in disputational theology, but he reflects at the same time a desire that theology be practical.[65] It made less and less sense for him to affirm a remotely decided scheme of predestination that was devised as an abstraction in the mind of God prior to lived existence. It was not that he could not grasp the logical scheme; it was rather that he came to distrust this epistemic system as an end in itself. Arminius judged the system to be inadequate to the object of its attention; indeed, it was beneath the dignity of God for theologians to propose such a notion of God at all. The double predestinarian scheme, as well as the character of God it implied, was increasingly offensive to Arminius.

As we shall note regarding his years in Amsterdam as a pastor, when Arminius was assigned the task of refuting those who called

---

[62] Cf. Heiko Oberman, *The Harvest of Medieval Theology* (Grand Rapids: Eerdmans, 1963).

[63] Cf. James D. Tracy, *Erasmus of the Low Countries* (Berkeley: University of California Press, 1996), esp. 55–57.

[64] St. Augustine, *On Christian Doctrine*, trans. R. P. H. Green (New York: Oxford University Press, 1997).

[65] Stanglin, 91ff. Indeed, his monograph argues for Arminius' theology being inclined toward the "practical." For Stanglin, this is especially important for the believer's assurance of salvation. He argues that Arminius is intent to counteract the "desperation" a believer experiences when assurance is unavailable, as is the case with all forms of supralapsarian soteriology.

Beza's scheme of double predestination into question, Arminius began by preaching an extended series of exegetical sermons on Romans. Indeed, as a student he had already made a first run at these expositions under the tutelage of J. J. Grynaeus in Basel. We know that Grynaeus shared Arminius' sympathy for Ramism, but we do not know what form Arminius' exegesis of Paul's letter took under Grynaeus' supervision. Details of their correspondence are scant, but we do know that Arminius remained in contact with the Basel professor when he returned to Geneva and also during later years back in Holland.

In Geneva there is another professor whose potential influence on Arminius is often overlooked, namely, Charles Perrot. He taught theology and presided at the student disputations on theological propositions. It seems that Perrot openly disagreed with Beza's extreme position on predestination and grace. He is quoted as saying: "Justification by faith has been preached up too much; it is time to speak about works."[66] Perrot's irenic spirit is reflected in advice to Arminius' friend Uytenbogaert prior to his departing Geneva to return to the Netherlands:

> Never assist in condemning any for not agreeing in every point of religion with the established church, so long as they adhere to the fundamentals of Christianity, and are disposed to maintain the peace of the Church, and bear with other of their brethren who do not reject the fundamentals of religion, though a little differing from them. For this is the way to avoid schism, and to arrive at the pious union and tranquility of the Christian Church.[67]

Arminius was highly thought of in Basel by a recognized leading faculty member, Grynaeus.[68] Arminius presented no less than eight public disputations in Basel (more than any other student during that period), and the majority of the disputations received an evaluation from Grynaeus noting "superlative performance."[69] Student disputations were generally followed by summary statements by the presiding

---

[66] Reported by Isaac Casaubon, professor of Greek at Geneva from 1582 to 1596, cited in a conversation with Uytenbogaert (April 20, 1610), from a letter to Uytenbogaert in Brandt, *History*, 2:72.

[67] Brandt, *History*, 2:72.

[68] *Rijker dan Midas*, 25–26.

[69] *Rijker dan Midas*, 343, cites Grynaeus, *Disputationes theologicae* (1584).

professor, perhaps offering a "definitive answer" to the presenting issue. At the disputation presented by Arminius on September 6, 1582, Grynaeus seems to have allowed Arminius a final word: "Let the Dutchman answer for me."[70] Grynaeus also appointed Arminius to lecture in his place during the "harvest holiday." Arminius lectured on the book of Romans. Grynaeus was in attendance at the lectures, and he afterward wrote in a letter that he was quite pleased with Arminius' performance.[71]

Before Arminius returned to the land of his birth in 1587, he traveled to Italy with a law student friend of his, Adrian Junius.[72] Arminius went to the university at Padua specifically to hear the famed Jacopo Zabarello.[73] Although Padua is not well known to the modern reader, in Arminius' day it was *the* place to study in Italy.[74] What Arminius actually encountered or may have learned during these brief months in Italy is not clear, so conjectures about such remain just that: opinions not rooted in good historical analysis. What we do know is that lots of conjectures were offered. Upon his return to the Lowlands, the trip to the heart of Roman Catholicism was used by his enemies against him—accusing him of kissing the ring of the Pope, implying inclinations toward Rome. The error of the youthful Arminius regarding Italy was not along religious but rather along personal, political lines. He did not ask the permission of his Amsterdam benefactors before making the journey, although it is quite likely that permission would have been granted. The fact that he did not "ask" was later used against him to imply devious design.

His return from Italy went by way of a return to Geneva, but Arminius was bidding Switzerland farewell. It is the opinion of F. J. Los that the Italian sojourn was "a disaster," and he is also convinced that Arminius was really no longer a true Calvinist when he assumed the pastorate in Amsterdam.[75] About this there is a range of opinion.

---

[70] *Rijker dan Midas*, 25; and Uytenbogaert, *Historie*, 312 (note: 1647 edn., with sequential pagination).

[71] *Rijker dan Midas*, 25n31.

[72] Peter Bertius, "Funeral Oration," in *Works*, 1:25–26.

[73] Cf. W. F. Edwards, "The Logic of Jacopo Zabarello (1533–1589)" (PhD diss., Columbia University, 1960), esp. chap. 1.

[74] Cf. *Rijker dan Midas*, 270n90.

[75] F. J. Los, *Grepen uit de Geschiedenis van Hervormd Amsterdam* (Amsterdam: J. R. Vrolijk, 1929), 52.

Generally speaking, there may be some warrant for Los' sentiment, if being a true Calvinist meant being in total sympathy with Beza's extreme predestinarian scheme. When Arminius arrived in Amsterdam in the fall of 1587, what might he have brought with him as residual effects of his years in Geneva? The words of Carl Bangs are tantalizing:

> Even during Arminius' stay in Geneva there were students who dissented from Beza's rigid Calvinism. Uytenbogaert has been mentioned; there were also Joannes Halsbergius, Cornelis Royenburgh, and the moderate Calvinists Franciscus Junius, Werner Helmichius, Jeremias Bastingius, Johannes Becius, Thysius, Adrianus Lymphaius, and Johannes Polyander. Geneva continued to produce opponents of strict Calvinism after Arminius had finished his work there, including Jacob de Graeff, Vorstius, Adriaan van der Mijle, Theophilus Rickwaert, Henricus Leo, Isaacus Diamantius, Nicolas Grevinchovius, Cornelius Burchvliet, Daniel Wittius, the later Remonstrant professor Stephanus Curcellaeus (de Courcelles), Johannes Arnoldus Corvinus, and Niclaes van Sorgen—all in the days of Beza himself. De Vries has called Geneva the "seedbed of Dutch Calvinism." It is almost as fitting to call it the "seedbed of Dutch Arminianism."[76]

This is, of course, an arguable point. The student who left Geneva to pastor in Amsterdam would soon be faced with the responsibility of spelling out what "Calvinism" was in his own land. He likely had a pretty good idea what it meant in Geneva and some other parts of Switzerland—but what did it mean in the Netherlands?

---

[76] Bangs, 77.

3

AMSTERDAM PASTOR (1587–1603)
and the
"FIRST ARMINIAN CONTROVERSY"

When Arminius went to Amsterdam, what kind of church did he pastor? Well, of course, it was Reformed theologically, but what did "Reformed" mean in Holland in 1587? The United Netherlands was a small country, but we will inquire whether theological inclinations were rather different in North Holland than in South Holland. Also, what were the dominant narratives in the recent history of a church in Amsterdam at this time? Even, one must ask, what did it mean for a clergyman to be confessionally Reformed? This related set of questions is crucial to an informed understanding of Arminius and the development of his thought during the first decade of his ministry. Indeed, the foundational lines of Arminius' theological trajectory were worked out during the years of his Amsterdam pastorate. Also, during those years of theological maturation, Arminius worked in conversation with multiple ecclesial, political, and social narratives that were crucial to Dutch life: the role of the Christian magistrates (city officials) in maintaining the welfare of the church (i.e., supervising care for the poor, maintaining church buildings, appointing ministers, paying their salaries, and assessing their effectiveness); the autonomy of the consistory (church council) that met as often as once a month; and the classis ("presbytery," a gathering of clergy representatives from other congregations in geographic proximity) that met every one to three months. Add to these the manner in which the Belgic Confession and the Heidelberg Catechism were to be used and the republican nature of the national government. Although not directly pertinent to our topic, Arminius had to deal with ongoing issues related to the prosecution and winding down of the war with Spain and the relative positions of the civil and military arms of the government. This constellation of complicated issues led Carl Bangs to refer to Amsterdam as Arminius' other alma mater, an appropriate word play given the ways in which the Amsterdam period was formative for Arminius at every level.[1] Interesting to note, the issue of predestination is not to be found among the many complex concerns that Arminius faced initially as a pastor.

Arminius arrived in Holland in the fall of 1587, reporting to the classis of Amsterdam on October 5. Even though both regional lay and clergy delegates were appointed to the classis, only clergy delegates were in attendance: ministers from Weesp, Loenen, Loosdrecht, Naarden, Muiden, Saerdam, and Amsterdam. The classis of Amsterdam would have had in hand the letters of commendation from Beza and Grynaeus in Switzerland. The classis' vote in favor of Arminius was unanimous.[2]

After the classis, Arminius appeared before the consistory (*Kerkeraad*) on November 12. The minutes report that the consistory was pleased, and they conveyed their approval to the local magistrates, the Amsterdam burgomasters.[3] The consistory met again early in February and heard the report that Arminius had been fully examined by the classis and was "well qualified" to be admitted to the ministry. After further examination on their part, the consistory ordered that he proceed to the preaching of a trial sermon on Sunday, February 7, 1588. It was further noted that the Amsterdam burgomasters were to be informed of the ecclesial decisions, and that Arminius would be appearing before the magistrates for their approval.[4] It is important to note that the Amsterdam church leaders did not strictly follow the Synod of Emden (1571) or the Synod of The Hague (1586) in their specific provisions that pastors would be called without *any* participation by the Christian magistrates. In Amsterdam the protocol was for the call to proceed "provided the burgomasters made no objections."

---

[1] Bangs, 83–109.

[2] *Protocollen*, 1:354 (October 5, 1587). From the manuscript entry in the *Protocollen*, it might be inferred that the classis' approval was February 1, 1588; however, it is more likely that the later date was the final approval of Arminius for appointment *after* the consistory process and the trial sermon, etc. Cf. Bangs, 110n3; and F. J. Los, *Grepen uit de Geschiedenis van Hervormd Amsterdam* (Amsterdam: J. R. Vrolijk, 1929), 52. Note: Bang's reference to 1:34 in note 3 as a reference to October 5, 1587, is problematic, as 1:34 refers to the year 1581. The minutes for October 5, 1587, are in 1:354–55. I suggest that Bangs' citation is a typographical error: 3[5]4.

[3] *Protocollen*, 1:361 (November 12, 1587).

[4] *Protocollen*, 1:370 (February 4, 1488).

None were made, and Arminius was confirmed as a *proponent*, candidate for pastor in Amsterdam.[5]

This seemingly small detail about the relationship between the consistory and the burgomasters is a window into the complicated ways in which politics and ecclesial life were inextricably intertwined. When one takes into account the pronouncements of the Synod of Emden and The Hague, combined with the requisite acceptable interpretation of the Belgic Confession,[6] it is apparent that potentially explosive amalgamations were at play. As a pastor, the two issues that Arminius could not avoid were the interpretation of the Belgic Confession and the relationship between church and state. These two were literally part and parcel of ministering on the larger ecclesial stage of Amsterdam, but we must also note that there were two quite different interpretations of these issues represented in the persons of Prince Maurits (Maurice) and Johan van Oldenbarnevelt. There was the more open-minded perspective called *rekkelijk*, and there was a more narrowly conceived set of interpretations labeled *precies*. In the earliest days of the republic, Prince William of Orange (William the Silent) was known to support the *rekkelijk* position. When William was assassinated at Delft in 1584, Prince Maurits (primarily a man of military expertise and perhaps not as politically perceptive and adept as his father) was appointed in 1585 as *Stadholder*, "lieutenant."[7] Upon the death of his

---

[5] In 1617 three decades later, in the heat of the controversies leading up to the Synod of Dort, a quite different version of Arminius' examination and call to the Amsterdam pastorate appears. Cf. Bangs, 111–13. By this time, with Plancius in the lead, Amsterdam, always the most influential congregation, became a gathering place for the more combative ministers to meet. These joined ranks to insist on a national synod to bring the Arminians (Remonstrants) in line. Cf. J. Keuning, *Petrus Plancius: Theoloog en Geograaf* (Amsterdam: van Kampen & Zoon, 1946), 44–47.

[6] The Belgic Confession was composed in 1559 by the French Protestant, Guido de Brès—assisted among others by Adrian Saravia, who took it to Geneva for approval. When it was not approved, it was nonetheless published in Rouen, France, in 1561. In 1563, Dutch and German editions appeared, and in 1566 slightly abbreviated editions appeared in Dutch and German. Cf. Gootjes, *Confession*.

[7] It is not logical to the modern reader that a "lieutenant" should function as national leader, but the Netherlands owed huge war debts to England. The politics are complicated, and it was in fact Robert Dudley, Earl of Leicester, who led the triumphal process through the Netherlands after the defeat of the Spanish. Cf. Jeremy Dupertuis Bangs, *Strangers and Pilgrims, Travellers and Sojourners: Leiden and the Foundations of Plymouth Plantation* (Plymouth, Mass.: General Society of Mayflower Descendants, 2009), 132–33.

older brother, Maurits acquired the title Prince of Orange and served as sovereign over the United Provinces. He moved steadily away from William's position supportive of the *rekkelijken*, and by the time of Arminius' later ministry in Amsterdam, Maurits seems to have had strong sympathy for the precisionists, who insisted that the church be empowered to order all its affairs without "interference" from the magistrates. Added to this insistence was the assumption that all the clergy engaged in such decisions were understood by the precisionists to be under the discipline of a binding doctrinal confession. After the death of Arminius, as we shall see, Maurits embodied these ecclesial preferences (adopted increasingly for calculated reasons) in a set of politically motivated decisions.

With this as a background, it is clear that the Amsterdam classis and consistory's sending their favorable recommendation of Arminius to the city magistrates for approval was a nod in the direction of the more liberally inclined *rekkelijken*.[8] Maurits' move to the precisionist side did not leave the more liberal side without strong representation in high political office, for the *landsadvocaat* (attorney general), Johan van Oldenbarnevelt, was decidedly inclined to less strict interpretative stances. If not openly a declared Arminian, he certainly never inveighed against the *rekkelijk* Arminians. Indeed, throughout North Holland (much less the case in South Holland), a strong majority of magistrates and a significant contingency of clergy were counted among the *rekkelijken*. The case has been made that the *rekkelijken* held the high ground of being the original shapers of Dutch Protestant ecclesial and political life, while the *preciezen* were the reactionary "late comers." It was not unusual to hear, "Wij waren er eerder dan gij!" (We were here ahead of you!)[9] While the issue of who came first and who got it right remains a warmly contested issue among historians, article 13 of the Union of Utrecht (1579), a document that united the provinces as a Protestant stronghold in the northern Lowlands, was unambiguous in its language about religious freedom: "Every particular person shall remain free in his religion, and no one will be pursued or investigated

---

[8] Cf. T. G. Kootte, ed., *Rekkelijk of Precies. Remonstranten en contraremonstranten ten tijde van Maurits en Oldenbarnevelt* (Utrecht: Rijksmuseum Het Catharijnenconvent, 1994).

[9] Cf. Marthe F. de Vries, "'Wij waren er eerder dan gij.' De historische legitimatie van de Remonstranten zoals door Johannes Uytenbogaert gegeven in zijn *Kerckeliike Historie*" (Doctorandus scriptie, Leiden University, 1988).

because of religion."[10] Even though these assertions applied explicitly to the province of Holland, and they were not accepted and applied universally across the United Provinces,[11] this document consciously followed the Pacification of Ghent (1576). The Union document was fundamentally a document of pacification between Protestants and Roman Catholics, and it is not technically correct to call it a Constitution for the United Provinces, although in many ways it functioned as such. The grand ideal of religious toleration enshrined therein, for which Holland eventually became famous, proved exceedingly difficult to "live into" initially. It succeeded remarkably well in pacifying Protestants versus Roman Catholics, but it did not do so well for many decades amid conflicts between *precies* and *rekkelijk* Calvinist Protestants. Even though the first national synod at Emden in 1571 favored a stronger role for the consistory (as it was coming from Geneva) in the call and placement of pastors, there was strong sentiment among the clergy in North Holland to push back against strict Genevan orthodoxy—favoring instead the writings of Bullinger, Melanchthon, Anastasius Veluanus,[12] and especially the sentiments of Erasmus on toleration.[13] There was in this period a genuine ambivalence about which direction to lean theologically and ecclesially.[14]

Tensions ran high about who came first and who got it right, and the tensions played themselves out publicly in strife between Prince Maurits and Oldenbarnevelt. In the final analysis, "might proved to

---

[10] Cf. *Unie, Eeuyvich Verbond ende Eendracht* (Utrecht: Coenraet Hendricksz., 1579) [Pamphlet, University Library of Utrecht, RARIORA.br.oct.75]. A modern edition may be found in Simon Groenveld, *Unie, Bestand, Vrede: Drie Fundamentele Wetten van de Republiek der Verenigde Nederlanden* (Hilversum: Verloren, 2009).

[11] Cf. Jeremy Dupertuis Bangs, "Dutch Contributions to Religious Tolerance," *Church History* 9, no. 3 (2010): 589–90.

[12] Ioannes Anastasius Veluanus, *Kort bericht in allen principalen punten des Christen geloves . . . und in des halven genant der leken wechwyser* (1554), in *Bibliotheca Reformatoria Neerlandica: Geschriften uit den tijd der hervorming in de Nederlanden*, ed. S. Cramer and F. Pijper (The Hague: M. Nijhoff, 1906), 4:123–76.

[13] Cf. Carl Bangs, "Arminius and the Reformation," *Church History* 30 (1961): 159.

[14] Cf. Alisdaire Duke, "The Ambivalent Face of Calvinism in the Netherlands, 1561–1618," in *International Calvinism, 1541–1715*, ed. Menna Prestwich (New York: Oxford University Press, 1985), 109–34; Joseph Leclerc, *Toleration and the Reformation* (New York: Association Press, 1960), 2:256ff.; and J. Lindeboom, "Erasmus' Bedeutung für die Entwicklung des Geistigen Lebens in den Niederlanden," *Archiv für Reformationsgeschichte* (1952): 43:1–12.

be right" (or at the least the winner). In 1618 Oldenbarnevelt was convicted of treason on trumped-up charges, and he was publicly beheaded at the age of seventy-one in the center of parliament (*Binnenhof*) in The Hague—having served his country for thirty-three years as attorney general.[15] While this was during the decade after the death of Arminius in 1609, the trial and execution were part and parcel of concerted attempts to remove the Arminians from every level of government and positions of influence in society. Once again, I am getting ahead of my story, but the point is clear: during Arminius' day, the admixture of religion and politics was a deadly concoction.

When Arminius began as a *proponent* (ministerial candidate on trial) conducting evening worship services in the Old Church of Amsterdam on February 7, 1588, his duties were to lead prayers and preach. The leading of these evening services continued for several months, and in July the formal consideration of his call and ordination was taken up again by the consistory. On July 21, the call of Arminius was unanimously approved, and his name was forwarded to the city, subject to the approval of the burgomasters.[16] One week later, on July 28, it was reported back to the consistory that the burgomasters had given their consent. With permission from the consistory Arminius was out of town, so the meeting to confirm his call did not take place until August 11. On that date, the consistory minutes confirm Arminius' call to be a pastor in Amsterdam. It was further noted that his ordination would take place at the time of the next communion service.[17] Bangs relates that for each communion celebration there was a service of preparation on the Saturday night before. This means that Arminius would have been ordained on Saturday evening, August 27, 1588.[18]

F. J. Los, typically inclined to be suspicious of Arminius and all things later called Arminian, raises questions about the sequence of events related to Arminius' ordination, and he also opens the door to the query whether, following the strict protocols of the *preciezen*, Arminius was required to sign the Belgic Confession.[19] During the years that

---

[15] For the life and influence of Oldenbarnevelt, see Jan den Tex's massive five volume *Oldenbarnevelt* (Haarlem: Tjeenk Willink, 1960–1972), and John L. Motley, *Het leven en sterven van Johan van Oldenbarnevelt* ('s Gravenhage: W. P. van Stockum, 1874).

[16] *Protocollen*, 1:404–5 (July 21, 1588).

[17] *Protocollen*, 1:409 (August 11, 1558).

[18] Bangs, 115.

[19] F. J. Los, *Grepen uit de Geschiedenis*, 55, 67. During his years as a pastor in

Amsterdam had been formally Protestant (since 1578), nine clergy had been called; however, they had all been previously ordained elsewhere. Arminius seems to have been the first to engage the entire ordination process in Amsterdam as a *proponent*.[20] There is no way to know whether the previous ministers had signed the Belgic Confession at the time of their ordination (although it is possible, depending on the town and classis), but there is no record in the *Protocollen* of the Amsterdam consistory that the question was even put to Arminius. Johannes Hallius, who came in 1581, seems to have been the only Amsterdam minister whose signature on the Belgic Confession is confirmed by the *Protocollen*. In connection with Arminius, is it the case that this never was a strict practice, or was this a case of forgetfulness on their part; or, was it the case that, in Bangs' words, "the practice had evidently been dropped" in Amsterdam?[21] Since the consistory minutes, usually very detailed in their record keeping, reflect that neither ministers nor deacons nor elders raised the issue about Arminius' signing the confession, perhaps the most reasonable conclusion is that the *rekkelijk* spirit typified the consistory. This does not mean that they did not hold the Belgic Confession in high esteem, but rather that they were confident their examination of Arminius and their experience of hearing him preach over several months had adequately revealed his clear gospel teaching. It may also have been the case that the Amsterdam consistory was aware that the authors of the Belgic Confession never intended it to be viewed strictly as a *regula fidei* to which signatures needed to be attached.[22] Plancius' biographer makes the point emphatically: "The earliest Reformers in our land did not possess a formal confession of

---

Amsterdam, Los evidently scoured the records of the Amsterdam Reformed Church looking for evidence that Arminius signed the Belgic Confession. Several times he poses the question, but he concludes that there is no record that he ever did—neither in a session of the classis or in a meeting of the consistory. He then points out in a minatory tone: "No one ever seems to have pointed this out to Arminius" (69). Arminius explicitly contradicts this in his *Declaration* (see p. 101, below).

[20] Cf. *Protocollen*, 1:89; *Amsterdam*, 1:155; F. J. Los, *Grepen uit de Geschiedenis*, 67–68. More accessible to the English reader is a succinct overview of these issues in Bangs, 116–19.

[21] Bangs, 116.

[22] Cf. Maronier, 78; and Christiaan Sepp, *Het Godgeleerd Onderwijs in Nederland* (Leiden, 1873), 1:265. Sepp, quoting an original composer of the confession, asserts: "Not one among us who had a hand in its composition ever intended this to be a rule of faith, but rather an affirmation of our faith as discerned from Scriptures."

faith, only the teaching of the gospel. In [the town of] Wezel, requiring a signature to the Confession was out of the question, whereas in Emden, it was required." He goes on to confirm that the original framers of the Belgic Confession explicitly warned against "mixing human and divine writings." This warning was dropped in the 1581 edition of the confession, and "ever so slowly the Gospel was no longer the primary guide for faith, being replaced with human explanations of the Gospel. In this process, religious compulsion eventually replaced freedom of conscientious interpretation."[23]

Bangs relates that there were probably five other ministers serving in Amsterdam at the time of Arminius' ordination, and of those five, four could be described as "moderate" Calvinists: Johannes Cuchlinus (Arminius' uncle by a later marriage in 1596),[24] Johannes Hallius,[25] Everhardus Hermanii,[26] and Johannes Ambrosius.[27] The fifth minister, Petrus Plancius,[28] was definitely counted among the *preciezen*, and he would prove to be for many years a thorn in the side of Arminius. Given his disposition, one cannot but wonder why Plancius did not raise the issue about Arminius not signing the Belgic Confession. Even if he felt that Arminius was safe, it was still a matter of proper procedure according to the Synods of Emden and The Hague. At the suggestion of other ministers at later dates, he was bold to accuse Arminius on several issues. Perhaps he would have been a solitary voice at Arminius' ordination, or perhaps he simply acquiesced to the positive, affirming spirit in which the ordination of Arminius was carried out.

When Arminius began participating in the regular preaching rotation, he would have preached in the Old Church as well as the New Church, but it is likely that most of his preaching was at the Old Church—the center of Amsterdam church life.[29] An important part played by a select group of listeners was to adjudicate the doctrinal soundness of the preaching. The ministers who were not preaching, as

---

[23] Keuning, *Petrus Plancius*, 16.
[24] *NNBW*, 2:353.
[25] *BWPGN*, 3:463–65.
[26] Everhardus Hermanii remains an obscure figure for whom I have not been able to locate a biographical essay.
[27] *NNBW*, 1:108.
[28] *BLGNP*, 1:291–95; *NNBW*, 4:1077.
[29] Bangs, 125.

well as the deacons, would sit in specially reserved seats in the front of the sanctuary. Any perceived deviation from sound doctrine became an agenda item at the regularly held consistory meeting the following Thursday. Bangs asserts, "By all accounts, Arminius was a popular preacher and was favored especially by the group which constituted the ruling element in Amsterdam, the merchant-regents who were the burgomasters and the council members."[30] With typical rhetorical flourish, Bertius offers the perspective: "Even the ministers and preachers of that city, the whole of them learned and eloquent men, rendered homage to his erudition, by ingenuously acknowledging that every time when they enjoyed the privilege of sitting under his ministry, they derived the greatest profit from his sermons."[31] In earlier years, it is reported that sermons may have lasted up to four hours; however, in Arminius' day, the expectation was approximately an hour and a half—only one hour on days when the city burgomasters announced a meeting afterward. The modern reader cannot help but wonder whether a sermon of one hour rather than four would not contribute to one's popularity.

Rather early on during his tenure, Arminius found himself in tedious circumstances. These were not a direct consequence of his preaching, but rather due to an external request to defend Genevan orthodoxy on the point of predestination. An exact sequence of events is difficult to ascertain with certainty, for there are a multiplicity of accounts that have survived.[32] In the minds of Arminius' less charitable accusers, he was cut from the same "liberal" bolt of cloth as Caspar Janszoon Coolhaes (pastor in Leiden during Arminius' student days) and Dirck Volckertszoon Coornhert, brought to Leiden by the city magistrates at that same time to write a defense of the magistrate's position regarding the role of magistrates in ecclesial matters.[33]

---

[30] Bangs 126.

[31] Bertius, "Funeral Oration," *Works*, 1:29.

[32] Bertius, "Funeral Oration," *Works*, 1:29ff.; Brandt, *Life*, 61ff.; Uytenbogaert, *Historie*, pt. 3, pp. 103ff.; Maronier, 60ff.; and Bangs, 138–52.

[33] See previous discussion, pp. 22–24. Coornhert had been brought into the Coolhaes fray in Leiden to defend the Erastian sentiments of the magistrates. After this, he and Coolhaes were often viewed as "two peas from the same bad pod." At the Synod of Middelburg in 1581, Coornhert's theological opinions were condemned. Cf. H. Bonger, *Leven en Werk van D. V. Coornhert* (Amsterdam: G. A. van Oorschot, 1978), 97–105.

During his Amsterdam pastorate, when Arminius' name began to be connected in negative ways with Coolhaes and Coornhert, the conflict had moved from defining Erastian-informed church polity to defining predestination. With specificity, Arminius was requested to support the doctrine of supralapsarian predestination put forward by his former teacher, Beza. Two ministers at Delft, Arent Cornelisz. and Reynier Donteklok, in the ongoing disputes that arose in connection with the troublesome Coornhert (troublesome to the strict *precies* Calvinists), published a piece that attempted to modify Beza's supralapsarian position into a more acceptable infralapsarian doctrine of predestination.[34]

It seems that Arminius was requested, both by his consistory in Amsterdam and then later by Professor Martinus Lydius, to write an apologetic defending Beza. Lydius had been a minister in Amsterdam until 1583, at which time he went to the newly established academy at Franeker in Friesland. By all accounts, Arminius was open to setting out his own thoughts on the issue, even if he did not intend to simply defend Beza's supralapsarianism. This is where the converging story lines in the various accounts are in conflict. In his "Funeral Oration," Bertius asserts that when Arminius began setting out his theology of predestination, he was a supporter of his former mentor:

> But while he was contriving a proper refutation, and had begun accurately to weigh the arguments on both sides, and to compare different passages of scripture together . . . he was conquered by the force of truth, and, at first, became a convert to the very opinions which he had been requested to combat and refute [infralapsarianism]. But he afterwards disapproved of them, as promulgated by the brethren of Delft, because he did not think the doctrine contained in them to be correct according to the scriptures. . . . [and finally he] turned towards those

---

[34] R. Donteklok and A. Cornelisz., *Responsio ad argumenta quadam Bezae et Calvini ex Tractatu de praedestinatione, in caput IX ad Romanus* [An answer to some of the arguments adduced by Beza and Calvin, from a treatise concerning predestination, on the ninth chapter of the Epistle to the Romans] (1589). This volume is referred to repeatedly by historians; however, I have not located a copy in any library. It is anachronistic to apply these terms to sixteenth century disputes, as they did not become customary until the seventeenth century, specifically during and after the Synod of Dort (1618–1619). At the risk of oversimplification, "supralapsarianism" may be interpreted to mean that God's decision to predestine took place prior to the fall; "infralapsarianism" infers predestination within the context of humanity's falling into sin. In both cases, these divine decisions took place in the mind of God prior to creation.

opinions which he finally embraced, and which to the close of his life he constantly maintained.[35]

The opinion of Bertius was taken over uncritically by James Nichols in the translation of Arminius' *Works*. In appendix E to the volume, Nichols embellishes the process by which Arminius changed his mind: "When further light from heaven was communicated to him, he abandoned without regret the sublapsarian scheme which he had recently embraced, and [he] entrenched himself within the scriptural stronghold of General Redemption."[36] Then Nichols goes even further to certify the magnitude of this supposed change of mind: "Arminius parted from the supralapsarian doctrines, which he had imbibed in his very boyhood, and which were afterwards confirmed and fixed in him by the authority and persuasive eloquence of the venerable Beza, who had magnified them into such importance as to make the recognition of them and of all their eventful consequences a *sine qua non* to salvation."[37]

This all sounds quite logical; however, it is a marvelous example of how a story twice-told eventually bears little resemblance to the events themselves. We have no record that supralapsarianism was "imbibed in his boyhood." Indeed, it is quite unlikely. Keep in mind that what it meant to be Protestant during Arminius' youth had nothing to do with disputes about the finer points of Reformed doctrine; it was about *not* being Roman Catholic. When Arminius was growing up, no more than one in ten people in the Netherlands openly identified themselves as Protestant, for there was considerable ambivalence among the general population about leaving the Roman fold.[38] There is also the fact that both of Arminius' adoptive parents after the death of his family were recently Roman Catholics in their personal history. When Rudolphus Snellius took the young Arminius with him to Germany, it was to the University of Marburg—a university whose guiding theological light was Philip Melanchthon. It was with Melanchthon's views on predestination that Arminius' own declared views would later be compared and identified by many. In short, there is nothing in Arminius' life story to support Bertius' and Nichols' fanciful accounts. In the

---

[35] Bertius, "Funeral Oration," 1:30.
[36] *Works*, 1:63.
[37] *Works*, 1:65.
[38] Alistair Duke, "Ambivalent Face of Calvinism," 109.

opinion of Carl Bangs, "There is no clear evidence that Arminius had ever accepted Beza's doctrine of predestination and its concomitants. Secondly, he [Arminius] makes no point of having undergone a theological transition."[39] Granting that Bangs is likely correct, this does not answer the question why Arminius was asked by both Lydius and his own consistory to take on both Coornhert and the Delft ministers in their mutually opposing positions. Lydius may have simply assumed that Arminius, so recently returned from Geneva, would be a mirror reflection of Beza on predestination—clearly a false assumption. In a letter that he wrote after the fact to Uytenbogaert, Arminius confides that for no less than seven years he had been "highly doubtful" (*anxie dubito*, lit: "anxiously doubtful") about Bezan predestination.[40] With regard to the request from the Amsterdam consistory, might we discern the hand of Arminius' senior colleague and later persistent nemesis, Petrus Plancius? In addition to being in theological disagreement with him, did Plancius perhaps entertain a bit of professional jealousy toward his increasingly popular and influential younger colleague? As early as 1591, we see Arminius gaining stature in Amsterdam as well as with important matters in the life of the larger church. In February of that year, the States of Holland convened a conference to draw up a new church order, and of the eight ministers chosen to serve on the commission, Arminius was the only clergy representative from the Amsterdam church.[41]

It is certain that Plancius played a key role in bringing before the Amsterdam consistory his disapproval of Arminius' exposition of Romans 7. The complaint was placed on the consistory agenda for January 2, 1592.[42] Arminius was not present at the first meeting of the consistory, but in order to settle the dispute as amicably as possible,

---

[39] Bangs, 141.

[40] Letter to Uytenbogaert (February 7, 1597), *Ep. Ecc.*, no. 19, p. 34.

[41] Cf. Letter of Arminius to Uytenbogaert (February 10, 1591), reproduced in H. C. Rogge, *Brieven en onuitgegeven stukken van Johannes Uytenbogaert* (Utrecht: Kemink, 1872), 1:8–9.

[42] Triglandius, *Geschiedenissen*, 284. Triglandius (1583–1654) became a minister in Amsterdam in 1610 (after the death of Arminius in 1609) and was named professor at Leiden in 1634. Triglandius was a bitter foe of Arminianism, and his "church history" was written as a rebuttal to the pro-Remonstrant (pro-Arminian) history published by Johannes Uytenbogaert in 1646, republished in multiple print editions in 1647 and beyond.

the decision was made to invite Arminius to a meeting on January 7. Arminius appeared with fellow minister Johannes Halsbergius as an ally, and at this meeting the records indicate that Arminius and Halsbergius insisted on a fair due process rooted in the assumptions of Erastian polity: they refused to discuss the dispute except in the presence of the Amsterdam burgomasters or their deputies, who were charged with oversight for the well-being of the church "as moderators and righteous arbiters."[43] If the matter were deemed by the consistory to be merely a matter of collegial dispute, then they were willing to meet in a closed session attended only by the ministers. This meeting, with neither burgomasters nor lay elders in attendance, was a gathering of the classis on either January 7 or 14, 1592. Plancius was blunt, and his accusations were many. He was not just concerned about the exegesis behind Arminius' preaching. He charged Arminius with being Pelagian, undermining the Belgic Confession and Heidelberg Catechism by being overly dependent on the early church fathers and holding inferior views on predestination, and harboring incorrect opinions on the perfectibility of humanity in this life.[44] Arminius responded by saying that his views on perfection had been so fully explicated in his public sermons that he felt no need to rehearse those opinions. Many of his fellow clergymen had already heard his position. He refused even to discuss predestination, because Plancius' complaint to the consistory was about his expositions on Romans 7, and there is nothing in Romans 7 that pertains specifically to predestination. Arminius evidently did give a defense of his teachings related to the other charges, denying guilt on every point. The meeting ended in something of a standoff: "Yes, you did." "No, I did not."[45]

---

[43] Maronier, 63; Triglandius, *Geschiedenissen*, 284; and Brandt, *Life*, 68. Note: When Brandt wrote his biography of Arminius, he seems to have possessed a manuscript account from Arminius (to which he frequently refers and cites) that has since been lost.

[44] "Perfectibility" in this context meant that by the grace of God through Jesus Christ, it is possible for the regenerated believer to observe perfectly the law. This was another of the accusations that had been directed at Dirck Coornhert, and not without some justification. Cf. B. Becker, "Coornhert, de zestiende-eeuwse apostel der volmaaktbaarheid," *NAKG* 19 (1926): 59–84. The article is also reprinted in D. V. Coornhert, *Op zoek naar het hoogste goed*, ed. H. Bonger (Baarn: Ambo, 1987), 133–59.

[45] This account is from Brandt, *Life*, 68–70.

Eventually, a truce between Arminius and Plancius was agreed upon by the two parties. It specified that Arminius was not aware that he preached or taught anything that contravened the confession and catechism; furthermore, he agreed to be vigilant in the future about staying within the bounds of Scripture as explicated in the two formulas of faith. Arminius also agreed to submit questions about difficult doctrinal issues to his colleagues, but with the proviso that if the issues could not be worked out among them at the classis level, then said questions would be forwarded to a national synod. In turn this plan of pacification stipulated that the classis would keep the peace privately as well as publicly and that it would desist from further accusations against Arminius.[46] With the endorsement of Arminius, this plan was presented to the consistory on January 17, but it did not enjoy a majority vote.[47] Since attempts to work this matter out at the classis level had failed, the dispute was forwarded to the burgomasters of Amsterdam. Plancius had succeeded in raising suspicions about Arminius' orthodoxy, and those accusations were taken to the highest level of arbitration below a national synod. Bangs calls this the "first Arminian controversy," but he notes with some mirth that forwarding the complaints against Arminius to the Amsterdam burgomasters was akin to "sending Bre'r Rabbit to the briar patch." Almost to a man the burgomasters were of a *rekkelijk* disposition, and several were close acquaintances of Arminius' father-in-law, Laurens Jacobsz. Reael.[48]

From the now-lost manuscript of Arminius, Caspar Brandt reports,

> The burgomasters had perceived with pain from their public ministrations, and that for a considerable time back, as well as from the complaints of several citizens, that they [the clergy] were not at peace among themselves. Dissensions of that kind must be checked in the bud, lest they should issue in results disastrous to the church, and even to the Republic itself. The honorable senators [burgomasters], therefore, in consideration of the office with which they were entrusted, wished and enjoined that the ministers would diligently apply themselves henceforth to the cultivation of peace and harmony, of which they had hitherto stood forth as an example to other Churches; and avoid giving any one occasion, by their

---

[46] Brandt, *Life*, 73–75; and Triglandius, *Geschiedenissen*, 284.
[47] *Protocollen*, 2:73; and Triglandius, *Geschiedenissen*, 284.
[48] Bangs, 145.

declamatory statements, to suspect that some serious contentions were fostered among them. But if they did happen to differ on some points, it was lawful for them to institute among themselves private and friendly conferences on such topics; only, they must see to it that these differences do not find their way from the Ecclesiastical Court [consistory] into the pulpit, and thence to the public. Should they fail in this duty, they [the burgomasters] would be obliged to have recourse to other remedies, that no harm might accrue to the Church and the Republic.[49]

At this point, we see in even bolder relief the issues related to which group is going to get the final say in matters. There was division among the ministers about accepting the pronouncement of the burgomasters. Johannes Ambrosius supported the sentiment of the magistrates regarding the importance of maintaining peace; however, he also supported the point that any minister whose teaching was suspect should be held accountable. This, of course, did not address the issue of who was going to decide to hold whom accountable or for what. In the course of the exchange, Arminius asked permission to speak. He admitted freely that his position on Romans 7 differed from that of some in the Reformed tradition. Contrary to Calvin and Beza, Arminius taught that the person described in Romans 7 is unregenerate, dead in trespasses and sin, yet capable of desiring to keep the Law. He was of the opinion that his interpretation was not contrary to the scriptural interpretations allowed by the Belgic Confession and Heidelberg Catechism.[50] Then Arminius made the point on polity that he would be forced to make time and again, namely, that if his doctrinal teachings were in any way contrary to acceptable Reformed doctrine, he was quite prepared to discuss the issue in the appropriate context— in the presence of the burgomasters or their assigned deputies, as they were the appropriate "righteous arbiters." The magistrates were the proper and final authority at the local church as well as the classis levels. One of Arminius' senior colleagues, Cuchlinus, who had been serving in Amsterdam for more than a decade, appealed to his seniority in service and pressed the point that these types of issues should be settled at the consistory level. This apparent stalemate among the

---

[49] Quoted in Brandt, *Life*, 81–82.

[50] Arminius pointed out that others before him had held an interpretation of Romans 7 similar to his, namely, Martin Bucer and Erasmus of Rotterdam, whom the Dutch Reformed held in high esteem. Cf. Maronier, 63–64.

ministers led the burgomasters again to go into executive session without the ministers present.

After the magistrates had conferred, the groups reconvened, and burgomaster Reynier Cant spoke for the magistrates.[51] It was their opinion,

> The Church Court [consistory] should allow this whole matter to rest, and permit whatever discussions had arisen out of it up to this time to be consigned to oblivion. A fresh conference upon it did not appear to them to be suitable, or likely to do good. They [the ministers] must henceforth be on their guard lest any of them should give vent to new doctrines from the pulpit. Should any of them have opinions in which they differed from other divines, and on which they boasted a profounder knowledge, it would be incumbent on them to reserve these to themselves, and to talk them over in a friendly manner with their compeers. Meanwhile, those who think differently, and who cannot be convinced of error, must be calmly forborne with until the points in dispute be decided by the authority of some council.[52]

In effect, Plancius suffered public rebuke in this admonition, as he had been the one to press public accusations in the consistory against Arminius. We might also say that Arminius was publicly vindicated, and that on two counts: the accusations of Plancius were found to have no merit, at least implicitly, since no judgment was entered against Arminius; secondly, his insistence that the magistrates had the right and duty to exercise oversight of the internal affairs of the church was upheld.[53] What seems also to be upheld by the pronouncement of the magistrates ("Meanwhile, those who think differently . . . must be calmly forborne with until . . . decided by the authority of some

---

[51] Reynier Cant and Arminius' father-in-law, Laurens Reael, had worked shoulder to shoulder to usher Protestantism into Amsterdam. Bangs reports that at the first Protestant communion service in 1566, they sat together at the first table served. Bangs, 145.

[52] Brandt, *Life*, 84–85.

[53] Multiple logics were applied to the rationale for Erastian versus consistory or classis-centered authority. Keuning, *Petrus Plancius*, 13, mentions a quite plausible reasoning: "The governing powers were not inclined to concede entirely to the church what seemed to be a reasonable request [self rule], as they feared that they might well end up in a situation that required them to uphold, even with force," decisions that had been made by the classis, consistory or synod.

council") is the possibility that there might indeed remain matters of doctrine to be clarified in the Reformed Church of the Lowlands. Bangs concludes: "Thus, the oligarchy stood firm (1) in its support of toleration, (2) in its support of its adopted son Arminius, and (3) in its support of its own role as the guardian of the peace of the church."[54] This may all be true, but it was not to be the final word in the first Arminian controversy.

Doctrinal controversy revived again in 1593 when Arminius was preaching on Romans 9. As Plancius was to recount the events years after the fact in 1617, a prominent layman in the Amsterdam congregation (Pieter Dirksen) refused to attend communion because "Arminianism" was being preached from the pulpit.[55] As the story is told by Plancius, burgomaster Claes Franszoon Oetgens joined Dirksen in this complaint, and the matter of Arminius' teaching was again referred to the consistory. This account seems to indicate that by early 1593 oppositional parties could be delineated in the Amsterdam congregation, with Petrus Plancius succeeding in getting at least one burgomaster, Oetgens, in the precisionist corner, while Arminius was supported by the majority of the magistrates. The political leader mentioned most often as joining with Arminius was the prominent merchant Jan Egbertszoon Bisschop, brother to Rem Bisschop (later an influential Remonstrant lay leader) and Simon Bisschop. Simon was later a student of Arminius at Leiden (known as Episcopius), and he would become the acknowledged spokesperson for the Remonstrants at the Synod of Dort.

The issue of Arminius' interpretation of Romans 9 was on the consistory's agenda for March 25, 1593, at which time it was asserted that public rumor indicated theological strife among the clergy. Arminius agreed that he had heard these rumors, but he enjoined that for his part he was being careful to observe the boundaries previously set out by the magistrates regarding respect for the confession and catechism. Rather than more innuendo and rumor, Arminius requested specificity from his accusers, as he was no more required to agree with their interpretations of Scripture and creed than they were to agree with his. Indeed, Arminius' words were more a demand than they were a request. At least one elder responded vociferously that Arminius

[54] Bangs, 147.
[55] *Protocollen*, 4:197.

was in league with a group of city magistrates to disrupt the peace of the church. This return to innuendo on the part of his accusers led Arminius to throw down the gauntlet. In no uncertain terms and at high decibels, Arminius proceeded to defend the authority of the city magistrates, and he made an explicit call for the names of his accusers along with the specific nature of their accusations—no more generalizations like, "You are disturbing the peace."

Arminius allowed that there was one point in his exegesis of Romans 9 that was not in strict conformity with typical Reformed interpretations, especially with regard to the marginal note in the Belgic Confession on verse eighteen: "So then he has mercy upon whomever he wills, and he hardens the heart of whomever he wills" (Rom 9:18).[56] Arminius points out that his taking this liberty for latitude of interpretation was not unusual, no more so than any other ministers took homiletically. This point was fully granted by his colleagues, but Johannes Cuchlinus made the point that in order for there to be peace in the church there had to be "agreement in all those points which constituted the hinge on which the articles of the Confession turned." No one contravened this opinion, and the discussion moved quickly to issues of ecclesial polity. There was no common ground here among them. Arminius and Halsbergius were again accused of being absolutely incorrect in their insistence that the magistrates were the final arbiters in all ecclesial matters. It was now totally out in the open that the heart of the disputes was fundamentally rooted in polity, at least as much as in doctrine. The key question, regardless of the dispute, was, "Who holds the power?" Evidently they agreed to disagree on this crux issue. Johannes Hallius directed a closing conciliatory statement to Arminius, and the meeting was adjourned with the hope for a harmonious way forward.[57]

If one assumed this would mark an end to the intrigue in Amsterdam, that would be a wrong assumption. Arminius' opponents were not inclined to rest from their accusations. A meeting of the consistory was held on April 22, 1593, without Arminius' being invited or even aware that the meeting was taking place. This time the consistory

---

[56] Arminius felt that typical interpretations undermined the integrity of God by implying capriciousness in decisions regarding mercy and hardening.

[57] Cf. Maronier, 64–75; and Bangs, 147–48. The dating of the events is from the *Protocollen*, 2:106; and Brandt, *Life*, 88–93.

decided to petition Arminius that he should declare openly and "without any circumlocution his opinion on *all* the articles of faith."[58] Arminius responded in kind to this rather extraordinary demand. He stood to answer and evidently quite loudly challenged anyone to come forward with an explicit reference to anything he had said in a sermon that would merit censure. Not a single person stood to accept this challenge, but one did offer the opinion that people like Martinists (Lutherans), Anabaptists (Mennonites), and even libertines (humanists like Coornhert) would be the only ones who would champion his exegesis of Romans. Indeed, they would "glory in his discourse." That being the case, surely it was a warranted conclusion that he was teaching something other than acceptable Reformed doctrine. Once again, Arminius requested to be given a concrete example, but the closest thing he got to an answer was totally inferential. The opinion of his opponents was that Arminius had been exceedingly guarded in his chosen language, using such ambiguous expressions that it was hard to pin down his exact meaning. Once again, Arminius demanded a specific accusation; however, none was given.[59]

At the following meeting of the consistory, May 27, the unpleasantness continued, and it again became clear that Plancius was the ongoing instigator of the conflict. Cuchlinus asked, "Now, where is Plancius?" Since he was the one to raise questions about the fitness of Arminius' teaching, it was now time for Plancius to declare his concerns to the consistory. His charges may be reduced to three headings: (1) In explicating Romans 9, Arminius taught that "no one was condemned except on account of sin," which seemed to exclude infants from condemnation, as they had committed no sin. In other words, the pristine dogma of predestination as taught by Beza was being undermined. (2) Arminius was inclined far too much in the humanist direction, teaching specifically that "too much could not be ascribed to good works, nor could they be adequately commended, provided no merit [to earn salvation] was attributed to them." (3) Arminius taught that angels are "not immortal."[60]

In reply, Arminius turned a Pelagian mirror on Plancius by asking, "What about original sin?" Aren't you forgetting the doctrine of

---

[58] *Protocollen*, 2:108; and Brandt, *Life*, 93 (emphasis added).
[59] *Protocollen*, 2:110; Brandt, *Life*, 94–95; and Los, *Grepen uit de Geschiedenis*, 52.
[60] Maronier, 74–75.

original sin when you say that infants are left out? Although this rhetorical move was not a checkmate, it did put Plancius on the defensive, and it allowed Arminius to avoid addressing directly the issue of predestination. With regard to the second question about good works, Arminius stood firm, not taking back a word or offering a qualifying remark. With regard to the immortality of angels, Plancius was placed once again in an awkward position. Arminius related to the consistory that he had never even touched on the topic of angelic mortality in a public venue. In a private conversation in Plancius' home, Arminius had observed that only God possesses immortality, and the life of angels is sustained only by divine sustenance. Without saying so, Arminius left the inference open that Plancius was opening the door to an eternal dualism. Plancius lost the debate in quite a bad fashion.

Plancius was defeated at every turn, but then Arminius went on to publicly declare a most important point with regard to interpreting article 16 of the Belgic Confession. The article itself he was perfectly willing to affirm, but he pointed out two possible interpretations. Article 16 is on "eternal election," affirming that God saves and preserves "all whom he, in his eternal and unchangeable council, out of mere goodness, hath elected in Jesus Christ our Lord." But here is the crucial question: does the "all" refer to those who believe, or is it an arbitrary divine decree to *bestow faith*? Arminius declared his preference for the first option (believers are the elect), rejecting the second option, knowing full well that this was Beza's position and the preferred position of his strict Calvinist opponents.[61]

Arminius had answered all of Plancius' accusations, but even more importantly, he had announced his position on the crux issue for interpreting Romans 9. It would be the undergirding hermeneutical key for all his exchanges with his supralapsarian colleagues at Leiden, and it would be the assumption that guided his assertions in his *Declaration of Sentiments*. The consistory found Arminius' statement on predestination acceptable. The meeting closed with a note of exhortation for fraternal peace until such a time as a general synod could be convened to ascertain the proper interpretation of article 16. There was peace in Amsterdam. Or one might more accurately say that the

---

[61] I did not find this exchange for May 27, 1593, in the *Protocollen* of the Amsterdam consistory. To my knowledge, it can be found only in Brandt, *Life*, 95–98, and it is reported by Maronier, 75–76.

concerns regarding Arminius were not brought again to the consistory for formal consideration.[62] It is also safe to say that no one entertained any longer the expectation that Arminius was going to write an apologetic defending supralapsarianism. He was on his way to defining with greater precision what historians of doctrine would label "Arminianism." On the issue of predestination itself, a close reading of his exegesis and the position he stakes out will lead to the conclusion that Arminius has been mostly misunderstood by modern interpreters. As Bangs has noted, "Arminius stands firm with Calvin in using the figure of predestination to give structure to his doctrine of salvation." He does not deny predestination; he affirms it and makes it central to his soteriology.[63]

In closing it should be noted that Arminius continued to minister in relative harmony with his classis colleagues for a full decade after these episodes, before he went to Leiden as a professor. We are also reminded that when the call to Leiden was formally on the table, the consistory as well as the classis supported him with praise. In a letter to Uytenbogaert shortly before his Leiden appointment, he wrote: "I am aware that I enjoy a good reputation among a number of ministers and [lay] elders. Only a few are less so inclined."[64] Little could he have anticipated that even in Leiden the "less inclined" would continue to pursue him—Plancius not the least among them.

---

[62] Maronier, 76.
[63] Bangs, "Arminius and the Reformation," 165–66.
[64] Maronier, 77.

4

THE LEIDEN YEARS
A Prelude to the *DECLARATION*

The foregoing chapters of this focused theological biography trace to a large extent the conflicts in which Arminius was embroiled. That will also be the case in this chapter describing the years immediately prior to Arminius' appearance before the States of Holland at The Hague in 1608. One should not conclude, however, that Arminius' life as a pastor and theologian was consumed with conflict. There were, to be sure, years of relative harmony, but the years characterized by harmony did not pave the path that led to The Hague *Declaration*. In the pages that follow, we will focus on the conflict between Arminius and Gomarus (1563–1641).[1] Professional relationships with other theologians and within the university at large paint a more congenial total picture than a focus on Gomarus alone would allow. Amid multiple points of controversy among academics who disagreed over theological issues, Stanglin reminds us: "There were moments of collegiality."[2] This seems to have been partially due to the fact that there was agreement among them that a peaceful coexistence even amid disagreements was best for the church as well as for the university. When the disagreements threatened to flow over into the church and larger society, the professors took the unusual step, surprising to some observers, to issue a public statement of congeniality on August 10, 1605.[3] The statement publicly affirmed that they "were not aware of any differences among the professors in the faculty that affected the foundations

---

[1] Bangs, 244–48, gives a concise overview of Gomarus' life. The *BLGNP*, 2:220–25, and the *BWPGN*, 3:285–301, provide biographical dictionary overviews. The standard biography of Gomarus remains that of G. P. van Itterzon, *Franciscus Gomarus* (The Hague: M. Nijhof, 1930). Stanglin, 33, 243, points out that all Arminius' colleagues in theology were supralapsarians, even if Gomarus was the most public of his opponents.

[2] Stanglin, 28.

[3] *Works*, 1:417.

of doctrine."[4] To this was added that they would be diligent to prevent such disputes among their students in the future. The reader is left to ponder what actually did happen to require a formal declaration of harmony among the Leiden professoriate when it was widely known that there were strong differences of opinion. This set of conflicts at the university was a prelude for what was to come.[5]

After Arminius accepted the Leiden post, he moved with his wife Lijsbet (nine months pregnant with their sixth child) in the early summer, 1603. As was the custom, public orations preceded his being awarded the professorial status of doctor in the acknowledged queen of all the sciences. These orations included: *The Object of Theology*, *The Author and End of Theology*, and *The Certainty of Theology*.[6] These were delivered with the usual pomp and circumstance, and no issues were raised at the time regarding their content. As we will have occasion to note later, these orations are more foundational to Arminius' theological agenda than hearers then or readers since have seemed to be aware. On July 10, he presented a closely argued disputation, "On the Nature of God." The disputation was quite lengthy even by the standards of the day. In various accounts of Arminius' life, teaching, and debates, those less favorably inclined to report positively on Arminius often accuse him of dissimulation, and even of hypocrisy in these early presentations. This public disputation would argue otherwise, for Arminius is clear on a crucial point about divine foreknowledge that distinguished his epistemology from that of many strict predestinarians, especially Beza and Gomarus. We can be fairly certain that he knew at this time that he was contravening Beza, and perhaps it only became clear to him over time that he had straightforwardly challenged a fundamental assumption in Gomarus' epistemology. One of Arminius' fundamental propositions centered on *scientia media*—a concept of "middle knowledge," which asserted that divine foreknowledge does not predetermine that which is known. God knows all things, but some things God foreknows are necessary, whereas some things that God foreknows are contingent: "Though the understanding of God

---

[4] P. C. Molhuysen, *Bronnen tot de Geschiedenis der Leidsche Universiteit* (The Hague: M. Nijhof, 1913–1924), 1:417.

[5] The story that I relate here is recounted with much more detail by Bangs, 252–93, and in less detail by Stanglin, 19–35, whose extensive footnotes are of special importance for specialists.

[6] *Works*, 1:321–401.

be certain and infallible, it does not impose any *necessity* in things, nay, rather it establishes in them a contingency."[7]

At the close of his oration *The Priesthood of Christ*, Arminius offers a prayer and a very generous expression of gratitude to Gomarus, among others, for approving his promotion the previous day. The expressions are perfunctory in the sense of expected, but there is no reason to believe they were not sincere. It is the words of gratitude chosen to address his senior colleague Gomarus that are noteworthy: "I thank you, Dr. Franciscus Gomarus . . . for this great privilege with which you have invested one who is undeserving of it. I promise at all times to acknowledge with a grateful mind this favour, and to strive that you may never have just cause to repent of having conferred this honour upon me."[8] There is little doubt in the ensuing years that Gomarus had his reasons for regretting Arminius' appointment, and Stanglin is exactly right when he notes, "Even if Gomarus was not thrilled with Arminius, his best opportunity to stop this appointment had passed."[9] Actually, Gomarus had made efforts to stop Arminius' appointment, but he simply was not up to the task. It seems that Gomarus was pressed by Plancius to protest Arminius' appointment, and Arminius insisted on a "friendly conversation" with Gomarus before he would accept the post.[10] The ups and downs of Arminius' relationship with Gomarus after his appointment are also related in a subsequent letter to Uytenbogaert. Arminius notes that at the moment he "lives in peace" with Gomarus and intends to continue doing so, as long as "no false prophet be discovered," a reference evidently to ministerial colleagues (Plancius and Hommius), who opposed his appointment and who continued to cause mischief.[11] Even though Gomarus and others remained less than pleased, the powers

---

[7] *Works*, "On the Nature of God," 2:123, subpoint 38 (emphasis added).

[8] *Works*, 1:432.

[9] Stanglin, 26.

[10] Cf. Brandt, *History*, 2:27; and Uytenbogaert, *Leven*, 19–20, where Uytenbogaert reports in some detail on Arminius' exchange with Gomarus. In his *Historie*, Uytenbogaert reports that after cordially shaking hands, Gomarus and Arminius went to a dinner feast with the university curators and other dignitaries (319). Triglandius, *Geschiedenissen*, tells a different story, namely, that Arminius was deceitful in his conversation with Gomarus, implying that otherwise Arminius' appointment could have been stalled (289). Triglandius' report echoes what can be found also in Gomarus, *Bedencken over the Lyck-oratie Petri Bertii* (Leiden: 1609), 43, as well as the *Acta der Nationale Synode 1618/1619*, both cited by Hoenderdaal, 8–9n2.

[11] Letter to Uytenbogaert (June 7, 1605), *Ep. Ecc.*, no. 77, p. 147.

that wanted Arminius in Leiden at the time of his appointment were greater than those who wished to keep him out.

Once again, we encounter an interpersonal intrigue similar to the one that played itself out in Amsterdam—only this time, Gomarus (often with other clergy and professorial colleagues in the background) replaces Plancius as Arminius' primary accuser. According to the Acts of the University Senate, Arminius was officially named professor on October 11, 1603. His supervision of public disputations and his own lectures began a few weeks later. Almost immediately conflicts arose. In early 1604, on February 7, Arminius was scheduled to present a disputation on the assigned topic of predestination.[12] Little seemed to be amiss in the immediate weeks after Arminius' public lecture; however, that all changed about eight months later. Gerard Brandt reports that on October 31, 1604, Gomarus, although he did not explicitly mention Arminius, delivered a lecture addressing the doctrine of predestination—a public presentation "out of his turn, and contrary to the method that had been agreed upon."[13] Arminius realized that Gomarus' audacity as well as the content of his lecture meant that Arminius' teachings were the intended target. He immediately wrote a letter to Uytenbogaert describing Gomarus' actions as "highly offensive," or as one might colloquially render *offensissimus*, "insulting."[14] To be sure, Gomarus' choosing to dispute publicly on a subject already covered by a colleague in the public disputation roster was a way of challenging Arminius, and Arminius decided to write a detailed point-by-point response to Gomarus.[15] Although Arminius was deeply wounded by this personal affront, he did not make public his refutation of Gomarus. It was not published until the year of his death, 1609, in a volume that included Gomarus' disputation.[16] Arminius' emphasis on contingency and the "middle knowledge" of God—by which it is asserted that those things which will come to pass will not occur by absolute

---

[12] "On Divine Predestination," *Works*, 2:226–30.

[13] Brandt, *History*, 2:31.

[14] Letter to Uytenbogaert (November 1, 1604), *Ep. Ecc.*, no. 74, p. 141.

[15] "Examination of the Theses of Dr. F. Gomarus Respecting Predestination," *Works*, 3:526–658.

[16] *Twee disputatiën vande goddeliicke predestinatie* (Leiden: Jan Paets Jacobszoon, 1609 and 1610). Arminius' answer to Gomarus was republished separately in 1613 and 1645; however, it was not included in his *Opera* in 1629, 1613, or 1635. It is, of course, in the English editions of Arminius' *Works*, 3:526-658, based on a 1645 Latin text.

necessity—are directly challenged by Gomarus in propositions 13 and 16 of his disputation. Appropriating logic parallel to that which we encountered in Beza, Gomarus defines the object of predestination to be humanity as "salvable, damnable, creable, liable to fall, restorable," with the result that the decree of election itself and all that follows happens by necessity in order to carry out the prior decrees of both election to salvation and damnation. According to Arminius, Gomarus is teaching explicitly an epistemology of definitive foreknowledge and necessary events: "For, as creable depends on the indeterminate and absolute omnipotence of God, so what is to be created depends on that omnipotence determined to creation by predestination of the will [of God]; and therefore cannot come before predestination, which is its efficient cause."[17] In other words, God's prescience is as it were a book on which God's will for predestinating has inscribed the things predestined that must of necessity occur. In Arminius' mind this way of interpreting foreknowledge is little short of a determinism that makes God responsible for all things, including sin itself. Arminius is not enlightened by Gomarus' distinction between sin as a "consequence" rather than as an "effectual cause." For Arminius the practical results are the same, and God is still responsible.[18] It is this implication that God is the author of sin that Arminius cannot abide. We might wonder in retrospect whether Arminius might have been well served to publish his refutation of Gomarus immediately; however, we must remember that Arminius was a new member of the faculty and Gomarus was a senior colleague. As confident as he might have felt himself to be in his own theological opinions, he might not have felt as secure in negotiating the political terrain of the university.

In the correspondence with Uytenbogaert,[19] as we have noted, Arminius expressed dismay at the obvious lack of collegial respect

[17] Thesis 13, as cited by Arminius in his "Examination of Gomarus," *Works*, 3:564.

[18] For a point-by-point discussion of Gomarus' theses (based on public disputations in 1599, 1601, and 1604), see W. Verboom, *De Belijdenis van een gebroken kerk* (Zoetemeer: Boekencentrum, 2005), 53–63, esp. Gomarus' distinction between sin as a consequence (Dutch: *gevolg*) rather than as the cause (Dutch: *effect* = *causa efficiens*). Verboom has a much better understanding of Gomarus than he does of the finer points of Arminius' theology. He oversimplifies Arminius to the point of caricature, especially in his charts on pp. 61–62.

[19] Letter to Uytenbogaert (November 1, 1604), *Epp. Ecc.*, no. 74, p. 141; and Brandt, *Life*, 201–2.

reflected in Gomarus' actions. In his mind he had done nothing to offend Gomarus, and he seemed to view Gomarus' actions in a similar light to those of Plancius in Amsterdam. The depth of Arminius' anguish over this is reflected in his comparing his pain to that of Jesus' betrayal, and he indicates his own willingness to die for the truth. He truly felt isolated in his new context, perhaps quite unlike how he felt in Amsterdam, where he knew the magistrates and a number of colleagues were in his corner. Since Bertius was probably the only colleague who agreed with him, this support was certainly not the case in Leiden: "Every one of his academic colleagues who conducted regular disputations in the Staten College was a supralapsarian."[20] As we shall see in his *Declaration*, this is the predestination theory against which Arminius directs all his energy. If Stanglin is correct about the predestinarian inclinations of Arminius' colleagues, then Arminius' preoccupation with supralapsarianism is all the more understandable—for it was certainly the form of predestination that his naysayers among the clergy were fostering. A fundamental source of conflict in the Reformed church was the doctrine itself, but that was invariably connected to a particular approach to the formal appropriation of doctrinal confessions. Gomarus' actions were a clear indication of this. Given how deeply Arminius was distraught over the conflict, and reflecting on how intentional Gomarus' actions seem to have been, it is not surprising that these issues eventually spilled over into local congregations.

Stanglin points out that "Calvin and Beza considered together are indeed mentioned frequently by Arminius . . . [but] if one wants to identify a certain theologian to whom Arminius is responding, we can find examples more proximate than the usual culprit Beza."[21] To be sure, but this should not lead to a frame of reference that misses three crucial points: (1) It was the Bezan doctrine that Arminius had been struggling with/against since at least 1590; (2) It was Bezan supralapsarianism that Arminius had been requested to support early in his Amsterdam ministry; and (3) It was Bezan predestination that informed to a great extent the forms of Calvinism that Arminius was encountering among his university colleagues as well as among the

---

[20] Stanglin, 33.

[21] Stanglin, 34.

[22] Gomarus studied in Heidelberg, but this does not rule out his holding a supralapsarian position essentially the same as Beza.

clergy.[22] Richard Muller has pointed out that Beza himself acknowledged that supralapsarianism need not be the confessional norm in Geneva, and Beza confessed that he had high esteem for Bullinger's infralapsarian position.[23] Such a willingness to countenance multiple opinions was all that Arminius was really asking for, but in the final analysis, this level of toleration was not to be. Arminius had begun his quest for such toleration during his Amsterdam ministry. As early as 1599, Arminius had given extended attention to "improving" William Perkins' celebrated piece on predestination. The extended apologetic counts more than 240 pages,[24] and it is widely recognized as crucial to Arminius' working out his own theology.[25] Arminius worked on this foundational document from 1599 to 1602. Dekker asserts that the essential structure of Arminius' theology on predestination was clearly in view when he received the call to Leiden, but in Leiden it became necessary for him to work these foundational assumptions out in detail in the face of challenges brought by all his colleagues. Arminius' public and private disputations reflect a refinement of his theological thinking, and in this regard Stanglin's assertion is on point.

In February 1605, Arminius was elected chief academic officer of the university, *Rector Magnificus*. This honor reflected the esteem Arminius enjoyed among his university peers (as he had been on the faculty only two years), but it also made him a much bigger target for those who desired to bring him down. Initially, his detractors adopted the highly dubious strategy of asserting that Arminius taught things in private to his students that he would never dare to proclaim in a public lecture or disputation. This innuendo spread beyond the university, and the Leiden pastor, Festus Hommius (1576–1612),[26] openly accused Arminius of introducing doctrinal innovations. Arminius addressed Hommius' allegations point by point, and he was momentarily silenced. According to Arminius' account of this set of events, during times of earnest prayer in the days that followed, despite Arminius' answers to his accusations, God "revealed" to Hommius that he had been correct in his initial suspicions. With due irony, Arminius wrote to

---

[23] Richard Muller, *God, Creation and Providence*, 19. See also, R. Muller, "The Christological Problem in the Thought of Jacobus Arminius," *NAKG* 68 (1988): 145–63.

[24] "Modest Examination of Dr. Perkins's Pamphlet," *Works*, 3:249–484.

[25] Cf. Bangs, 209; and Dekker, *Rijker dan Midas*, 36–38, esp. 37n103.

[26] *BLGNP*, 2:251–54.

Uytenbogaert: "Well done, worthy investigator of the truth! As if God, forsooth, grants his Holy Spirit at one prayer in such large bestowals as to impart the ability to judge, in matters so great, without any liability to error!"[27]

At the risk of repetition, we will trace in the next few paragraphs some events that Arminius also covers in his *Declaration*. We relate these because we can provide more historical detail than Arminius chose to include in his speech before the States of Holland. The bulk of these events occurred during 1605 when Arminius was *Rector Magnificus*, and they are part of the extended context in which Arminius was refuting the accusations of Festus Hommius. It was as if an avalanche of accusation was coming down on Arminius, and it became almost full-time work to refute the innuendo and to answer all the allegations. Matters were personally complicated because Arminius' health was becoming fragile. As if the physical threats were not enough, there was also the emotional toll taken on him by the inferences that he was poisoning the minds of his students with subversive doctrine. One of Arminius' students, Joannes Narsius, had come to Leiden with financial support similar to that which Arminius had previously enjoyed. Prior to his arrival in Leiden, Narsius had been examined by the Amsterdam leaders in early 1604. They were evidently pleased with what they heard, and they approved his financial aid to study with Arminius. It was not unusual for a classis to place a chosen student under the guided supervision of a specific professor, and it is important to keep in mind that the magistrates who funded the scholarship were not beholden to the area ministers for their decision.

Here Plancius seems to enter the picture again. Evidently under the assumption that studying with Arminius would corrupt Narsius' theology, the Amsterdam ministers were persuaded to compose a set of test questions that Narsius would have to answer to their satisfaction, a plan approved by the consistory of Amsterdam on January 13, 1605. Narsius would have been by this time for some months under Arminius' supervision in Leiden. Several issues are at play in the interrogatory, but the crux issue is in question three, namely, "Whether whatsoever things come to pass contingently in respect of man . . . [whether they] also come to pass thus contingently in respect of providence and of the

---

[27] Letter to Uytenbogaert (May 20, 1605), *Ep. Ecc.*, no. 77, p. 145; cited also by Brandt, *Life*, 211–12.

divine decree." Even leaving open the issue whether the question was designed to be a trap, it was certainly a trickily worded question. If a person's belief is contingent, then God's decree is dependent on man's choice and by definition cannot be absolute. Perhaps he conferred with Arminius (we do not know), but Narsius recognized the potential trap, and he answered with careful precision:

> I have to request, brethren, that, seeing the word *contingently* is not to be found in the Sacred Volume, nor in the Belgic Confession, nor yet in the Palentine [Heidelberg] Catechism, and is moreover used in a variety of senses by scholastic writers, you will submit to rest satisfied with this my confession: "Nothing seems to pass by chance; but whatsoever things come to pass, whether of great accounts or small, whether good or bad, are subjected to the government and direction of Divine Providence; in such a manner, indeed, that those things which seem to us to be uncertain, and to happen by chance, nevertheless in respect of the most wise and omnipotent providence of God, and his eternal decree, happen certainly and immutably; although, of evil itself, which is committed, he is in no respect the author."[28]

Arminius had taught his student well. Narsius' answer reminded the ministers that both the Belgic Confession and the Heidelberg Catechism were silent on the disputed issue of contingency, and Narsius with his shrewd response also was able to avoid making God responsible for evil and the origin of sin. Neither Narsius nor Arminius was served well in this entire affair. It only served to enhance suspicions about Arminius' heterodoxy, and Narsius was not accepted as a pastor in Amsterdam. He later sided with the Remonstrants, but he served only very briefly as a minister, if ever at all officially.[29]

The second incident involving a student, Abraham Vlietius, took place on April 30, 1605. Arminius does not mention this in his *Declaration* because the student took the step himself in a public disputation to openly challenge Gomarus' assumptions. It actually occurred with Gomarus presiding at the public disputation. Gomarus' reaction was bitter and perhaps even retaliatory. Rather than engaging the arguments set forth by the student, as one would normally expect of the

---

[28] Cited in Brandt, *Life*, 215 (emphasis original).
[29] Cf. Joannes Tidemann, *De Remonstrantsche Broederschap* (Amsterdam: Y. Rogge, 1905), 336–38.

presiding professor, Gomarus proceeded to accuse Arminius of putting the student up to it by arming him with his line of argumentation. Gomarus was joined by his allies in attacking the student for doing something improper by disagreeing publicly with the professor overseeing the disputation. Fearing for the well-being of the student, who had not formally transgressed any rule of public disputation, Arminius wrote a letter of support for Vlietius:

> That Abraham Vlietius, in a disputation concerning Divine Predestination held on the 30th April, 1605, was bound, from the office he then undertook in the college of disputants, to offer objections; and that, in objecting, he kept himself within the bounds of modesty and advanced nothing unworthy either of himself or his auditory, and consequently gave no just occasion of complaint, I hereby testify as requested.
>
> > Jacobus Arminius
> > Rector of the University for the time being,
> > And myself an eye and an earwitness[30]

As rector of the university, Arminius was an easy target to use as a way of keeping the issue of Calvinist orthodoxy in the forefront, mostly because of his supposed heterodoxy. If his public statements could not be used to support the suspicions, then his private instructions to his students had to be examined. Those who mistrusted Arminius' teachings took steps to protect their students from hearing Arminius at all. Some even changed the times for regularly scheduled lectures to conflict with those of Arminius, and they required the students dependent on their goodwill for scholarships to attend the rescheduled lectures. When Johannes Cuchlinus (Arminius' uncle by marriage, who had from the beginning opposed his Leiden appointment) took this unusual step, Arminius pointed out the impropriety of the move. He appealed to the magistrates to reprove Cuchlinus, and the lecture times were reset.[31]

It was now clear that the suspicions were not to be kept within the academic lecture halls. As Arminius reports in his *Declaration*, he was visited on June 30, 1605, by five ministers from the synods of

---

[30] Cited by Brandt, *Life*, 220.

[31] Letter to Uytenbogaert (May 2, 1605), *Ep. Ecc.*, no. 76, p. 143; and Brandt, *Life*, 220–21.

North and South Holland: from North Holland, Jacobus Rolandus (Amsterdam) and Joannes Bogardus (Haarlem); from South Holland, Franciscus Lansbergius (Rotterdam), Libertus Fraxinus (The Hague), and Daniel Dolgerius (Delft). Even though they appeared at Arminius' door as "deputies" from their respective synods, Bangs asserts that "no mandate for their visit is indicated in the minutes of the preceding sessions of the synods."[32] Nevertheless, they explained that their visit was occasioned by persistent rumors circulating throughout the region to the effect that candidates for the ministry were giving novel responses to the classis when being examined for the ministry. They also asserted to Arminius that he was named as the authority for their answers. Surely, they implored him, that as a minister who had himself overseen examination sessions for ministry candidates, he understood that it was their duty to protect the integrity of Reformed theology. To this end, they had come to request a "friendly conversation" with him. Arminius reports this exchange in his *Declaration*.[33] But the important points to note at this juncture are twofold, as Arminius points out: (1) The students themselves were responsible for answers they gave before the classis; and (2) As a Leiden professor, he was accountable to the university curators for his work at the university, not to the regional synods and certainly not to representatives of those bodies who came calling privately at his door. On these procedural points, Arminius was obviously correct, but his ministerial colleagues were not pleased. Arminius recognized the ploy at play in this visit, and he perhaps guessed that his colleagues Gomarus, Trelcatius, and perhaps even Plancius were behind the visit.

His appeal to proper procedure put the issue aside for the moment, but he knew it was not going away. Arminius was now fully aware that he was being pursued from all sides, so he took an active step to keep the peace. He held a public disputation (July 23, 1605), "On the Free Will of Man and Its Powers."[34] Arminius left no room for his accusers to assert his believing that sinful humanity has any capacity to exercise "free will" in connection with salvation: "In this state the free will of man towards the true good [salvation] is not only wounded, maimed, infirm, bent, and weakened, but it is also imprisoned, destroyed and

---

[32] Bangs, 268.
[33] For this and other visits, see 91ff., below.
[34] "On the Free Will of Man and its Powers," *Works*, 2:189–96.

lost." The will toward salvation "has no powers whatever except as excited by divine grace."[35] When humanity is graciously regenerated, love for the good is exercised and good deeds are performed, but all of this is possible only by the enabling of the Holy Spirit, and these deeds, coming after regeneration, make no contribution to the salvation received. These are strong statements that are in full accord with Reformed orthodoxy; however, as Bangs points out, these strong assertions did not deal with certain important topics: "There is nothing there about the universal call of the gospel and its effects on the bound will. Such a universal and effective call [as distinguished from specific elective predestination] is not denied; it is simply not discussed."[36]

Arminius' accusers were quite less than satisfied, for they recognized that he had omitted key disputed points. Two days after the public disputation, Arminius wrote to his friend, Adriaan Borrius,[37] to explain his strategy:

> I transmit you my theses on free will, which I have composed in this [guarded?] manner, because I thought that they would conduce to peace. I have advanced nothing which I consider at all allied to a falsity. But I have been silent upon some truths which I might have published, for I know that it is one thing to be silent respecting a truth and another to utter a falsehood, the latter of which it is never lawful to do, while the former is occasionally, nay very often, expedient.[38]

Arminius was making a sincere effort to keep the peace in the university as well as in the church, by emphasizing those points that he knew were common ground, without raising the issues he knew were disputed with his colleagues. One has to wonder whether Arminius remembered the words written to Uytenbogaert a few years previously: "I wonder whether we can win this." This query was certainly sustained when, only five days after delivering his disputation, he was visited (July 28) by two representative deputies from the Leiden consistory. Burgomaster Foy van Broekhoven and Professor Paulus Merula were on assignment from the local congregation to urge Arminius "in

---

[35] "On the Free Will of Man and Its Powers," *Works*, 2:192.

[36] Bangs, 269.

[37] Borrius was one of the first signers of the Remonstrance in 1610 and a Remonstrant later driven into exile after the Synod of Dort.

[38] Letter to Adriaan Borrius (July 25, 1605), *Ep. Ecc.*, no. 78, p. 147.

gentle terms" to meet with his professorial colleagues in the presence of the church consistory to discuss doctrinal differences. Evidently the tone of this visit was in stark contrast to that of the "synodal deputies" the previous month; however, despite their congeniality, on procedural grounds Arminius stated that he was not prepared to do this, as he technically would have required permission of the university curators to participate in such a gathering. Merula, a professor, and van Broekhoven, a Leiden curator and burgomaster, appreciated fully Arminius' rationale, and the request was not pursued further. Confirmation that parties on both sides of the issue were attempting to keep peace in the faculty is evidenced by the fact that they all signed the previously mentioned document (August 10, 1605) affirming that there was no fundamental difference of opinion among them on any matter that touched the "foundations" of doctrine. As has been noted, "surprise" is the only word to describe the reaction from many quarters. It was reported that Gomarus "could easily have been induced to cultivate peace with Arminius, but for the importunity of the churches and their deputies."[39] As to which among the ecclesial representatives might have "importuned" Gomarus to do other than preserve peace, the best educated guess points the finger at Petrus Plancius.[40]

There were points of strong disagreement in the Leiden faculty over soteriology. In connection with salvation, there were fundamental differences on Christology. These are not small matters, so the question remains for the modern reader how the faculty could sign a public pacification. It is perhaps our point of vision that makes for such a conundrum. Even for the professional historian, it is difficult to ignore the subsequent history: the Remonstrant controversy in 1610, the Synod of Dort in 1618, the banishing of the Remonstrant ministers from the Netherlands in 1619, the later evolution of Remonstrant theology away from the strongly Calvinist frames that Arminius affirmed, even

---

[39] Brandt, *Life*, 25. See also Hugo Grotius, *Ordinum hollandiae ac westfrisiae pietas*, critical edition with English translation and commentary by Edwin Rabbie (1613; Leiden: Brill, 1995), 150–51. Grotius notes that the supreme magistrates from the States of Holland were not aware of anything in these disputes that would lead to the "violation of ecclesiastical peace."

[40] Bangs, 270. Keuning, *Petrus Plancius*, 29–30, supports these suspicious about Plancius. He describes Plancius' role as a player in a "religious war" and notes that Plancius takes the warfare to the pulpit in multiple sermonic discourses over a period of time.

as he was trying to find his way on predestination—trying to affirm the doctrine in such a way that it did not render God responsible for sin and evil, nor nullify human accountability and freedom. All of this is there for us, but we must be reminded that these things were not in the minds of the signatories on the statement of harmony. Also, their theological purview was not as expansive as the range of disciplinary vision that characterizes the modern theological landscape that now includes the influence of the natural sciences as well as the social sciences. Still, theology in the sixteenth and seventeenth centuries was the recognized "queen of all the sciences," and it covered a large territory. Across this spectrum, there was a great deal of agreement in the Leiden faculty, and Stanglin's comment regarding the 1605 truce is appropriate: "Yet because of the vast areas of agreement, the faculty could sign the declarations of unity such as the 1605 statement, and they could work together for the common cause of training students and building up the church. Arminius and his colleagues survived in such an environment by establishing and working together with a curriculum that, with few exceptions, ran smoothly."[41] It was not the case that their disagreements did not affect foundational doctrine, but what they were saying to the public was, "This is an internal matter among colleagues who for the most part manage to get along with each other." There was pressure from all sides for the faculty to put the best face possible on these issues, so they took steps to do just that, even if the effects were not to be long lasting. We must also not forget: Arminius publicly affirmed both election and predestination, even as he was approaching these honored emphases differently than his colleagues.

At the end of that summer (August 1605), the Synod of South Holland met in Rotterdam to discuss a *gravamina*, a formal request from the classis of Dordrecht pertaining to the disputes in Leiden. The decision was made to follow proper procedural steps by asking the university curators to mediate among the professors regarding their views on the controverted issues.[42] Nine questions were composed, and the curators were petitioned to submit these questions to the professors, requiring them to answer. The university curators refused, asserting that such matters were best handled by a national synod. Here again we see the suggestion that a national synod was in order, a sentiment

---

[41] Stanglin, 32.
[42] *APPS*, 3:236–37, art. 24.

that was gaining ground on all fronts.⁴³ In Arminius' report of this incident, he says the entirety of this process was carried out with such a high degree of secrecy that it occurred without his knowledge.⁴⁴ Notwithstanding Arminius' perspective, credit must be given to the Synod of South Holland for following proper procedure in connection with matters that were of grave concern to them; however, the position of the university curators was a difficult one. If they granted the request, they would weaken the integrity of the university against outside interference and thereby open the door to the potential imposition of dogma within the university. The concerns of both parties were legitimate, but the university curators had the final say, and the answer was, "No!"

Some important details that Arminius does not report in his *Declaration* come to light in his correspondence with his trusted friend Uytenbogaert.⁴⁵ Although we do not know how, the nine questions came into Arminius' possession at some point, and he wrote out precise answers to them—certainly realizing that he would need to respond at some point in the future. To each question, he not only wrote a response but also a counter question, with added commentary on the entirety of each point. In his letter to Uytenbogaert, Arminius recounts various definitions of faith that are amenable to him. In the process, he makes use of the typical Reformed distinction between "historical" and "saving" faith—the distinction between the historical fact of Christ as Savior and the actual salvation of believers: "If therefore I believe, as I am bound to do, that Christ is constituted Savior, that is, possesses the power, ability and will to save, and if I thus through faith deliver myself up to him, I shall in this case actually obtain salvation from him, that is, remission of sins, the Spirit of grace, and life eternal." All the theological disputants would likely affirm this statement,

---

⁴³ On March 15, 1606, the States General did issue the formal call for a General Synod, but as the subsequent events reveal, the road to this synod was a rocky path. The synod did not convene until 1618 at Dort.

⁴⁴ See p. 94, below.

⁴⁵ Letter to Uytenbogaert (December 31, 1605), *Ep. Ecc.*, no. 81, pp. 150–52. Bangs, 271, dates the letter January 31, 1606, and Nichols (*Works*, 1:179–80) dates it as January 31, 1605. They cannot both be right, and Dekker, *Rijker dan Midas*, 45n144, asserts that they are both wrong. He is correct. Arminius closes the letter by wishing Uytenbogaert a "Happy New Year" and signs off, "*Pridie Kal. Januarii* 1605" ("the day before" the first day of January, or New Year's eve).

but they would speak differently about *how* this faith is received and appropriated. Arminius is knowingly drawing fine lines of theological distinction, but his intention is clear: historical faith saves no one, but historical faith becomes saving faith when it is *exercised*. No one need be left merely with historical faith, but unless faith is exercised, it remains ineffectual, merely a *fides* (mental assent to veracity) but not a *fiducia* (abiding trust in the saving reality).[46]

In the December 31 letter to Uytenbogaert, we encounter an overview of his detailed response to the nine questions submitted to the university. In *Rijker dan Midas*, Dekker outlines these as follows, in question form:[47]

1. Does election precede divine foreknowledge of faith, or does foreknowledge of faith precede election?
2. Does it follow from God's predestinating all things that God is the author of sin?
3. Does the Fall in and of itself lead to guilt deserving eternal death, or do actual acts of sinning that result from the Fall lead to deserving eternal death?
4. Are the good deeds of the unregenerate performed out of natural abilities so pleasing to God that He confers on them supernatural and salvific grace?
5. Can God rightfully expect faith from a human being who is devoid of the capacity for such faith? Does God bestow on all to whom the Gospel is preached "sufficient grace" (*gratia sufficiens*) that they can believe if they will?
6. Is justifying grace the result and the pure gift of God alone? And does this pertain only to the elect?
7. Can a true believer be assured of salvation, and is it the believer's responsibility to attain this certainty?
8. Can the elect and true believers temporarily suffer the loss of their faith?
9. By the grace of God, can true believers fully observe the law of God?

Arminius' questions rhetorically imply that the way his opponents conceive predestination means that God is responsible for sin (question

---

[46] Letter to Uytenbogaert (December 31, 1605), *Ep. Ecc.*, no. 81, pp. 150–52.

[47] *Rijker dan Midas*, 45–46. These questions are my translation from Dekker and from Arminius' letter.

two). Time and again Arminius returns to this point, and it is foundational to his presuppositions in his *Declaration*. Questions one, five, and six above also play key roles in his polemic before the States of Holland, as well as in many other places in Arminius' apologetic.

Arminius' term as *Rector Magnificus* ended on February 8, 1606, and he used the high lectern in his final address for an impassioned plea on reconciling dissension.[48] He highlighted how religious conflicts are potentially always the most destructive, because they touch the deepest areas of human commitments. In the final analysis, he suggested that conferring together is the only constructive way forward. He called also for a national gathering, "an orderly and free convention of the parties that differ from each other, where, after the different opinions have been compared and the reasons weighed in the fear of the Lord, let the members deliberate, consult, and determine what the word of God declares concerning the matters in controversy, and afterwards let them by common consent communicate the result to the churches."[49] Arminius seems to have been calling for a national synod as well, but the Erastianism that informed all his proposals in the past is abundantly clear:

> The chief magistrates who profess the Christian religion will summon and convene a synod by virtue of the official authority which they possess by divine mandate and according to ancient Jewish practice, which was afterwards taken over by the Christian church and was continued nearly to the ninth century, until the Roman Pontiff began, through tyranny, to arrogate this authority to himself. Such a procedure is required by the public good, which is never committed with greater safety to the custody of any one than to his whose own interests are not involved.[50]

Six assumptions explicitly undergird Arminius' suggestions: (1) Under the direction of God the magistrates possess the power of supreme mandate; (2) This practice is in harmony with ancient Jewish practices; (3) This practice was faithfully followed by the early church; (4) To deny this process is to deny ancient biblical practice by substituting an appropriation of power by lesser authorities; (5) As parties with no vested interest, magistrates are the most appropriate parties to

---

[48] "On Reconciling Religious Dissensions Among Christians," *Works*, 1:434–541.
[49] "Reconciling Religious Dissensions," *Works*, 1:473. English modernized.
[50] "Reconciling Religious Dissensions," *Works*, 1:473–74.

oversee disputes; and (6) For the ultimate good of all, religious peace and tolerance are required.

Arminius is not only unwilling to forsake his Erastianism, he is also pressing for Holy Writ to be the final arbiter in all doctrinal matters. Let all parties "be absolved from all other oaths directly or indirectly contrary to this [divine word] by which they have been bound either to churches and their confessions, schools and their masters, or even to princes themselves (except in matters of their proper jurisdiction)."[51] Despite all that has gone before, Arminius is proposing an idealistic (naïve?) path under the assumption that the majority of all foundational doctrines will be agreed upon as "supported by clear testimony from Scripture." It is his fondest hope that "brotherly love" may exist, or at the very least, where there are remaining differences, "party zeal" will not lead to bitter dispute. Indeed, he warns that the wrath of God would be upon those unwilling to live into the peace that is at their disposal: "Faith should be by persuasion and not by compulsion," for "nothing is less religious than to force religion."[52] Whether Arminius really wanted a national synod at this time is difficult to say. What is clear is that he used the highest pulpit in Leiden to call for a synod along the lines already set down by the States General a decade before in 1597: a synod designed to review and possibly revise the Belgic Confession, and possibly even the Heidelberg Catechism. It is certain that Arminius assumed the synodal deputies would be furious at this prospect, for that was not what they had in mind when they called for a national synod. In this assumption he was absolutely correct, for the prospect of such a set of guidelines would undermine if not destroy the propositionalist approach the strict *preciezen* Calvinists relied upon.

Before concluding these introductory chapters, one final crucial set of conflicts should be reviewed to prepare the way for a well-informed reading of Arminius' *Declaration*. Much mention has been made of Beza, but no mention of Calvin as a valued conversation partner for Arminius. Late in the spring of 1607, Arminius was accused of requiring his Leiden students to read the Jesuits as well as the theological opinions of Dirck Coornhert. We may remember that Coornhert was, in the minds of the *preciezen* Calvinists, quite liberal. Evidently,

---

[51] "Reconciling Religious Dissensions," *Works*, 1:522.
[52] Lactantius, *The Epitome of the Divine Institutes*, chap. 54, and Tertullian, *To Scapula*, chap. 2, respectively, quoted in Bangs, 278.

Arminius experienced this widely circulated but false rumor as adding insult to injury. He wrote to burgomaster Sebastian Egbertszoon, a friend in the Amsterdam church, that these accusations were pure falsehoods:

> So far from this, after the reading of Scripture, which I strenuously inculcate, and more than any other (as the whole university, indeed, the conscience of my colleagues will testify) I recommend that the *Commentaries* of Calvin be read, whom I extol in higher terms than Helmichius himself, as he owned to me, ever did. For I affirm that in the interpretation of the Scriptures, Calvin is incomparable and that his *Commentaries* are more to be valued than anything that is handed down to us in the writings of the Fathers—so much so that I concede to him a certain spirit of prophecy in which he stands distinguished above others, indeed above all.[53]

Even as he was dealing with this fresh round of personal accusations, Arminius was also designated to participate in formal preparatory conversations to prepare for the much-anticipated national synod. The session of the Preparatory Convention convened in The Hague on May 26, 1607, and Arminius joined with Uytenbogaert and Gomarus among more than a dozen others in this preparation.[54] The States of Holland had given the Preparatory Convention eight general questions to decide in order to set out the parameters for the expected General Synod. On the initial five questions, dispositions were rather easily reached—including the provision that the synod would convene during the early summer of 1608 in Utrecht (which did not happen).

Question six was a completely different matter: "Should the delegates be bound only by the Word of God?" Only four delegates voted a simple *yes*. The other thirteen delegates pressed to add the Belgic Confession and the Heidelberg Catechism as binding authorities. The *yes* ballots came only from Arminius, Uytenbogaert, and two ministers from Utrecht (where toleration had been the norm since the Union of Utrecht in 1559): Everhardius Bootius and Henricus Ioannis. In the minds of the four dissenting ministers, the inclusion of the confession and the catechism would assume a priori that these documents were comprehensively conformable to Scripture and that there would be no

---

[53] Letter to [Sebastian] Egbertsz. (May 3, 1607), *Ep. Ecc.*, no. 101, p. 185.

[54] Johannes Bogerman, from Leeuwarden (Friesland) was a delegate, and he later presided at the Synod of Dort in 1618–1619.

way for the Scriptures to judge them. The human documents would become de facto authoritative.

On question number eight, there was also serious division, the point being whether the purview of the synod would include the process of revising the Belgic Confession and the Heidelberg Catechism. At length, the majority decided that, should the synod itself so choose, revisions could be placed on the table; however, the vote did not allow that this provision for revision would be part of the preparatory stipulations.[55] A loss on these two points was a defeat for Arminius, Uytenbogaert, and the ministers from Utrecht. It was also a clear indication that the idealism outlined in Arminius' final address as *Rector Magnificus* was never going to be attained.[56] Arminius wrote to Egbertszoon, "There is nothing . . . which certain zealots leave unattended here and elsewhere, both at home and abroad, in Germany and France, that they may remove an insignificant creature like me from my chair and put me to silence."[57]

From closer to home, and this time not from Amsterdam or Leiden, another accuser appeared, this one from the university at Franeker in Friesland. Professor Sibrandus Lubbertus (1555–1625)[58] was making sure that negative reports about Arminius were being spread as well across the English Channel. In July 1607, Lubbertus wrote a letter to Andrew Melville (successor to John Knox) at St. Andrews, Scotland. The letter did not reach Melville because he was detained in the Tower of London, so it fell into the hands of the Earl of Salisbury. The earl recognized that this was a church affair, so he forwarded the letter to the archbishop of Canterbury. The archbishop gave the letter to the Dutch ambassador to England, who in turn placed it in the hands of the attorney general of Holland, Oldenbarnevelt. As Oldenbarnevelt was supportive of Arminius, he gave the letter to Arminius' close friend, Uytenbogaert.[59] The letter was a major embarrassment, more for its itinerary than for its actual content, which proved to be rather unsubstantial. Arminius and Uytenbogaert jointly wrote a response

---

[55] Cf. Brandt, *History*, 2:40–41; and Brandt, *Life*, 281.
[56] When the National Synod finally convened at Dort in 1618, the *rekkelijk* Remonstrants were not even seated as delegates. They only appeared as the "accused."
[57] Letter to Sebastian Egbertsz. (May 3, 1607), *Ep. Ecc.*, no. 101, pp. 184–85.
[58] *BLGNP*, 1:143–45.
[59] See Bangs, 291, for his description of the itinerary of this letter.

to Lubbertus in April 1608.[60] The mistaken accusations in Lubbertus' letter were so many that they characterized it as having as many errors as it had sentences. Among other inaccuracies, Lubbertus was still accusing Arminius and Uytenbogaert of insisting on revising the Belgic Confession and the Heidelberg Catechism, even though it was a matter of public record that they had agreed to omit this request from the synodal agenda submitted to the States General by the preparatory conference. Lubbertus' letter was little more than unsubstantiated gossip, and easily refuted at factual levels. Of course, what could not be undone by the correction of factual errors was the harm done by the circulation abroad of the negative letter. The negativity only added momentum to an impulse that was already at play in Holland with regard to Arminius' public image.

When the Synod of North Holland convened in June 1607, fear of heresy abounded, and the synod formally decided that all ministers were to expound the Heidelberg Catechism every Sunday afternoon.[61] The Synod of South Holland took similar steps, and the response of the classis of Gouda was to declare the Heidelberg Catechism unsuited to the instruction of their youth, it being too abstract and technical. Later that year, 1607, the ministers of Gouda published "A Short Instruction for Children of the Christian Religion." It was characterized by grammatical simplicity and references were made almost exclusively to Scripture. At some point, Arminius expressed his approval of this booklet written by Hermannus Herberts. The simple step of preparing a catechism for children set off a fresh round of accusations against Arminius as being a culprit who inveighed against the catechism. Caspar Brandt expressed dismay that such a simple book could lead to even more controversy,[62] but such was the explosive ecclesial atmosphere during the final months that led up to Arminius' appearance before the States of Holland at The Hague. The prelude to Arminius' appearance on October 30, 1608, was a conference on May 30, 1607, when both Arminius and Gomarus made presentations to the High Court. Subsequently, they were requested to submit

---

[60] Letter to Sibrandus Lubbertus (April 13, 1608), *Ep. Ecc.*, no. 104, pp. 190–96. In this jointly authored letter, Arminius and Uytenbogaert cite continually from Lubbertus' missive pointing out the inaccuracies and falsehoods.

[61] *APPS*, 1:418, art. 22.

[62] Brandt, *Life*, 296.

in writing what they had presented orally. Arminius requested subsequently that he might do both: appear before them in person with an oral report as well as a written presentation. Arminius received an affirmative reply to this request on October 20, 1608, so he had ten days to make final preparations for his written and oral presentations—his *Declaration of Sentiments*.

PART II
DECLARATION OF SENTIMENTS

VERCLARINGHE
IACOBI ARMINII
Saliger ghedachten,

In zijn leven Professor Theologiæ binnen Leyden:

Aengaende zijn ghevoelen, so van de Predestinatie, als van eenige andere poincten der Christelicker Religie; daerinne men hem verdacht heeft ghemaeckt:

Eerst mondelingh ghedaen in de volle vergaderinghe vande H.H. Staten van Hollant ende Westvrieslandt, opden 30. Octobris 1608 ende daer nae schriftelick aen hare Mo. E. overgelevert.

𝕭tgegheven / by de Weduwe van den Overleden / ende haere Broeders.

TOT LEYDEN,
Ghedruckt by Thomas Basson, Boeckverkoper in t' Musijck-boeck. Anno 1610.

BIBLIOTHEEK
SEMINARIUM DER
REMONSTRANTEN

The digital files of the 1610 *Verclaringhe* are courtesy of the Special Collections Library at the University of Leiden, with the cooperation of Mr. Ernst-Jan Munnik.

A DECLARATION OF THE SENTIMENTS OF JACOBUS ARMINIUS*

Professor of Theology at the University of Leiden

Regarding his sentiments on predestination and other doctrines[1] of the Christian Religion[2] about which his opinions have brought him under suspicion.

Initially delivered orally[3] in a full assembly of the States of Holland

---

* The lead title reads literally: *Declaration of James Arminius, of Blessed Memory*, this last phrase being a common insertion regarding a deceased person held in high esteem. The insertion of definite and indefinite articles is purely for English grammatical purposes. I have retained the traditional insertion of "sentiments" from the first subtitle, which may be interpreted as a double entendre: Arminius' theological expositions as well as his personal perspective on the totality of the events surrounding the theological controversy in which he found himself embroiled from the earliest days of his pastoral ministry in Amsterdam (August 27, 1588), with special reference to his years as professor of theology in Leiden—July 1603, to the delivery of his *Declaration* in 1608.

[1] Lit., "points."

[2] Here Arminius uses the phrase "Christian Religion"; however, throughout the *Declaration* we will encounter *religion* as a word standing alone. This always means *Christian Religion* or the *Christian Faith*. With rare exception, I have simply sufficed to translate it as "religion." Modern connotations about comparative religion or religious studies were simply not part of a theological frame of reference in the sixteenth century.

[3] The English translation that appears in all editions of Arminius' *Works* is from a Latin translation (not done by Arminius himself) from the original manuscript in sixteenth-century Dutch. When the *Verclaringhe* was published in 1610, it included a rather lengthy preface. This was clearly rooted in an apologetic being carried on from both sides of the predestinarian disputes as a result of a "pamphlet warfare" that was already breaking out. A print version of Arminius' original manuscript, housed in the Collection of the Remonstrant-Reformed Church (Rotterdam, 2201, no. 29, City Library), was published by the late Prof. dr. G. J. Hoenderdaal, *Verklaring van Jacobus Arminius* (Lochem: De Tijdstroom, 1960). Many of the critical notes from Hoenderdaal are taken over with some modification in this translation. Other critical annotations have been added, as well as clarifying notes for the English reader. Strictly speaking, it may not be linguistically accurate to refer to the language of this period as "middle Dutch," as the period in which Arminius lived and worked was actually a bridge era in the language's evolution. This is reflected in the

and West Friesland on October 30, 1608, thereafter in writing to the Noble Lords of government.[4]

LEIDEN

Published by the Widow of the Deceased and her Brothers
Printed by Thomas Basson, Bookseller at the Music-Book,[5] 1610

SECTION ONE

A Personal History

To my Supreme Governors, the Noble Lords of the States of Holland and West Friesland:

After the Conference with Gomarus[6] convened at your command here in The Hague in the presence of four Ministers of the Gospel,[7] under the oversight of the Counselors of the Supreme Court, the results of that gathering were reported to you. Reference in that report regarding the nature and importance of the controversy between us has led to your requesting the two of us, along with those four ministers, to appear in your honored

---

explanatory notes of the language dictionary composed specifically for middle Dutch: *The Middelnederlandsch Woordenboek*, 9 vols. (The Hague: M. Nijhoff, 1885–1929), 1:viii, where specific reference is made to the centuries "approximately" 1200–1500. Continual reference has been made to the *Middelnederlandsch Handwoordenboek*, ed. J. Verdam and C. H. Ebbinge Wubben (The Hague: M. Nijhof, 1932, 1976).

[4] The abbreviation "Mo.E." in the manuscript is the equivalent of expanded expressions that occur several times in the course of the document—*Edele, Vermogehende, Hoochwijse, seer voorsienighe Heeren*: "Noble, Influential, Most wise, perspicacious Gentlemen." While this list of adjectives may be offensive to modern sensibilities, it is important to remember that the sixteenth- and seventeenth-century Netherlands was an era of polite titles. Also, there was an Erastian form of national governance in which oversight on the part of magistrates was comprehensive of both civil as well as religious matters. These attributions, seen in their context, are not so much fawning as they are expressions of hope that such comprehensive knowledge and wisdom would indeed be the case in matters of governance. With this setting in view, these various expressions will be rendered simply: *Noble Lords*.

[5] The printer's mark of an open book of music on the original title page of the 1610 edition visually represents Basson's place of business, "bookseller in [the house named] the Music-Book." Thanks to Jeremy Bangs for making this known to me.

[6] This conference before the Supreme Court of the States of Holland took place on May 30, 1607.

[7] The ministers in attendance were Joannes Becius from Dordrecht, Wernerus Helmichius from Amsterdam, Johannes Uytenbogaert from The Hague, and Hermannus Gerardi from Enkhuizen.

presence so that you might reveal to us what you consider to be of significant importance.

Subsequently, Franciscus Gomarus declared that the theological differences between us were of such import that he would not dare to appear before God holding such opinions.[8] Furthermore, he asserted that unless proper steps were taken to prohibit the consequences of these theological differences in our native land, armed chaos would ensue with provinces, churches, cities, and even private citizens taking up arms against one another. To these sweeping allegations I made no reply, except that I was not conscious of holding any such atrocious religious sentiments as those described by him. I also expressed the hope that I would never be the cause of division in God's church or of division in our native land. By way of confirmation, I added that when summoned to appear before this assembly, I was prepared to make a full and open statement of all my theological opinions, not leaving until this was fully done.[9]

You, Noble Lords, after careful deliberation on my offer, now deem it proper to summon me here in your presence in order that I might fulfill that pledge.[10] So I appear before you now with a clear conscience to keep that promise. For some time sinister reports about me have been widely circulated at home and abroad,[11] indicating that I have consistently refused (despite frequent requests) to make a full statement of my theological opinions. Because these negative reports have given rise to no small amount of difficulties, I humbly request to be allowed frankly to clarify some important related matters.

The Account of a Conference Proposed to Me, Which I Refused[12]

On June 30, 1605, three clergy representatives from the Synod of South Holland came to me at Leiden. They were Francis Lansbergius, Libertus Fraxinus,

---

[8] In the original English translation, the words attributed to Gomarus are in quotation marks; however, the indication of a direct quote does not appear in either the Dutch manuscript or the 1610 edition. This should not be taken to mean that Gomarus did not utter these words, as he is cited as offering this opinion on multiple occasions, including in the minutes of the Synod of Dort a decade later. Throughout the previous English translation from the Latin manuscript, quotation marks are imported. The quotation marks are not in the original manuscript, and they do not appear in this translation unless there is a direct citation noted. Likewise, other incidental/editorial items from previous English versions are omitted.

[9] Uytenbogaert, *Historie*, 16–17, provides textual evidence for this.

[10] See chapters 3 and 4 and the reference to the text of this invitation in Uytenbogaert, *Historie*, 446 (consecutively paginated edn.). Other sources (especially the introduction to the *Acta*) seem to assert (erroneously!) that Arminius appeared "uninvited" before the States of Holland in 1609.

[11] An exchange of letters that resulted from these rumors may be found in *Ep. Ecc.*, nos. 101–15.

[12] These types of section headings, intended to assist the reader, are not in the original

and Daniel Dolegius (of blessed memory), each of them the minister of their respective churches in Rotterdam, The Hague, and Delft. They were accompanied by two representatives elected from the Synod of North Holland, namely, Johannes Bogardus from Haarlem and Jacobus Rolandus from Amsterdam.[13] They told me that it had been reported to them that some Leiden students, during the course of their examinations by the classis for admission to the Christian ministry, had given answers that were novel and, in some cases, in conflict with the received teachings of the church. These students asserted that they had learned these opinions from me. Based on this, they requested that I enter into a "friendly conversation" with them to determine whether there be any truth to these allegations, in order to remedy the situation.[14]

I responded that I did not deem such a course of action to be prudent. Such a step would inevitably lead to continual requests for such friendly interviews every time a student gave a strange response to a question and then hid behind the excuse that he had learned the answer from me. I suggested that a more prudent course of action would be that when a student under examination gave an answer that seemed to be in opposition to the Belgic Confession or the Catechism, if that student asserted that he had learned this opinion under my tutelage, then that student should appear before them in my presence. Furthermore, I was prepared to travel at my own expense to any location designated by the examining ministers for such a confrontation, the obvious result being that when this had happened a couple of times, it would become evident whether there be any truth or mere slander in these assertions.

When Franciscus Lansbergius, speaking for the delegation, continued to insist on a conference, I offered yet another reason why I did not deem such a conference to be wise. They had come to me as elected representatives of their respective synods with the expectation that they would bring back a full report of our exchange. I pointed out to them that I was not at liberty to consent to their requests without the express knowledge and permission of

---

manuscript. They first appeared in the 1610 edition of the *Verclaringhe*, and are also in Hoenderdaal's edition. My headings are often phrased differently and also placed differently in the text.

[13] Bangs, 268, notes that the ministers were likely acting on their own, for no mandate for their visit is indicated in the minutes of the preceding sessions of the synods. Arminius refers to them as *deputanten* (deputies or chosen representatives). We do not know if they led Arminius to believe that they were deputized, or whether he simply assumed this to be the case.

[14] It seems that when the students of Arminius appeared before the classis of Amsterdam, they were questioned sharply and expected to give answers that were formulaic in nature. An example of this may be found in Uytenbogaert, *Historie*, 327. The *classis* minutes indicate that a candidate named Narsius was admitted in 1604, but then required to undergo a second examination in writing in 1605. See pp. 72–74, above.

my superiors, whom I and they were equally bound to obey.[15] Furthermore, it would not be to my advantage to leave the report of our conversation entirely to their discretion.

They had likewise no cause or reason to make these requests, my being unaware of ever having propounded, either at Leiden or in Amsterdam, anything that was contrary to the Word of God, the Belgic Confession, or the Catechism of the Churches of the Netherlands. No one had ever brought a [formal] complaint against me, and I was confident that no charge against me could be sustained if said accuser were required to prove his accusations, or lacking such proof, to admit his error.

A Conference Proposed by Me, Refused by the Clergy Representatives

I then proposed to the clergymen that if they would be willing to set aside their status as deputies of their respective synods and converse with me on equal footing, then I was prepared to enter immediately into conference with them. The understood conditions of such an exchange would be: (1) They would explain their position on each point, and I would explain mine; (2) They would offer their objections to my opinions with reasons, and I would do the same; (3) They would attempt to refute my theological positions and my reasons, and I would in turn try to refute theirs; (4) If we should reach an understanding, then the issues would be resolved; if not, then no report would be made to anyone, and the entire affair would be placed in the hands of a national synod.

When they refused my proposal and were in the process of leaving, I suggested that they offer the same opportunity for a "friendly conference" to my colleagues Gomarus and Trelcatius, bless his memory,[16] because it did not seem to me that I had given cause for making such a demand on me any more than either of my colleagues. I reinforced this request with several arguments too lengthy to repeat here. The deputies responded that they would relay the request for a conference to my colleagues, and they stopped in again before leaving Leiden to report that they had done so. This is the first request about which there has been much discussion. The reporting by some was quite

---

[15] Arminius is pointing out to them what they actually knew: theirs was an Erastian society. His appointment as a Leiden professor came first and foremost under the purview of the university curators and the government in The Hague. Even matters of doctrine were not to be handled without the express knowledge and permission of these "superiors."

[16] Lucas Trelcatius passed away on September 12, 1607. Brandt, History, 2:79. The manuscript reads: "p.m.," *piae memoriae*. Trelcatius was appointed professor *extraordinarius* only three days after Arminius' appointment, perhaps a move by the university curators to balance the theological tendencies in the faculty. Trelcatius was known to hold supralapsarian views.

inadequate, leaving out my stated positions as well as my reasons [for not acquiescing to the requests].

Another Request Made to Me

A few days later, July 28, 1605, a similar request came to me from the Consistory of the Church of Leiden, with the proviso that should I approve, other persons would also be requested to appear; however, should I not approve, the matter would be laid to rest. I related to Mayor Brouckhoven and the late Merula, both having come to me as Elders of that congregation, that I could not grant such a request. I provided reasons that completely satisfied them, and thus the matter was laid to rest.

A Request from the Deputies of the Synod of South Holland to the Curators of the University of Leiden

On November 9, 1605, deputies from the Synod of South Holland, Franciscus Lansbergius and Festus Hommius, along with several associates, presented nine questions to the Curators of the University of Leiden with the request that the Professors of Divinity be required to answer them. The Curators answered that they did not approve that questions be posed to Divinity Professors in this manner. Furthermore, if anyone was of the opinion that anything of an improper nature was being taught at the university, that concern should be forwarded to a national synod (which, it was hoped, would be convened within a short period of time).[17] Upon receiving this denial of their request, the deputies from South Holland requested permission themselves to propose said questions to the Divinity Professors so that they could hear what the professors freely offered of their own accord as a response to the questions. This request was also refused. This entire affair occurred [in such a clandestine manner] that I was totally unaware even of the presence of the deputies, although I did become aware shortly thereafter of their visit.[18]

A Fourth Request

An entire year passed before I was again questioned about these matters. However, just before the meeting of the Synod of South Holland at Delft in

---

[17] The decision by the States General in The Hague to hold a national synod is dated March 15, 1606; however, no date was set at this time. Cf. Uytenbogaert, *Historie*, 329 (consecutively paginated edn.).

[18] For Arminius' full response, see his "Apology against Thirty-One Defamatory Articles," in *Works*, 1:733–70. The difference between nine questions and thirty-one articles is the result of continued expansion of suspicions and questions.

1607,[19] Jan Barentszoon (the pastor in Delft), Festus Hommius from Leiden, and Dibbetius from Dordrecht (deputized by the Synod of South Holland) came to me inquiring whether I was making progress in my refutation of the Anabaptists.[20]

After I attempted to answer them, we had a lengthy exchange. Just as they were about to leave, they asked me to reveal to them my considered opinions on the subject of religion so that as deputies of the synod they could relay my thoughts and satisfy the synod[21] regarding such matters. I refused to comply with their request because, in my opinion, this could not be done conveniently—nor to anyone's advantage—other than at a national synod, which we hoped to convene soon, following consent from the Noble Lords of the States General. I promised I would make every effort to declare at that time the entirety of my sentiments in such an open manner that no one might have occasion to complain that I was trying to hide anything. I concluded by saying that each individual is the best interpreter of his own words in such matters, and that I was not inclined to rely on their ability to make a faithful report. After this, we parted ways.

Private Requests

In addition to these requests, several clergymen have privately suggested that I declare my views to a session of the synod. Others entreated me to disclose my views to them so that they might consider them "in the fear of the Lord," and they promised to keep the content of our exchange to themselves. To the former I gave my rehearsed response that they had no reason to request such an account from me any more than from other clergy. To the latter request, from one of the more influential among them,[22] I proposed on three different

---

[19] This was a meeting of the Provincial Synod of South Holland, not the national synod previously mentioned.

[20] The request from the Synod of South Holland for Arminius to refute the Anabaptists dated back to 1600 when Arminius was still pastor in Amsterdam. In letters from Arminius to Uytenbogaert dated January 26 and May 26, 1600, it is evident that Arminius was occupied with the project. Cf. *Ep. Ecc.*, no. 52 (January 26, 1600) and 53 (May 26, 1600), in *Works*, 1:135–36. See also *Works*, 1:174–83, for a translation of the letter to Uytenbogaert (October 1, 1602), no. 56, contra Bangs, 173, who dates the letter October 10. These letters indicate that Arminius feared that his opponents were looking for carelessly worded pronouncements on regeneration, free will, and predestination.

[21] Lit., "brethren."

[22] Lit., "not from one of the less influential." The identity of this clergyman is not certain. In 1605 Plancius preached a fiery sermon against Arminius in Amsterdam. Cf. *Ep. Ecc.*, 80. In a letter dated June 7, 1605, Arminius wrote to Uytenbogaert regarding a conversation with Festus Hommius about his invitation to Helmichius that the two of them should have a conversation about the main points of Christian doctrine. Cf. *Ep. Ecc.*, 77.

occasions to participate in a conference concerning all the main points of religion—a gathering at which we would determine the best means possible for establishing truth and refuting falsehood. I suggested also that this should be done in the presence of the principal leaders of our country. He refused my proposals. To others who entreated me, I gave various answers. In some cases I simply denied the request, but to others I gave some limited responses, depending on whether the persons were known to me. In general it was my experience that whenever I revealed any opinion, even when that person had received it in confidence, affirmed the truth therein, and pledged to keep the content of our exchange to himself, that material was immediately reported to others.

The Preparatory Convention

In addition it is also necessary for me to report a letter campaign that has been taking place in our country and abroad. These letters assert that even when requested this in a most cordial manner, I refused to give a public account of my opinions on the Christian faith to a preparatory convocation convened in The Hague by the Noble Lords of the States General in June 1607.[23] It is reported that I remained steadfast in my refusal even when assured that every possible precaution would be taken to handle this matter in ways that met my satisfaction. Presented in this manner, I understand that many responded negatively because it was felt that I should have given greater deference to that assembly of divines from all the Provinces. So, I now find it necessary to relate how this sequence of events took place.

Prior to my departure from Leiden for this convention in The Hague, five articles were sent to me, evidently already circulating in the provinces and read by some ministers and ecclesial assemblies. These articles purported to contain my sentiments on several key points of the faith: predestination, the fall of Adam, free will, original sin, and the salvation of infants. When I read through them, the style of writing convinced me that I knew the identity of

---

[23] This preparatory convocation in anticipation of the national synod was of considerable importance because it was the first time that the conflicted groups met one another face-to-face in a public arena. The differences fell along lines of both agenda and procedural guidelines. Arminius and Uytenbogaert, along with two ministers from Utrecht, brought a minority report to the States General, while the majority were represented by thirteen clergy from across the United Provinces. From the very outset there was considerable unrest across the provinces to the announced intention by the States General that the national synod would convene a conversation around a review of the Belgic Confession and the Catechism of the Churches of the Netherlands. Given the general state of unrest, it is understandable that this planned national synod did not take place until 1618, by which time the political climate had changed considerably.

the author.[24] Because he was present at the gathering in The Hague, I confronted him and made public my opinion that he had composed the articles. He did not bother to deny it, but rather asserted that the articles had not been distributed as *my articles*,[25] but rather as points of doctrine on which Leiden students had held public disputations.[26] I challenged him, pointing out that he knew all too well that when such things were distributed, I would be the one held finally accountable[27] even though I was blameless with regard to their content. They not only failed to reflect my theological judgments, but even worse, they were in my view not in conformity to God's Word.

Because the exchange took place in the presence of only two other persons, I deemed it wise to make mention of this affair in the convention itself. When I did so, several persons in attendance who previously had read them admitted that they had assumed the documents reflected my sentiments. After this occurred, we placed our signatures on the proceedings so that an account could be handed over to the Noble Lords of the States General. Just as the convention was about to be dismissed, I implored them to remain just a bit longer to hear something else I wished to say. When they agreed, I proceeded to outline the contents of the five articles I held in my hand, articles that had been distributed by a member of that convocation into different provinces, namely Zeeland and Utrecht (which I knew for certain). Furthermore, I was certain that these had been read by some ministers in public venues where it was assumed that they represented my sentiments. I further affirmed to all those present, with a clear conscience and before God, that the articles were not from my hand and that they did not contain my sentiments.[28] Twice I repeated this solemn vow. I earnestly requested of my colleagues that they not rush to give credence to every negative report about me as if it actually reflected my opinions.[29]

In response, a member of the convocation asserted that it would be well for me to identify the portions of the articles to which I would give my

---

[24] Wernerus Helmichius, a co-pastor in Amsterdam, may have been the composer. Cf. Hoenderdaal, 12–13. The list of points by which Arminius was brought under suspicion was expanded later to number thirty-one.

[25] Emphasis added.

[26] See the discussion about "disputations" in Stanglin, 37–46. Stanglin highlights the key functions of disputations: (1) They provided a "snapshot" of the professor's opinion at a particular time on a specific topic; (2) They provided an appropriate context for the professor to set out his opinions; and (3) They provided the professor with the opportunity to defend his position, while offering others the chance to challenge his position.

[27] Lit., *dootschult*—responsible to pay burial costs for the deceased.

[28] In the manuscript there is an additional marginal note: "Indeed, they do not conform to the Word of God, not a single one of them as they are presently composed."

[29] Lit., "came from me."

approval as well as the portions that I disavowed, so that they might have better insight into my sentiments. A second member openly concurred with this request. I replied that the convocation had not been called into session for this purpose and that we had already detained one another long enough, because the Noble Lords of the States General were awaiting our answers. So we parted ways. No one attempted to continue the meeting, nor did anyone assert that the reasoning set forth for adjourning the meeting was anything other than equitable. Indeed, there were a number present at the assembly (as I understand it) who declared afterwards that it was never the intention of the convocation to discuss doctrine, and that if doctrine had become a point of order, they would have immediately recused themselves. This indicates to me that it was never the case that I was being called upon for such a declaration at this gathering.

My Reasons for Refusing a Conference

This, Noble Lords, is an accurate narrative of the conferences and interviews that the brethren have requested of me, along with my refusals. From this account it seems apparent to me that there is no reason to bring accusation against me on account of my responses, especially when one considers their requests, the manner in which the requests were delivered, and the nature of my refusals, which were always accompanied by a rationale. Their request for a public declaration of my opinions regarding the faith was unwarranted, for I have never made doctrinal pronouncements that were contrary to God's Word or to the Confession and Catechism of the Belgic Churches—nothing that would give cause for suspicion of me any more than of another clergyman. I have maintained and continue to affirm that I am prepared to consent to a formal enquiry at a provincial or a national synod so that the truth might be discerned, as long as it is apparent that this would be fruitful. Their choosing to send officially designated representatives to request my opinions was clearly prejudicial against me, for we may assume that deputies would not be sent to invite a man into conference unless it were already determined in the synod that he had given strong grounds for such an interview. Therefore, I did not deem it wise to consent to such a conference, since that very act would render me suspect, a tacit admission that my teachings were irregular. The reasons for my refusal were:

FIRST, since I am not under the immediate jurisdiction of either the Synod of North or South Holland, and because I have other superiors to whom I am required to give account,[30] it would have been improper for me

---

[30] As a Leiden professor, Arminius was accountable first and foremost to the curators of the university.

to consent to a conference with synod deputies without the advice and express consent of my superiors. To be sure, a conference of this type was not incumbent upon me as part of the ordinary discharge of my duties, and there was no clear indication from the deputies that said conference [in 1605] was to be *privata collatio*, an entirely private exchange, for they would not agree to set aside their official status as deputies of the synod. Had this exchange occurred, I would have been acting in disobedience to my superiors by acquiescing to the proposed conference. I wish the brethren would remember that even though every minister of a synod is subject to the jurisdiction of that synod, he should not enter into an official exchange with members thereof without the knowledge and consent of the magistrates by whom he is governed. No magistrate has ever allowed a minister within their jurisdiction to formally engage with deputies from the churches without prior consent, and when such did occur, the magistrates chose to have their own deputies present at the conference. Let us not forget what happened at Leiden in the case of Coolhaes,[31] at Gouda with the late Hermano Herberts,[32] at Horn in the case of Cornelius Wiggeri,[33] and at Medenblick in the case of Tako Sybrants.[34]

SECONDLY, I was dissuaded from entering into conference because I realized that it would not be level ground for an exchange, and equality is a prerequisite between those who would confer. (1) They came armed with deputized authority, while I was simply a private citizen; furthermore, I was well aware of the power that people employ when they are operating under the sanction of formal authority. (2) There were three of them, including two deputies from the Synod of North Holland. On the other hand, standing alone, I not only had no one with whom to confer, but there was also no other person to witness the interview who, had it been allowed, could be ready to give an account on my behalf. (3) The deputies were not acting on their own behalf, but rather at the behest of their superiors, required as such to contend to the utmost for the religious sentiments set down by those who had religious authority over them. This dictated that the deputies were not left to their own discretion to accept the validity of any arguments that I might offer, regardless of the cogency of my sentiments or their ability to refute them or to accept them as valid. Given this situation, I did not see how such a conference

---

[31] Caspar Coolhaes was living in Amsterdam at the time, having been dismissed from the ministry. Because it was believed that these ministers taught contrary to the Belgic Confession and Heidelberg Catechism, formal inquiries had been initiated against each of them. Cf. Hoenderdaal, 13n15. Extended biographical information can be found about these accused clergy in the footnotes, *Works*, 1:602–5.

[32] Herberts died on February 23, 1607.

[33] Cf. *NNBW*, 7:1321.

[34] Cf. *NNBW*, 5:868.

could proceed with mutual advantage, which ought to be the case in such an exchange. For my part, since I was completely at liberty to speak solely according to the dictates of my conscience, I suppose I might have gained some advantage by witnessing to the truth[35] of those things my convictions allowed without speaking prejudicially against anyone else. You, Noble Lords, would have been able to discover the merits of this perspective if your deputies had been present at the Preparatory Convention.

My THIRD REASON is that it was unavoidable that the account of this exchange with the synod would have been detrimental to me, whether or not I was present for the report. In my absence it could easily have happened through the omission or the addition of certain words, or through the alteration of words, sentences, or order—whether through misunderstanding or faulty memory or prejudice—that something would be reported in a manner quite different than what actually transpired. Indeed, had I been present, it would have been extremely difficult for me to address inconsistencies, because a greater authority would have been given to the deputies of the synod than to me. In conclusion, had I accepted their offer, I would have implicitly conveyed to the synod an authority over me that it does not actually possess. In the discharge of my assigned duties, it would be impossible for me to transfer oversight to the synod without manifest disrespect toward those persons placed over me by our common Government.

I was compelled by necessity as well as equity to reject the terms on which this conference was offered. Despite my convictions about these matters, the deputies had opportunity to gain the information they desired. If they had been willing to accept the private exchange of opinions that I proposed, they could have learned my sentiments on every article of the Christian faith. In addition, this exchange would have been much better suited than a public one to promote our mutual edification and instruction. In my opinion, a private conversation is most conducive for each person to speak freely and openly, more so than under the formal constraints of a deputized interview. There need not have been any reluctance on their part, for each of them was at liberty, if he so chose, to engage in a private conversation with me. When making this offer to them, I did require that the content of our private conversation would remain entirely confidential, with not a word ever to be divulged to another living person. I have no doubt that if they had consented to the private conversation, one of two things would have been the result. We would have arrived at a mutually satisfactory conclusion, or we would have concluded at

---

[35] Hoenderdaal, 58, substitutes a verb form of *getuigen*, "to witness," whereas the manuscript has a form of *overtuigen*, "to convince oneself."

the very least that our disagreement presented no immediate danger to the truth necessary for salvation and piety, or to Christian peace and unity.[36]

Inaccuracies Regarding My Refusal to Issue a Declaration of Sentiments

Considering all of this, I cannot fathom how they complain that I refuse to make a public declaration of my sentiments and make so much noise about it at home and abroad, accusing me of introducing novel, impure, and false doctrines into the Church and into the Christian faith.[37] If I do not openly profess my sentiments, how can they know what harmful opinions I might introduce? How could I be introducing falsehoods when I am not explaining my sentiments? If the suspicions being brought against me are simply groundless, it is uncharitable to entertain them At the very least, they should not be ascribed such great importance. But it is insinuated that I disclose some of my opinions without making a full disclosure, and it is averred to be quite apparent where my sentiments lead from the few things I do care to make clear.[38]

To this I would simply respond: Can any of the sentiments that I have openly declared be demonstrated to be in contradiction either to the Word of God or the Confession of the Churches of the Netherlands? If the latter be the case, then formal charges should be brought against me, for by my own signature on that document I vowed never to expound any opinions contrary to the Confession.[39] If the former can be demonstrated, that any of my opinions are contrary to the Word of God, then my blame is even greater. I should be required to recant or to resign my position, especially if the main points of doctrine are detrimental to the honor of God and the salvation of humankind. But if it be the case that the sentiments that I am accused of advancing are found neither to be contrary to the Word of God, nor in conflict with the Confession to which I have referred, then neither the direct consequences of these opinions nor those that indirectly result from said opinions can possibly be construed as being contradictory to the Word of God or to the Belgic

---

[36] Arminius was consistent in his willingness to make a public declaration of his theological opinions; however, he was equally insistent that he should not be required to do this in the setting of an ecclesial trial, as he was not actually under the supervisory jurisdiction of his ecclesial peers.

[37] See the previous discussion, pp. 84–85, for the situation of Lubbertus and others sending letters that had the potential to bring the University of Leiden into disrepute. The letter to Sebastian Egberts (May 3, 1607), *Ep. Ecc.*, no. 101, p. 185, also provides details about Arminius' concerns.

[38] Cf. Letter to Sebastian Egberts (May 3, 1607), *Ep. Ecc.*, no. 101, p. 185.

[39] Arminius is here contradicting what later historians have been unable to verify independently, namely, that he signed the Belgic Confession at some point. See previous discussion, pp. 48–49.

Confession. Following the rule of the Schoolmen, if a doctrine leads to false practice then the doctrine itself is false, and vice versa. Therefore, one of two courses of action should have been followed: Either formal charges should have been filed, or the rumors should cease. I prefer one of these, but I do not fear the other. Although thirty-one derogatory articles[40] against me have been widely distributed, even into the hands of highly influential people,[41] it may be discerned through the inconsistency and lack of substance in their composition that they do me an injustice.

The Principal Reasons I Refused to Engage the Deputies

Some might say that for the sake of avoiding trouble and to satisfy a large number of ministers, you should have made an open and straightforward declaration of your sentiments on the whole subject of religion—so that you might receive proper instruction or in order that they might be adequately prepared for a mutual conversation. My hesitation to proceed in this manner was based on three concerns:

First, I feared that a declaration of my sentiments would lead to the initiation of a formal inquiry. Second, I feared that a statement of my opinions would have led to public discussion and refutation in the pulpits of the churches and the academic exercises of the universities. Third, I feared that my opinions would be spread to universities and churches abroad with the intention of oppressing me by gaining from them a statement of condemnation. From the [thirty-one] articles that have been widely distributed and from the writings of certain individuals in response, it can be clearly demonstrated that my fear of these consequences was well founded.

With respect to the edifying instruction that I might have received from such a disclosure, it is important to keep in mind that not only I but many others have formed particular perspectives on the subject of religion.[42] Attempts to instruct one another are not constructive unless they occur when all are

---

[40] These represent expansions of the original articles distributed prior to the preparatory conference in May of 1607, leading up to the proposed national synod.

[41] In his manuscript Arminius adds the annotation: "To each of whom I have given a written response."

[42] Regarding such steps, the esteemed Piscator had suggested corrections to his students at Herborn for the Heidelberg Catechism. Cf. Uytengobaert, *Historie,* 333. Piscator's suggested corrections are noted in a letter from Poelenburg to Hartsoecker, *Ep. Ecc.,* no. 92. In Arminius' own context, it is interesting to note the extensive exchange between Becius of Dort and Uytenbogaert. Cf. Uytenbogaert, *Historie,* 335-46. The history of such scholastic disputes is a long one. A decade later the formal conclusion of the Synod of Dort was postponed due to disagreement over exactly what was to be included or excluded in their revision of the Belgic Confession. Cf. Gootjes, *Confession,* 148-59.

assembled to discuss them openly with the express purpose of reaching a definitive opinion. With respect to my colleagues being adequately prepared, the best chance of this happening will be when each and every person has presented their views to the entire assembly and every perspective has been taken into account.

SECTION TWO

The Theological Declaration

Noble Lords, having refuted those objections made previously against me, I now present my case.[43] Because my appearance is in obedience to your request, second only to God to whom utmost obligation is due, I am confident that no prejudice against me or my stated opinions[44] shall result from what I have to say.

On Predestination

THE FIRST and most important article of religion on which I offer my view, which for many years has engaged my attention, is the Predestination of God—the election of some to salvation and the reprobation of others to damnation. I begin with what is taught orally and in writing on this point by some in our churches as well as at the University of Leiden.[45] Then I will declare my own views on the matter and follow with my opinions of what others have put forward.

On this article of religion there is no consistent and uniform opinion among the teachers of our churches. From their writings we can determine that some espouse the most extreme form of the doctrine, as follows:

I. By an eternal and immutable decree, God has predestined certain individuals to eternal salvation and others to eternal damnation—persons whom he was not viewing as already created or even as fallen. This eternal decree was made with no regard for righteousness or sinfulness, obedience or disobedience, but solely according to his good pleasure to demonstrate the glory[46] of his justice and

---

[43] In his manuscript Arminius has drawn a line through: "as I am legally required to do by the Magistrates over me."

[44] The words related to prejudice against his opinions are written in the margin, replacing the stricken words: *men my sulx geensins*, literally, "men shall for such by no means."

[45] Reference to the University of Leiden is a marginal annotation.

[46] The manuscript (p. 7) reads, *eerlijkheydt*; Hoenderdaal, 64, is in error when he says

mercy; or as others assert, to demonstrate his saving grace, wisdom, and sovereign power.

II. In addition to this decree, God has preordained certain established means by which to obtain these ends, this too by an eternal and immutable decree. These means necessarily follow by virtue of the prior decree, and they necessarily bring the one who has been predestined to the end that has been foreordained. Some of these means belong to both the decree of election and the decree of reprobation, while others are restricted to the one decree or the other.

III. Three means are common to both decrees: The first is the creation of humankind in an upright state of original righteousness—in the image and likeness of God, righteous and holy. The second means is to allow the fall of Adam—the foreordination of God that humanity would sin and become corrupt. The third is the resultant loss or removal of original righteousness and likeness to God's image—a creature left under the dominion of sin and condemnation.

IV. The logic is that unless God had created humanity, he would not have had anyone upon whom to bestow eternal life or to assign eternal death. Unless he had created them righteous and holy, he would himself have been the cause of sin, which would mean he had no right either to punish them to the praise of his justice, or to save them to the praise of his mercy. Unless they had themselves sinned, and by the demerit of sin rendered themselves deserving of death, there would have been no way for God to demonstrate either justice or mercy.

V. There are also three means preordained to establish the decree of election: The first is to ordain Jesus Christ as Mediator and Savior, through whose merit and virtue and by his power, lost righteousness and life would be restored to the elect, and to them only. The second is the vocation of the elect to faith—outwardly by the Word and inwardly by the Holy Spirit working in the mind, affections, and will. So powerful is this operation of the Spirit that the elect will of necessity yield assent and obedience to the divine initiative, for it is not possible for the elect to do otherwise than to believe and

---

it reads *heerlykheyt*. The *Verclaringhe* (1610), 10, reads *eerlijkheyt*. Perhaps Hoenderdaal was influenced by his reference to H. Y. Groenewegen, *De Remonstrantie op haren 300sten gedenkdag in den oorspronkelijken vorm uitgegeven* (Leiden: 1910), 9, where Groenewegen notes that the *Remonstratie* of 1610 actually did read *heerlyckheyd syner rechtveerdicheyt*. Verdam's dictionary of Middle Dutch notes that both *heerlykhyd* and *eerlykhyd* come from the same root word; indeed, both carry the connotation of "honor" as well as "glory."

be obedient. From this arise both justification and sanctification through the blood of Christ and his Spirit, and from them together arise all good works—all of these manifestly by the same force and necessity. The third is that provision which keeps and preserves the elect in faith, holiness, and zeal for good works: the gift of perseverance. The benefit of perseverance is not only that believing and elect persons do not freely and willfully commit sin, but neither do they fall away totally from faith and grace. Likewise, neither is it possible for them to sin with a full and perfect will or to totally or finally fall from faith and grace.

VI. Vocation and perseverance belong only to the elect who are of an adult age. For children of believers and saints who depart this life before an accountable age, God employs a shorter way of salvation. Provided they are counted among the elect, known only to God, he bestows salvation on them through Christ and saves them through his blood and the Holy Spirit without actually ever bestowing faith and perseverance on them. This God does through the promise of the covenant of grace: I will be a God to you, and to your seed after you [Gen 17:7].[47]

VII. The means by which the decree of reprobation to eternal death is accomplished may be divided between the parts that belong to those who are rejected and reprobate, whether they live to adulthood or die before an age of accountability, and the parts that are proper only to some of them. The means common to the reprobate is to leave them in their sinful state by denying them that saving grace which is sufficient and necessary to salvation, the result being that they are left in sinfulness. This denial of grace consists of two parts: The first is that God did not will that Christ would die for them or become their Savior. This is not according to the antecedent will of God (as

---

[47] There was no standard Dutch language version of the Bible until *De Statenvertaling* in 1637. This was commissioned by the Synod of Dort in 1619, to be done by a team of translators following the methods for the Authorized, the King James Version. The *Statenvertaling* became the "Authorized Version" in Dutch because it had to be authorized by the States of Holland before the scholars could do their work. The delay between recommendation in 1619 and the publication in 1637 was related to the extensive required scholarly work combined with the slowness in the approval process by the States of Holland. Scriptural references and allusions are found throughout Arminius' manuscript; however, he very seldom indicates that he is quoting, and he seldom supplied the reference—even when he is quoting an entire verse. The scriptural references are supplied by the editors of the *Verclaringhe* (1610), and in some cases I have added additional citations. When Arminius references a short phrase in his biblical references, I have simply translated his words; when there is a full verse reference, I have used the Revised Standard Version.

some would call it), nor is it in reference to his sufficient will. Neither should it be attributed to the value of the cost of reconciliation, because this price was not offered for reprobates, either with respect to the decree of God, or its virtue and efficacy. The second part of this denial of grace is that God is unwilling to communicate the Spirit of Christ to the reprobate, and without such a sharing they can be made neither partakers of Christ nor recipients of his benefits.

VIII. The means that belong properly only to some of the reprobate is the act of hardening [of the heart], which happens to those adults who have frequently and maliciously sinned and broken the law of God, or because they have rejected the grace of the Gospel. In order for the hardening of the heart to occur, the conscience must first be illumined by knowledge and conviction of the righteousness of the Law, which by its very nature demonstrates their unrighteousness and renders it inexcusable. There is also another hardening. God calls the sinner through the preaching of the Gospel, but this call is powerless and insufficient both with respect to God's provision as well as the actual response. The call may be merely an external one which the hearer neither desires nor is able to obey. Or it may be an internal one that excites some hearers' understanding and inclines them to accept and believe what they are hearing; however, this is no more than the common faith before which the devils quake. Other hearers of the call are so enticed that they desire in a certain measure to taste the heavenly gift. Among all that hear the call, these are the unhappiest of all. Because, having been lifted so high, they then fall the hardest. This is unavoidable, for they will of necessity return to their vomit and fall away from the faith.

IX. The means attendant to the decrees of election and reprobation assure, on the one hand, that the elect will be saved, it being impossible for them not to believe, and on the other hand, that the reprobate are damned, it being impossible for them to believe. This results from the absolute intention of God antecedent to all things, including all possible causes or things that can result from those causes.

For some who advocate this perspective on predestination, this is foundational to Christianity, salvation, and its certainty. They suppose these opinions to be the only true source of consolation that can bring peace to the conscience of believers; furthermore, the praise of God's grace is so dependent on this that any contradiction to this doctrine necessarily deprives God's grace of its deserved praise and glory—for the merit of salvation is then attributed to free will, human strength and power—in a word, Pelagianism.[48] For these reasons the purveyors of this predestination labor diligently to preserve the purity of this doctrine in God's Church and to oppose any variation of teaching that they consider an innovation.

My Sentiments on This Scheme of Predestination

In my opinion, if I may speak with freedom in an attempt to form a better judgment, this doctrine as formulated contains many falsehoods, inconsistencies, and contradictions, too many to recount within our time constraints. I shall therefore restrict my remarks to a global frame of reference and point out four principal points that are the most prominent and far-reaching in their implications. Once those are set out, I will endeavor to explain briefly my judgments regarding them:

I. That God has absolutely and with precision decreed to save certain human beings by his mercy and grace, but to condemn others according to his justice. God has chosen to do this without any regard for the righteousness or sinfulness, obedience or disobedience that might be present in the lives of either the elect or the reprobate.[49]

II. That God, in order to execute this decree, determined to create Adam and all humanity in him both pure and righteousness. He also ordained that they would commit sin so that they would be deprived of original righteousness, incur guilt, and deserve eternal condemnation.

III. That God decreed both the decision to save some as well as the means to attain that end. He willed not only to save them, but to bring them to faith as well as to assure that they would persevere in that faith. This God accomplishes by a grace and power that is irresistible, so that it is impossible for the elect to do otherwise than believe, persevere in the faith, and be saved.

IV. That those whom God has foreordained to perdition by his absolute will, he has also denied the grace that is necessary and sufficient for salvation. He does not confer this grace on them, and the result is that they are denied any capacity to come to faith and be saved.

---

[48] Pelagius (AD 354–420/440) was most famously opposed by St. Augustine, who did praise him for his sincerity and piety. The teachings of Pelagius were openly opposed at the Council of Diospolis in 415 and formally condemned at Carthage in 418.

[49] The manuscript has a partially illegible note in the margins, from which the following words are legible: "frequently the expressed opinion of Rev. Gomarus on this point."

*I. This Doctrine Is Not the Foundation of Christianity,
of Salvation, or of Certainty*

In the fear of the Lord, after thorough examination and contemplation on these four points, I offer the following with regard to this doctrine of Predestination:

I. This doctrine of predestination is not the foundation of Christianity,[50] of salvation, or of its certainty. (1) This doctrine of predestination does not correspond to the decree of God by which Christ is appointed to be the Savior, the head, and the foundation of those who will be made heirs to salvation. This decree [Christ appointed as Savior] is the sole foundation for Christianity. (2) The doctrine as formulated is not that doctrine by which, through faith, we as living stones are built up into Christ, the chief cornerstone, joined with him as members of the body connected to their head.

II. This doctrine is not the foundation for salvation. (1) This predestination does not correspond to that decree of the good pleasure of God in Christ Jesus on which our salvation solely rests and depends. (2) This doctrine of predestination is not the foundation of salvation, for it is not the power of God to salvation to everyone that believes [Rom 1:16], because in this plan the righteousness of God is not revealed from faith to faith [Rom 1:17].[51]

III. This doctrine is not a foundation for the certainty of our salvation. (1) The certainty of our salvation is: Those who believe will be saved [Mark 16:16]; and, I believe, therefore, I shall be saved. (2) For this doctrine of predestination embraces within itself neither the first nor the second part of the syllogism—a point recognized by those who say, "We do not intend to say that a knowledge of the doctrine of predestination is the foundation of Christianity, or that such knowledge is on par with knowledge of the Gospel as necessary for salvation."[52]

---

[50] In the manuscript the word "Christianity" is replaced with "Christendom." For modern connotational reasons, "Christianity" is retained.

[51] Implicit and explicit references to Romans are sprinkled throughout Arminius' *Declaration*, which is not surprising when we remember that, after being "requested" by supervisory ministers in Amsterdam to prepare a defense of traditional teachings on election and predestination, Arminius preached expository sermons on Romans for thirteen years, from November 6, 1588 to September 30, 1601.

[52] Arminius gives no indication whom he is quoting here. Could he be invoking statements by his teacher in Geneva, the esteemed Theodore Beza, that other theories of predestination were acceptable? The identification of the supralapsarian doctrine with salvation itself is specifically rejected by Gomarus. He taught that it was the superior interpretation of God's saving activity, but Gomarus allowed that the doctrine did not constitute the actual saving work of God.

II. The Doctrine of Predestination Does Not Contain the Gospel, or Any Part Thereof

The essence of the Gospel is wrapped up in an injunction to repent and believe, accompanied by a promise to bestow forgiveness of sins, the grace of the Spirit, and life eternal. This teaching is found in the preaching of John as well as Christ as it has been delivered to us in the Gospels by the Apostles of Christ after his ascension. This doctrine of predestination belongs neither to the admonition to repent and believe, nor to the accompanying promise. No, this doctrine does not in any way describe the characteristics of people whom God has predestined, which is, properly speaking, Gospel doctrine. It is characterized by a mystery known only to God, the one who predestines. Shrouded in this mystery are the identities of the particular persons as well as the total number God has decreed to save and to condemn. From this I conclude that knowledge of this doctrine of predestination is not necessary to salvation, either as an object of belief, hope, or performance. This has been admitted by a learned man [Gomarus] in the following words taken from the theses he proposed in his public disputation:

> The Gospel should not simply be called the book or the revelation of predestination, except in a particular sense. It does not prescribe the number nor does it define the form, i.e., it neither declares how many persons in particular, nor (with few exceptions) who they are. It describes only in a general way the ones whom God has predestined.[53]

III. This Doctrine Was Never Affirmed in a General or Special Council[54]

In the first six hundred years after Christ, this doctrine was never decreed or affirmed in any Council, either general or special. This did not happen at the Council of Nicaea in which a sentence was handed down against Arius in favor of the deity and consubstantiality of the Son of God. It did not happen at the first Council of Constantinople in which a decree was passed against Macedonius, affirming the deity of the Holy Spirit. Nor did it happen at the

---

[53] This essentially reflects the eleventh proposition in Franciscus Gomarus, *Twee disputatiën vande Goddelicke Predestinatie vertaelt uyt het Latijn* (Leyden: Jan Paets Jacobszoon, 1609 and 1610). Cf. "Examination of the Theses of Dr. Francis Gomarus Respecting Predestination," *Works*, 3:556–57. Also, from the very first line in the preface to the 1610 edition of Arminius' *Verclaringhe*, it is clear that the publication is a response to Gomarus' publications.

[54] The Dutch word translated "special" is *particulier*. The reference is to "provincial councils" that were convened in the early church to handle disagreements and conflicts at the regional or "provincial" level.

Council of Ephesus regarding the Son of God, which condemned Nestorius in favor of the unity of the persons. It also did not happen at Chalcedon, which condemned Eutyches and affirmed that in our Lord Jesus Christ there are two natures, each distinct in their essence. Nor did it happen at the second Council of Constantinople, in which Peter, Bishop of Antioch, and Anthymus, Bishop of Constantinople, along with others, were condemned for asserting that the Father had likewise suffered. And it also did not happen at the third Council of Constantinople, at which the monothelites were condemned for asserting that there was only one will operative in Jesus Christ. Furthermore, this doctrine was not discussed or confirmed in any of the special councils of the Church, such as that at Jerusalem, at Orange, or even at Mela in Africa, which condemned Pelagius' errors.[55] The Augustinian doctrine of predestination was so far from being affirmed in those councils that when Augustine's contemporary Celestinus, the Bishop of Rome, wrote to the Bishops of France and condemned the Pelagian heresy, he concluded his epistle with these words:

> the more profoundly difficult parts of the questions that occur in this controversy, as they have been treated in some depth by those who opposed the heretics. Because we affirm that the content of the previously mentioned rules [of the Apostolic See] are amply sufficient to teach us to confess the grace of God.[56]

We cannot be certain what he understood to be the more profoundly difficult issues, other than Augustine's doctrine of predestination. With regard to the Rules laid down by Celestinus in that epistle, which had been set out in the three preceding Special Councils, we shall have no difficulty in agreeing about them, especially with regard to the points necessary to affirm the doctrine of grace in opposition to Pelagius and his errors.

---

[55] Two councils convened in 416 condemning Pelagius, one at Carthage and another at the lesser known Mela (Mileve, Milevitano). The death of Pope Innocent I led to the reinstatement of Pelagius for a brief period, but he was condemned with finality at Carthage in 418.

[56] Cf. St. Prosper of Aquaitaine, "Official Pronouncements of the Apostolic See on Divine Grace and Free Will," in *Ancient Christian Writers*, vol. 31, *Prosper of Aquaitaine: Defense of St. Augustine*, trans. P. de Letter (Westminster, Md.: Newman Press, 1963), 185. Footnote 23 on page 232 notes that previous scholars (Arminius in this case) attributed the document to Pope Celestine I. The full quotation in the modern translation reads: "As to the more profound and more difficult points in the topical problems of our day which were treated at length by the opponents of the heretics, we neither mean to scorn them nor need we expound them here. For a profession of faith in the doctrine on the grace of God, from whose action and mercy nothing whatever may be withdrawn, we consider simply sufficient what the writings of the Apostolic See, as given above in these articles, have taught us."

IV. The Divines of the Church Have Not Affirmed This Doctrine as Orthodox

During the first six centuries after the birth of Christ, this doctrine has never been brought forward and approved, even by the sympathetic Doctors of the Church. It was not affirmed by a single one of the primary and keenest defenders of grace against Pelagius. Among these may be counted St. Jerome, Augustine, the author of "The Calling of the Gentiles," Prosper of Aquitane, Hilary, Fulgentius, and Orosius. This is clearly apparent from their writings.

V. This Doctrine of Predestination Is Not in Harmony with the Confessions of the Reformed Churches

This doctrine neither agrees with nor corresponds to the "harmony" of those Confessions that were published in one volume in Geneva to represent the Reformed and Protestant churches. When one carefully reads that Harmony of Confessions,[57] it is apparent that many of the confessions do not address predestination in this way. Some of them address the topic briefly, but even then they do not address the main points of doctrine under dispute that I have set out above. Also, no confession of faith proposes this doctrine in the formulation that I have described. The confessions of Bohemia, England, Wirtemburgh, the first Helvetic [Swiss] Confession, and that of the four cities of Strasburg, Constance, Memmingen, and Lindaw make no mention of this form of predestination; and the confessions of Basel and Saxony need only four or five words to cover the subject. The Augsburg Confession addresses it in such a manner that the Genevan editors of the Harmony felt that annotations of warning on their part were necessary. The last of the Swiss Confessions, to which a great number of the Reformed Churches have subscribed their assent, likewise speaks of predestination in such a manner as to lead me to wonder how it could ever be adapted in such a manner as to conform with the doctrine of predestination that I have described above. Yet, this is the Swiss Confession that has received the approval of the Churches of Geneva and Savoy.

VI. This Doctrine Is Not in Agreement with the Belgic Confession or the Heidelberg Catechism

With a minimum of contention or even trivial objection, it may be appropriately doubted whether this doctrine agrees with either the Belgic Confession or the Heidelberg Catechism.

---

[57] [Jean Francois Salvert], *Harmonia confessionum fidei, orthodoxarum ac reformatorum Ecclesiarum* (1581).

1. In the 14th Article of the Belgic Confession, we affirm that man "willfully subjected himself to sin and consequently to death and the curse, giving ear to the words of the devil."[58] From this I conclude that humanity did not sin on account of necessity due to a preceding decree of predestination, a conclusion diametrically opposed to the doctrine of predestination that I am opposing.
2. In the 16th Article, dealing with eternal election, we read: "God then did manifest Himself such as He is; that is to say, merciful and just: merciful, since He delivers and preserves from this perdition all whom He in His eternal and unchangeable counsel of mere goodness has elected in Christ Jesus our Lord, without any respect to their works: just, in leaving others in the fall and perdition wherein they have involved themselves."[59] It is not obvious to me that these words are consistent with the doctrine of predestination that I am opposing.
3. In the 20th question of the Heidelberg Catechism, we read: "Are all men, then, saved by Christ as they have perished in Adam?"[60] And the answer is: "No, only those who by true faith are engrafted into Him and receive all His benefit." From this I conclude that God has not absolutely predestined anyone to salvation, but that in predestining them, he views them as believers in Christ. This deduction is in open conflict with the first and third points of predestination as described above.
4. Furthermore, in the 54th question of the Heidelberg Catechism, it is asked: "What do you believe concerning the 'Holy Catholic Church'?" To which is answered, "That out of the whole human race from the beginning to the end of the world, the Son of God, by the Spirit and Word, gathers, defends, and preserves for Himself unto everlasting life a chosen communion in the unity of the true faith." In this sentence "preserves for Himself unto everlasting life" stands in mutuality with "in the unity of the true faith" in such a manner that the latter [true faith] is not subordinated to the former [preserves...unto everlasting life]. This subordination would be required in the logic of the position that I oppose, and

---

[58] A. C. Cochrane, ed., *Reformed Confessions of the Sixteenth Century* (Philadelphia: Westminster, 1966), 2:432.

[59] Cochrane, *Reformed Confessions*, 2:433–34.

[60] In Arminius' *Declaration*, the questions from the Heidelberg Catechism are not reproduced; but they are added here so that the answers might be seen in their larger context. See *Reformed Confessions of the Sixteenth Century* under the respective "Questions."

it would read: "The Son of God calls and gathers unto himself, by his Word and Spirit, a company chosen to eternal life in order that they would believe[61] and agree together in the faith."

Since these are the actual statements of our Confession and Catechism, no good reason can be put forward by those who defend these aforementioned sentiments on predestination to force these doctrines on their colleagues or on the Church of Christ; nor should they be offended and place it in the worst possible light when something is taught in the church or university that does not exactly correspond to or is in opposition to their position.

VII. This Doctrine Is Repugnant to the Nature of God

I assert that this doctrine is repugnant to the nature of God, especially with regard to those attributes by which he performs and manages all things: his wisdom, justice, and goodness.

1. It is repugnant to God's wisdom in three ways. (1) Because it represents God as decreeing something for a particular purpose that is not good, nor could it ever be good: namely, that God created something for eternal damnation in order to praise his justice. (2) Because it teaches that the end goal of this divine predestination is to demonstrate the glory of God's mercy and justice. But this glory cannot be demonstrated except by an act that is inherently contradictory to his justice and mercy, because God has determined that man would sin and be miserable. (3) Because it changes the twofold wisdom of God as it is displayed in the Scriptures by reversing the order. This doctrine asserts that without having foreseen the circumstance of Christ's death, God has with specificity predetermined to save humanity by the mercy and wisdom encompassed in the Word of the cross of Christ. This is established without any possibility of salvation by the wisdom[62] revealed in the law or infused into humanity when created—the impossibility of salvation being humanity's own fault. This is asserted in the face of Scripture's clear declaration that it pleased God by the foolishness of preaching to save them that believe, that is, by the Word of the cross, when in the wisdom of God the world did not know God through wisdom [1 Cor 1:21].

---

[61] In the manuscript there is a notation, "be born again."
[62] The manuscript has the marginal notation, "wisdom of God, wisdom of God as revealed in the law."

2. This doctrine is repugnant to the justice of God with regard to that attribute by which God loves righteousness and hates iniquity, and also with regard to God's consistent and constant desire to render to everyone that which is due to them. It is at odds with the first of these ideas of justice for the following reasons: (1) Because it affirms that God has absolutely willed to save certain individual persons and has decreed their salvation with no regard for their righteousness or obedience. From this it may be properly concluded that God loves such creatures far more than God loves his own justice.[63] (2) It also opposes another dimension of God's justice because it affirms that God wishes to subject humanity to misery. This misery could have no justification other than as a punishment for sin, but since God [in this scheme] does not view the creature as a sinner, the creature could not be seen as deserving either wrath or punishment. So in this manner God has attributed to the creature that which does not properly belong to it, indeed, something that leads to the creature's greatest injury. This is then another act directly opposed to God's justice: God robs himself of that which rightfully belongs to him [justice] and then imparts to the creature that which does not rightfully belong to him [damnation],[64] but which brings great misery.

3. This doctrine is also repugnant to the goodness of God. Goodness is an affective disposition in God to communicate his goodness, insofar as his justice sees fit and allows. But according to this doctrine, God has solely of his own sovereign accord willed the greatest evil on his creatures. From all eternity God has preordained evil for them and predetermined to impart it to them, even before considering any good gift. The teaching is that God wills first to damn, and then in order to accomplish this, God wills to create. Creation, then, is the first act of goodness flowing from God towards his creatures. These assertions are in stark contrast to those that reflect the expansive goodness of God by which he confers benefits not only on the unworthy, but even on the evil, the unjust, and those who are deserving of punishment—the example of our heavenly Father whom we are commanded to imitate [Matt 5:45].

---

[63] Marginal note reads, "which is in direct contradiction to his justice."

[64] The reader should keep in mind here that Arminius is drawing the logical conclusions from a supralapsarian scheme of predestination that sets out the salvific decrees prior to creation and prior to the fall. Since in the supralapsarian scheme humanity has not yet been created and has not yet fallen, there can be no consideration of either actual sinfulness or requisite deserved punishment.

VIII. This Doctrine of Predestination Is in Conflict with Human Nature

This doctrine of predestination is contrary to human nature, being created righteous and holy[65] in the divine image with knowledge of God—created with freedom of will and with a disposition and aptitude for the enjoyment of eternal life. These three aspects may be deduced from the following concise exhortations: "Do this and live" [Rom 10:5], and "But of the tree of the knowledge of good and evil you shall not eat, for in the day that you eat of it you shall die" [Gen 2:17]. Were humanity to be deprived of these characteristics [freedom, inclination to enjoy eternal life, and capability of enjoying eternal life], such admonitions would be incapable of moving persons to obedience.[66]

1. This doctrine is inconsistent with the divine image, which consists of the knowledge of God and holiness. In accordance with this knowledge and righteousness, the creature was enabled and empowered—even under obligation—to know God, and to love, worship, and serve him. But by the intervention, or rather the priority of this predestination, it was preordained that humanity was made defective and that humans would sin. This resulted in humanity neither knowing God, loving, worshipping, nor serving him. It also meant that the creature could not perform those duties that being created in God's image enabled, empowered, and even obligated him to do. This scheme is tantamount to saying that God created humanity in his image, in righteousness and true holiness, but God also foreordained and decreed that the creature would become impure and unrighteous. Indeed, humanity would be made conformable to the image of Satan.

2. This doctrine is inconsistent with the freedom of the will, in which and with which humanity was originally created. It prevents the exercise of freedom by requiring and predetermining the will first to do specifically one thing or then quite another thing. This means that God may be blamed[67] for either of two things: creating humanity with freedom of the will, or then, after creating them as free agents, hindering the use of that freedom. In the first case, God is guilty of deficient consideration, and in the latter case

---

[65] "Holy" is a marginal addition in the manuscript.

[66] The last part of this paragraph, beginning with the reference to Romans 10, is written in the manuscript margin.

[67] Hoenderdaal follows the published *Verclaringhe*, which changes Arminius' "is to be blamed" to the conditional "may be blamed"—substituting *soude* for *is*. This should not be construed to weaken Arminius' opinion about the issue.

God may be charged with mutability—and in both cases God is charged with doing harm to humanity as well as to God's own self.
3. This doctrine of predestination is prejudicial with regard to the creature's divinely endowed inclination and capacity to enjoy the blessing of eternal life. This scheme of predestination has predetermined that the greater part of humanity shall not receive salvation but shall fall into everlasting condemnation. Since this predetermination took place prior to the decision to create humanity, the creatures were deprived in an a priori fashion of the desire for that with which they were naturally endowed by God. This great privation is not as a consequence of any sin or demerit on their part, but totally and completely as a result of this scheme of divine predestination.

IX. This Predestination Is Diametrically Opposed to the Act of Creation

1. By virtue of its intrinsic nature, creation is a communication of that which is good; however, creation is not a communication of good when its purposive intent and design is set up to attain a predetermined reprobation. That which is good may be judged and determined to be good according to the mind and intention of the donor and according to the goal or purpose for which it is bestowed. In this instance, the intention of the donor would have been to damn, an act that could only affect created beings, and the goal of the creative act was the eternal damnation of those beings. In which case, creation was not a communication of any good, but rather a preparation for[68] the greatest evil—according to the very intention of the creator and the actual result of the event as designed. For such an event, the words of Christ are appropriate: "It would have been better for that one not to have been born" [Matt 26:24].
2. Reprobation is a hateful act that springs from hate. But the act of creation did not grow out of hatred, and it should not be construed as a way or means to accomplish the decree of reprobation.
3. Creation is a perfect act of God that declares his wisdom, goodness, and omnipotence. It is therefore not subordinate to the purposes of any other preceding work or action of God. Creation

---

[68] The manuscript reads *ofte toebereydinge*, "or a preparation." Hoenderdaal follows the published *Verclaringhe: maar eene voorberydinghe*, "but rather a preparation." The two nouns had essentially the same meaning in the sixteenth century.

should be viewed as that act of God that necessarily precedes and is antecedent to all other actions that he can possibly decree or undertake. Unless God had designed a prior act of creation, he could not have decreed to undertake any other act. Until he had performed that act of creation, he could not possibly have completed any other act.

4. All actions of God purported to lead to the condemnation of his creatures are strange and alien to him, because God would be consenting to them through a cause that is itself extraneous to him. But rather than being alien to God, creation is an act quite proper to him. It is eminently an action most appropriate to him. It is an act to which he could be moved by no other external cause. Indeed, it is the primordial act of God, and until it was completed, nothing could have any actual existence except God himself. For everything else that has being came into existence through this act.

5. If it be the case that God willed the execution of the decree of reprobation through the act of creation, then God was more inclined to the act of reprobation than to that of creation. Consequently, the creator derived greater satisfaction from the condemnation of his innocent creatures than from the act of creation.

6. And finally, creation should not be viewed as a way or means to accomplish God's absolute design to damn: (a) Because creation was complete, it was within the creature's power to remain obedient to God and not commit sin; and, (b) To make this obedience possible, God had, on the one hand, bestowed on humanity sufficient strength, but, on the other hand, God had also placed sufficient impediments. This circumstance is clearly and diametrically opposed to the scheme of predestination under consideration.

X. *This Doctrine Is in Open Hostility to the Nature of Eternal Life*

This doctrine is openly hostile to the nature of eternal life, especially the nomenclature with which it is described in the Scriptures. It is described as "the inheritance of the children of God" [Titus 3:7], but only those who "believe in the name of Jesus Christ" [John 1:12] are the children of God according to the Gospel. It is also called the "reward of obedience" [Matt 5:12] and the "labor of love" [Heb 6:10], as well as "the recompense of those who fight the good fight and who run well, a crown of righteousness" [Rev 2:10; 2 Tim 4:7-8]. From these Scriptures it is clear that God has not by an absolute decree, apart from any consideration or regard whatever for faith and obedience, appointed any person to eternal life or predetermined that it would be their destiny.

XI. This Predestination Is Opposed to the Nature of Eternal Death

This doctrine of predestination is also opposed to the nature of eternal death and to the nomenclature used to describe it in Scripture. For it is called the "wages of sin" [Rom 6:23] and "the punishment of everlasting destruction that shall be meted out to them that do not know God and refuse to obey the Gospel of our Lord Jesus Christ" [2 Thess 1:8-9]. It is the "fearful prospect of judgment, and a fury of fire prepared for the devil and his angels, a fire that will consume the adversaries" of God [Heb 10:27]. God, therefore, has not by an eternal decree prepared eternal death for any person without regard to sin and disobedience.[69]

XII. This Predestination Is Inconsistent with the Nature and Characteristics of Sin

This doctrine of predestination is inconsistent with the characteristics and nature of sin in two respects: (1) Sin is described as disobedience and rebellion, neither of which may justly be applied to any person who has been placed under an unavoidable necessity of sinning by a preceding divine decree [1 John 1:3-4]. (2) Sin is the meritorious cause of damnation, and it moves God to condemn justly. God is moved to damn due to hatred for sin. So sin cannot be a mediate cause by which God carries out the design or decision to damn.

XIII. This Doctrine Is Destructive to the Nature of Divine Grace

This doctrine is contrary to the nature of divine grace, and to the extent that such is possible, it destroys grace. Regardless of the pretenses under which it is asserted that this kind of predestination is admirably suited and even necessary to establish grace, it destroys it in three ways:

1. Because grace is interwoven with the nature of humanity in such a way as not to destroy the freedom of the will, but rather to give it proper direction and to correct its depravity, it allows the creature to devise actions of his own accord. In stark contrast, this predestination introduces a type of grace that hinders free will and takes it away.

---

[69] I am following the *Verclaringhe* (1610), 22; and Hoenderdaal's amended text, 82. The manuscript (p. 15) interpolates these words: "an exclusion from resting in the Lord, which only occurs by divine edict due to unbelief and disobedience."

2. The representation of grace in Scripture describes it as capable of "being resisted" [Acts 7:51] and "received in vain" [2 Cor 6:1]. It is possible for the creature to "avoid yielding assent to it and to refuse all cooperation with it" [Heb 12:15; Matt 23:37; Luke 7:30]. On the contrary, this predestination asserts that grace is an irresistible force and operation.
3. In accordance with the primary intention and design of God, grace is conducive to the good of those persons to whom it is offered and by whom it is received. This doctrine, however, brings along with it the assertion that grace is offered to certain among the reprobate without effect. It is offered with sufficiency to illuminate their understanding and to excite within them a taste for the heavenly gift, but this is done to accomplish the end and purpose of their mighty fall—that they will be plunged into an abyss in proportion to the height to which they were elevated. And this is done so that they may both merit and receive the greater damnation.

XIV. This Doctrine Is Injurious to the Glory of God

This doctrine of predestination is injurious to the glory of God. God's glory consists neither of a declaration of liberty or might, nor of a demonstration of anger and power—except as the demonstration of such may be consistent with justice and the continual preservation of God's goodness. The consequence of this doctrine of predestination is that God is the author of sin, as can be demonstrated by four arguments:

1. In a simultaneous act of punitive justice and mercy to demonstrate his glory, God has precisely decreed salvation for some and damnation for others—neither of which was done nor could have possibly been done unless sin entered into the world.
2. This doctrine teaches: in order that this double decree could take place, God ordained that humanity would of necessity sin and become sinful.
3. This doctrine asserts that God has denied to humanity, or has withdrawn from the creature, the grace sufficient and necessary to avoid sin, and this deprivation took place prior to the first sinful act. In view of the nature in which humanity was created, the practical implication of this is that God prescribed a law simply impossible for the creature to keep.
4. This doctrine ascribes to God certain internal and external actions operative on humanity—actions that are both mediated by way of the influence of other creatures, as well as unmediated influence:

divine operations that entail the necessity to commit sin. This is what the schoolmen call *necessitas consequentis, et rem ipsam antecedens* [a consequential necessity antecedent to the thing itself]. This law of necessity totally destroys the freedom of the will. This causal action is attributed to the primary and chief intention of God without any foreknowledge of an inclination, will, or action on the part of humanity.

From these premises we may conclude that God is the one who truly commits sin; because, according to this doctrine, God incites the creature to sin through an irresistible action according to his own divine purpose and primary intention—all this without the creature being inclined to disobedience through any prior sin or warranting defect.

From this we may also conclude that it is God alone who has sinned. Since the creature is compelled to perpetrate a deed that has been prohibited, forced to sin by an irresistible force, it cannot be asserted that the creature himself has sinned. From this it is a legitimate conclusion that this sin is no sin at all, since that which God does can by definition not be a sin, nor may it be labeled as sin.

There is another method by which this doctrine is detrimental to the honor of God, but for the time being I will let it be.

XV. *This Doctrine Is Dishonorable to Jesus Christ as Savior*

This doctrine is highly dishonorable to Jesus Christ our savior, because (1) It entirely excludes him from the decree of predestination that foreordains the ultimate result. This predestination affirms that humanity was predestined to be saved prior to Christ's being predestined to save them, and thus it assumes that Christ is not the foundation for election. (2) By relegating him to a subordinate cause, it denies that Christ is the meritorious cause for the salvation prepared for us—but forfeited [through disobedience]. This subordination makes him merely a servant and instrument to administer salvation. This conclusion is in congruity with the opinion that in the first supreme decree God has absolutely willed the salvation of certain persons, and on this decree all other divine decrees are consequent and dependent. If this be true, then it would have been impossible for that salvation to be lost. Since it could not be lost, it was also not necessary through the meritorious work of Christ, the only one foreordained as savior, for it to be repaired, regained, and found anew.

XVI. *This Doctrine Is Hurtful to the Salvation of Humanity*

This doctrine is also hurtful to the salvation of humanity, because:

1. It prevents that salvific and godly sorrow for sins that have been committed, since that sentiment cannot exist in those who have no consciousness of sin. It is obvious that the person who commits sin, due to the unavoidable necessity of the decree of God to commit that sin, will have no conscious awareness of sin: "For godly grief produces a repentance that leads to salvation and brings no regret" [2 Cor 7:10].
2. It removes all holy concern about turning from sin to God. It asserts that the recipient is as passive as a corpse and can do none other—not only in connection with feeling and hearing God's calling and awakening grace, but also with regard to yielding and obeying. It teaches that the predestined will of necessity sense the grace that stirs internally, but also that the recipient must yield and convert, or more precisely, be converted. It is clear that such a person cannot produce within the heart or conceive in the mind such Godly solicitude, unless he has previously experienced this irresistible force. Even if one were to produce inward Godly concern, it would be totally in vain. By definition, it cannot be a genuine solicitude in the heart when it was produced by an irresistible force in accord with the absolute purpose and intention of God to affect salvation [Rev 2:5].
3. It hinders all zeal and careful regard for good works in the converted, because it declares that the regenerate can perform only a specified good, no more and no less. The believer that is compelled by this saving grace must work and cannot discontinue working; however, the one who is not compelled by the same grace can do nothing and will, of necessity, cease all attempts [Titus 3:14].
4. It extinguishes the zeal for prayer, an efficacious means instituted by God for asking and obtaining all kinds of blessings, especially the salvation that comes from God [Luke 11:1-3]. Prayer cannot possibly be a means to ask for and receive this salvation, since it was predetermined by an immutable and inevitable decree that the elect would receive salvation. Prayer can only be a service to God,[70] because the absolute decree of predestination has determined who shall be saved.
5. This scheme of predestination removes the salutary fear and trembling with which we are commanded to work out our salvation [Phil 2:12]. It asserts that the elect cannot either totally or finally

---

[70] Lit., "service of God rendered to Him."

fall away from faith and grace, because the one who is elected and believes cannot sin with that full and entire willingness with which sin is committed by the ungodly.

6. This doctrine produces an inward human despair of being able to perform what duty requires. It also obstructs our obtaining the goal toward which the inward desires are directed. This despair is the result of several specific teachings: (a) It is taught that the grace of God needed to do good has been denied to the majority of humanity by an absolute and preemptory decree of God. (b) It is taught that this grace is denied to many because an equally absolute divine decree has determined to confer on them damnation rather than salvation. (c) Thus taught, it is hardly possible that any other result will ensue other than what has been previously decreed: the individual who can only with great difficulty presume to count himself among the elect, must finally come to the conclusion that he is included among the damned. This awareness can only lead to despair regarding the hopelessness of performing righteousness and receiving salvation.

XVII. *This Doctrine Inverts the Order of the Gospel*

This doctrine inverts the order of the Gospel of Jesus Christ that requires repentance and faith and promises everlasting life to those who convert and believe [Mark 1:15, 16:16]. But it is stated in this decree of predestination that God bestows conversion and faith on specific persons through an irresistible force because God wills to save them. According to the Gospel, God threatens eternal death on the impenitent and unbelieving [John 3:36]. These threats contribute to the purpose God has in view, namely, that by such means the creature will be deterred from unbelief in order that God may save him. But this decree of predestination teaches that God chooses *not* to confer on certain individuals that grace necessary for conversion and faith because he has specifically decreed their condemnation.[71] The Gospel teaches, "God so loved the world that he gave his only Son, that whoever believes in him should not perish but have eternal life" [John 3:16]. But this doctrine teaches that God so loved those whom he had specifically elected to eternal life that he gave his Son to save them alone, and by an irresistible force in them produced the faith in Christ necessary for salvation. In short, the Gospel is this: fulfill the command and you shall obtain the promise; believe and you shall live. This doctrine, however, places these words in God's mouth: "Since it is my will to

---

[71] Emphasis added.

bestow eternal life on you, it is my will to give you faith."[72] Surely, this is a real and manifest inversion of the Holy Gospel.

XVIII. This Predestination Is Hostile to the Ministry of the Gospel

This predestination is hostile to the ministry of the Gospel because:

1. If God awakens the creature that is dead in trespasses and sin by an irresistible force, that one is not a servant together with God [1 Cor 3:9], nor can that person be an instrument of grace and the Spirit to preach the Gospel, any more than a creature could be an instrument of grace in the original creation, or a minister of the bodily resurrection from the dead.
2. Through this scheme of predestination the ministry of the Holy Gospel has been tainted with the stench of death unto death for the majority of those who hear it [2 Cor 2:14-16]. Indeed, according to the primary design and precise intention of God, the Gospel has become an instrument of condemnation without any consideration of prior human rebellion.
3. This doctrine teaches that when baptism is administered to non-elect children, even though they are the offspring of parents that believe and are part of God's covenant people, this sacrament is a seal of nothing and is entirely useless. Even though the sacrament was administered in obedience to the divine command, it is of no positive benefit to the child. This negative result is in accordance with the primary and specific intention of God, without any culpability on the part of the children to whom the sacrament is administered.
4. This doctrine hinders public prayers from being offered to God in a becoming and suitable manner. Prayers cannot be offered with suitable faith and confidence that they will be profitable to all the hearers of the Word when among the hearers there are those whom God is willing to save, but also those whom, by his absolute, eternal, and immutable will (antecedent to all things and all causes), it is his pleasure and will to damn. When the Apostle Paul commands prayers and supplications to be made for all, he adds this reason, "This is good, and it is acceptable in the sight of God our Savior, who desires all to be saved and to come to the knowledge of the truth" [1 Tim 2:3-4].

---

[72] I have followed the text in the *Verclaringhe* (1610), 26, and Hoenderdaal, 88. The manuscript reads: "this doctrine says: because I will give you the promise, therefore, will I make sure that you shall fulfill the command."

5. The implications of this doctrine may quite easily lead pastors and teachers to become slothful and negligent in the exercise of their ministry. This doctrine implies that their ministering diligence cannot profit anyone except those whom God has specifically willed to save, for these cannot possibly be damned. It further implies that their negligence in ministry would be harmful to none except those whom God absolutely wills to be lost, and these will of necessity most certainly be lost.

XIX. *This Doctrine Subverts the Foundation of Religion*

This doctrine subverts the foundation of religion in general and the Christian religion in particular. Considered as a whole, the foundation of the Christian faith is rooted in the twofold love of God, without which there neither is nor can be any [Christian] religion. The first is a love of justice, which is the source of God's hatred of sin. The second is the love for humanity, endowed by God with reason. In the matter before us, this love acts according to the Apostle to the Hebrews, "[And without faith it is impossible to please God, for] whoever would draw near to God must believe that he exists and that he rewards those who seek him" [Heb 11:6]. God's love for justice is made known in that it is not God's will to bestow eternal life on any except on those who seek him; God's love of humanity consists in the divine willingness to bestow eternal life on those who seek him.

A mutuality exists between these two kinds of love. The love that God extends to humanity cannot come into play unless it is permitted by God's love of justice. This implies that God's love for justice is the more excellent of the two; however, love for the creature abounds, except where the love of justice would prohibit its expression. The consequence of this is demonstrated by God's condemning humanity on account of sin. God clearly demonstrates this love relationship in the original created order; however, this does not imply that God's love for the creature supersedes his love for justice. Had this been the case, God would have manifested a stronger aversion to the eternal misery of the creature than to the creature's disobedience. The abundant place for divine love is clear because God condemns no person for any reason other than sin, and God saves the multitudes of humanity who are converted from sin. In the divine dispensation, this salvation would not be possible unless it was God's will to allow an abundant scope for his love toward the creature under God's judgment, to the extent this is permitted by his justice.

The proposed doctrine inverts this order and mutual relationship in two ways: (1) This happens first when it is stated that the Lord God wills to save specific individuals without any reference to the creature's obedience.

It places God's love for humanity prior to his love for justice, and as such reflects that God loves humanity more than justice. It thereby manifests a stronger aversion to human misery than to their sin and disobedience. (2) The other way in which this doctrine violates the order and mutuality [of justice and love] is the assertion that God wills to damn certain particular people without manifesting in his decree any consideration of disobedience. This detracts from God's manifest love for humanity, a love the creature is rightfully due. This doctrine implies that God hates the creature, but this hatred is not caused by or rooted in either his love of justice, nor in his hatred of iniquity. But is it not the case that sin is the primary object and the only meritorious cause of God's hate?

The powerful capacity that this teaching possesses to subvert the foundation of religion may be illustrated by the following parable: Let's suppose a son would say, "My father loves justice and fairness so much that, even though I am his beloved son, he would disinherit me if I were to be disobedient. If I desire to receive my inheritance, it is incumbent on me carefully to cultivate obedience." But suppose another son says: "My father's love for me is so great that he absolutely has resolved to make me his heir. Therefore, there is no need for me to be consistently obedient, because, according to his unchangeable will, I will remain his heir. Indeed, rather than risking my not being his heir, my father will draw me by an irresistible force to obey him." This is contrary to the words of John [the Baptist]: "Do not presume to say to yourselves, 'We have Abraham as our father'; for I tell you, God is able from these stones to raise up children to Abraham" [Matt 3:9].

The Christian religion is anchored foundationally in this twofold love. The state of humanity, created in the image of and in good favor with God, has been altered due to willful disobedience, so that humanity is by its own fault in a state of sinfulness and enmity toward God. (1) The love of justice, on which the Christian religion rests, is, first, that justice which God declared once and for all in Christ. It was God's will that sin would not be forgiven in any other way than by the blood and death of his Son, and that Christ would not come before Him in any other way as advocate and intercessor except when sprinkled by his own blood. Furthermore, God's love of justice is manifested daily in the preaching of the Gospel truth that it is God's will to grant a communication of Christ and his saving work to humanity, but only to those who convert from sin and believe in Christ. (2) The second point of the twofold love, on which the Christian faith is founded, is God's love for miserable sinners, that love by which he gave his Son for them and constituted Christ as Savior of those who are obedient to him. This love for sinners and the required obedience does not rest on the rigor and severity to which God is supremely entitled, but according to his grace and mercy. To this is added the promise of forgiveness for sin, provided the fallen sinner earnestly repents.[73]

The proposed doctrine of predestination is opposed to this foundational twofold order of love in two distinct ways: First, by asserting that God has such a great love for certain sinners that it was his will absolutely to save them before he had provided a way of forgiveness through Christ Jesus and before he had also satisfied his love of justice. Prior to both of these, God willed their salvation in his own foreknowledge and according to his determinate purpose. This completely overturns the twofold order of divine love by teaching that it is God's pleasure that satisfaction should be paid to his justice because he wills specifically to save such persons. This is tantamount to making his love for justice, manifest in the saving purposes of Christ, subordinate to his love for sinful humanity, whom it is his will absolutely to save. Secondly, this logic opposes the twofold love by asserting that it is the will of God specifically to damn certain sinners without any consideration of their unrepentant state. What has become of the full and complete satisfaction in Christ that demonstrates both God's love of justice and his hatred of sin? In this full and complete satisfaction, nothing other than the condition of repentance can hinder the possibility of divine mercy to the sinner. This is the case, of course, unless some person should choose to assert (as is done in this case) that it has been God's will to act towards the greater part of humanity with the same (or even worse) severity than he exercised towards the devil and his angels. Actually, the severity toward the damned would be greater since neither Christ nor his Gospel has the capacity for any greater blessing to them than to the devils, because the avenue of grace is as much closed against them due to the sin of our first parents as it is against the evil angels. Yet, each of those angels sinned freely and voluntarily, whereas humans have sinned only in their parent Adam.

In order that we may understand more clearly the nature of this twofold order of love as the foundation of all religion, especially the manner in which mutuality exists between the two orders, it is profitable for us to pay close attention to these words of the Apostle to the Hebrews: "[And without faith it is impossible to please God, for] whoever would approach him must believe that he exists and that he rewards those who seek him" [Heb 11:6]. Herein are two foundational assumptions of religion in opposition to the two pernicious, fiery darts of Satan, each of which by itself is able to overturn and destroy true religion. One is carelessness [*securitas*] and the other is despair [*desperatio*].[74] Carelessness is operative when one allows oneself to

---

[73] Lit., "gets up again."

[74] The original English versions miss the theological connotation of this word completely, rendering the Latin *securitas* literally as "security." Arminius' meaning is "false security,"

Portion of manuscript (p. 24) in which Arminius sets out his fourfold decree of predestination. Digital file courtesy of the Rotterdam City Library archive, filed as hs.2201.

be persuaded that regardless of how inattentive he may be to the worship of God, he will not be damned and is certain to obtain salvation. Despair reigns when a person is persuaded that no amount of reverence toward God will lead to a positive reception from God. When either of these deadly dispositions is operative, it is impossible for true and proper worship of God to follow. Both of these, however, are overturned by the apostolic teaching that when one firmly believes that God will bestow eternal life on those who seek him—but

---

which leads to "carelessness" in maintaining relationship with God. See the insightful discussion in Stanglin, 150–81.

that he will inflict eternal death on those who do not—one cannot on any account indulge himself in [the false security that leads to] carelessness. Likewise, when one believes that God is indeed the rewarder of those who diligently seek him, by applying himself to the search, he will not be in danger of falling into despair.[75] The foundation of the former kind of faith, by which one firmly believes that God will bestow eternal life on all who seek Him, is that God loves justice more than he loves humanity. This prioritizing of justice is the only adequate protection against carelessness. At the same time, the foundation for the latter kind of faith, one that dares to believe that God will undoubtedly reward those who diligently seek Him, is that great love for humanity which neither can nor will prevent God from effecting salvation for the sinner—unless God be hindered by his greater love for justice. Yet, this latter love is so far from operating as a hindrance to God's becoming a rewarder of those who diligently seek Him, that, on the contrary, it promotes in every possible way the bestowal of that reward. Those persons, therefore, who seek God can by no means indulge in a single doubt concerning his readiness to reward. And it is this which acts as a preservative against despair or distrust. This being the case, as we have set it out, God's twofold love, and the mutuality that each part bears toward the other, serve together to form the foundation of religion, without which no true religion can possibly exist. Any doctrine, therefore, that is in open hostility to this twofold love and to the relationship that mutually exists between them, subverts the foundation of all religion.

XX. *This Doctrine of Predestination Rejected*

Finally, this doctrine of predestination has been rejected by the majority of Christians in ancient as well as modern times. Passing over references to the earliest church, the facts themselves declare that the Lutherans and Anabaptists, as well as the Roman Church, hold this teaching to be false. Even though in the earliest days of the Reformation, Martin Luther and Philip Melanchthon held the doctrine in high esteem, they later moved away from this version of the doctrine. The change in Melanchthon is quite evident in his later writings, and Luther's followers contend that he refined his opinion on the subject rather than entirely abandoning his earlier position. Melanchthon himself asserted that the doctrine differs little from the concept of Fate to be found among the Stoics. His opinion may be found in many of his writings, but especially in a letter addressed to Gaspar Peucer, where he writes: "Laelius writes to me that the controversy in Geneva regarding Fate as taught by the Stoics has led to one individual being imprisoned because he happened

---

[75] At this point in the original manuscript, six lines are illegible due to a line drawn through them.

to differ from Zeno. O unhappy times! when the doctrine of salvation is obscured by such strange disputes."⁷⁶

The Danish churches embrace a doctrine quite opposite to this, as may be discerned from the writings of Nicholas Hemmingius in his treatise on universal grace (*de Liber Gratia universali*),⁷⁷ in which he declares that the issue between himself and his opponents consisted in the determination of two fundamental points: "Do the elect believe?" or, "Are believers the true elect?"⁷⁸ Hemmingius is of the opinion that those who hold the former opinion are in agreement with the Manicheans and Stoics, while those who hold the latter position are in harmony with Moses and the prophets, with Christ and his Apostles.

In addition, this doctrine is viewed so negatively by many in our land that they have declared their unwillingness to continue attending our churches. A few others have joined our churches, but under protest that they cannot possibly affirm this doctrine. On account of this doctrine, our churches have been deserted by quite a few persons who agree with us on this issue. Others have threatened to leave unless they are assured that the Church holds no opinion such as is described here.

There is not a single doctrine that the Papists, Anabaptists, and Lutherans oppose with greater intensity. Each in turn places our churches in a bad light and attributes a foul odor to our doctrinal teaching, bringing into disrepute all the doctrines we profess. They likewise affirm that of all the blasphemies against God that the mind can conceive or the tongue may express, there is no doctrine that can reasonably be deducted from our Doctors as ugly as this.

And finally, of all the difficulties and consequences that have arisen among our churches since the Reformation, there is none that has not had its origin in this doctrine to a greater or lesser degree. We recall the controversies that arose in Leiden with respect to Caspar Coolhasius [Koolhaes], at Gouda in that of Herman Herberts, at Horn with respect to Cornelius Wiggerts, and at Medemblik in the affair of Tako Sybrants—controversies in which this was a major issue. These are not the least among the motives that have led me to give my most diligent attention to this point of doctrine, especially to prevent

---

⁷⁶ Cf. Phillip Melanchthon, "No. 5040, C. Peucero," in *Opera Quae Supersunt Omnia*, ed. Carolus Gottlieb Bretschneider, vol. 7, *Epistolae, Praefationes, Consilia, Iudicia, Schedae Academicae* (Saxony: Schwetschke & Sons, 1840), 932: "Lelius mihi scribit tanta esse Genevae certamina de Stoica necessitate, ut carceri inclusus sit quidam a Zenone dissentiens. O rem miseram! Doctrina salutaris obscuratur peregrinis disputationibus."

⁷⁷ Nicholas Hemmingius (Niels Hemmingsen), *Tractatus de gratia universali* (Haffniae: Ioannes Alburgensis, 1591).

⁷⁸ In the margins of the manuscript Arminius puts the questions this way: "Do we believe because we have been elected?" or, "Are we elected because we believe?"

our churches from suffering any more damage, causing Papacy to increase. The Papacy has been the benefactor. All pious teachers earnestly desire the destruction of the kingdom of the Antichrist, and we work earnestly with every available resource to that end.

Briefly stated, these are my views on this doctrine of predestination. In good faith, I have attempted to extract the teaching of the authors without adding a single word not clearly indicated in their writings. Some of our Doctors, however, state the issue regarding God's predestination in a somewhat different way. In cursory fashion I will touch on the two modes they employ.[79] Among them, the following points are prevalent:[80]

1. In an eternal and immutable decree God determined within himself, according to his own good pleasure and to the praise of his glorious grace, to grant to the smallest portion of humanity the blessing of participation in his grace and glory. At the same time, also according to his good pleasure, he passed over the majority

---

[79] Arminius describes two interrelated points regarding predestination. He begins with what may be called "single predestination," whereby some persons are chosen for salvation while others are simply passed over. The elect are chosen but the rest of humanity is simply not included. This version of predestination is linked closely with God's omniscience. Arminius prefers an emphasis on foreknowledge (*praescientia*). It is within the context of connecting predestination to omniscience that the second part of the doctrine becomes apparent, a position that came to be known as "infralapsarianism." That is, "within the context of the fall," expressed in linear fashion, after the fall God decided who would be counted among the elect, still passing over the great majority of humanity. Thus, there are two complementary parts to the doctrine of single predestination. Arminius demonstrates that when one reasons consequentially through the logic of this softer doctrine of single election, it is in the final analysis no different than "double predestination" in its practical outcome. Not even the Synod of Dort (1618–1619) is absolutely clear on these points, although it is clear from the *Acta* of the synod that the delegates (especially from outside the Netherlands) demonstrated a preference for the softer infralapsarian version of the doctrine. With regard to the conflicted nature of the protracted debates at the synod, see the thirty-second sitting (December 14, 1618), where the Remonstrants prefer an emphasis on the blessing of election rather than on the awful decision to damn—seemingly indicating that they are confronting a version of double predestination. This was certainly the case with Gomarus. Indeed, this was also the case during Arminius' own lifetime. Cf. Hoenderdaal, 96n26.

[80] There is an explanatory note in previous English translations that is written in the first person, giving the impression that it is from the hand of Arminius. It is neither in the text nor in the margins of Arminius' manuscript, but the explanatory note reads as follows: "In the animadversions [unfavorable commentary] on the preceding scheme of Predestination, I have often called it 'Supralapsarian'; but it is more properly styled, in the language of that age, 'Creabilitarian opinion,' and that which follows in the text, as the 'second kind of Predestination,' is a modified Supralapsarianism and the 'third kind' is 'Sublapsarianism.'" This formal supra- and sublapsarian language did not enjoy wide use during Arminius' lifetime, but became somewhat standard usage after the Synod of Dort in 1618–1619.

of humanity, leaving them spiritually dead—incapable of participating in things divine. By overlooking them, a demonstration of divine liberty, God chose not to share with them any part of that divine grace through which their human nature, to the extent that its original integrity was preserved, might be strengthened, or by which, if that original integrity was corrupted, it might be restored. Furthermore, when humanity followed the divine plan to sin and deserve death, God punished them with eternal death as a demonstration of his justice.

2. Predestination should be examined with regard to its end and in connection with the means by which that end is obtained; however, these persons use the word predestination with a specific reference to election and set it over against reprobation. With respect to its goal of salvation as a demonstration of God's grace,[81] humanity is viewed entirely in its raw state as an undifferentiated mass. But then with respect to the means by which God would accomplish his saving purpose, humanity is viewed as guilty in Adam and dying a deserved death of his own doing.

3. With regard to the decree concerning ultimate goals, the following lines of thought or steps are important: (a) Divine *prescience*, by which God foreknew those whom he had predestined; and (b) Divine *predetermination*, by which God foreordained the salvation of those persons whom he had foreknown: first, by electing them from all eternity, and secondly, by preparing for them saving grace in this life and glory in the world to come.

4. The means by which this predestination is carried out are: (a) Christ himself; (b) An efficacious call to faith in Christ, from which justification takes it origin; and, (c) The gift of perseverance in faith to the end.

5. To the extent that we understand their scheme of reprobation, it consists of two acts: A *passing by* and *prior damnation*. These actions are prior to all things and constitute the cause of all things in themselves or anything that might arise out of them. In other

---

[81] Previous interpreters seem to have read a cognate of *beroemd* here, leading to the translation "salvation and the glorious grace of God." The *Verclaringhe* (1610), 32, reads: *berovinghe van Godts ghenade*, "plundering of God's grace," which could be a scriptural allusion to Exodus 12:35-36—a reference to "plundering the Egyptians" of their riches. The gift of salvation is a plundering of the riches of divine grace. However, in the Latin edition, we encounter *illustratio*, which would indicate *betooninghe* in the manuscript, p. 22. This informs my choice for "demonstration of God's grace."

words, this set of decisions has been made without regard to sin, but simply views humanity absolutely as an undifferentiated mass.

6. Two means are foreordained to obtain this act of bypassing the majority of humanity: (a) Abandoning humanity in a state of nature capable only of animal instincts; and (b) The denial of supernatural grace, by which their nature (if in a state of integrity) might be strengthened and (if in a state of corruption) might be restored.

7. Even though this pre-damnation is antecedent to all things, by no means does it exist without foreknowledge of the causes of damnation. It views the mass of humanity as sinful in Adam, liable to damnation and perishing through the necessity of divine justice.

8. The means ordained for the execution of this prior damnation are: (a) Just desertion (*Iusta desertio*), a justified abandoning through a trial (*Explorationis poena induratio*) after which God chooses not to confer grace, or after which examination a deserved punishment, when God takes away from humanity all his saving gifts and delivers them over to the power of Satan; (b) The second means is the hardening [of the heart], with the attendant consequences of the actual damnation of the persons beyond hope of salvation.[82]

Still others declare their opinion on predestination in a somewhat different manner, a third kind of predestination, with the following main points:

1. When God willed within himself from all eternity to make a decree by which he would elect a certain portion of humanity to salvation and reprobate the rest, he viewed the human race not only as they would be created but at the same time as fallen and corrupt, and for that reason worthy of condemnation. Among those in this fallen and cursed condition, God determined purely through grace to liberate and save certain individuals as a demonstration of his mercy; however, he resolved within himself at the same time to leave the rest in a state of damnation as a demonstration of his justice. In both cases God acted without the least consideration of repentance or faith in those whom he elected, or with regard to the impenitence and unbelief in those whom he damned.

2. The special means that relate specifically to the execution of both election and reprobation are the very same as those we have already delineated in the first of these kinds of predestination—with the exception of those means that are common both to election and

---

[82] Lit., "damnation of reprobate humanity."

reprobation. This third perspective on predestination does not view the fall of humanity as a foreordained means to accomplish predestination, but rather as the established occasion for making the decree.

These two positions differ from the first, as far as I can discern, in that neither of them describes the creation or the fall as a mediating cause foreordained by God for the execution of the prior decree of predestination.[83] And yet, with regard to the fall, these two theories do not exactly correspond. In the second theory of election, with regard to its goal, both election and the passing over of the greater portion of humanity (the first stage of reprobation) are placed chronologically prior to the fall. In contrast, the third theory does not allow any part of election or reprobation to take place until after the fall. In an attempt to avoid the accusation of making God the author of sin, the authors of the two latter schemes of predestination have studiously avoided the high degree of abstraction[84] present in the first description of predestination. This may be so; and yet, if we look closely at the second and third formulations on predestination in connection with other theological opinions set forth by the same authors, we shall discover that the logic of their opinions requires that Adam's fall into sin cannot possibly be interpreted in any other way than that it is the necessary means for carrying out the prior decree of predestination.

Both formulations of the doctrine contain two obvious assertions as to why this is the case. First, we encounter the assertion that God determined, by the decree of reprobation, to deny to humanity that grace necessary to undergird the created nature whereby it might not be corrupted by sin. In other words, God decreed not to bestow that grace necessary to avoid sin. From this it necessarily follows that the transgression of humanity was the result of an imposed law. The fall into sin is therefore a means ordained for the execution of the decree of reprobation.

The second reason is contained in the twofold nature of reprobation: the passing over and ensuing damnation. In the logic of the predestining decree, these two parts are connected by a necessary mutuality. All those passed over by God when grace was conferred are damned as a result. Indeed, no others are damned except those who are passed over in the dispensation of grace. It follows logically that sin is the necessary result, and sin leads to reprobation. If the result of sin could be any other than reprobation, it might possibly happen that a person who had been passed over in the dispensation of grace actually avoided sin. If sin were actually avoided, then that person would not be liable

---

[83] After this, two lines in the manuscript are marked through.
[84] Lit., "not to climb as high."

to damnation, since sin is the sole meritorious cause of damnation. The result is an absurdity—some individuals might be neither saved nor damned. We see then that the objection against the first position is true also of the second. Despite every effort, it fails to avoid it [making God the author of sin], falling into a palpable and absurd self-contradiction—in much the same way as the first predestination theory.

The third theory of predestination does a better job of avoiding these objections, except that its adherents, even as they are saying the right things about providence and predestination, are employing certain expressions that require the necessity of the fall. And this necessary fall into sin cannot possibly have any other origin than a decree of predestination. One of these expressions is related to the divine permission by which God is said to permit sin: "Permission is the withdrawing of that divine grace by which God (when God executes the decrees of his will through rational creatures), either does not reveal to the creature the will by which he wills that an action be performed, or God does not bend the will of the creature to yield obedience to the divine will." To these assertions the following are added: "And thus it happens that the creature commits sin through necessity, yet freely and willingly."[85] As they are stated, these assertions are not in harmony with the permission by which God permitted Adam to sin. Indeed, it also follows from these assertions that not only the first sin, but all other sins as well are committed through necessity.

Similar to this is the idea put forward by some that sin declares the glory [*heerlijkheid*] of God because it requires God to demonstrate both mercy and punitive justice. This cannot occur unless sin and its consequent misery—or at the very least a degree of requisite misery in the world for sin—is necessarily introduced in order to declare the glory [*eerlijkheid*][86] of God. When the fall of Adam is laid down as the necessary means for executing the prior decree of predestination, creation itself is likewise laid down as a means subservient to the execution of the same decree. For the fall cannot be a necessary consequence of creation except through the decree of predestination. Predestination is not placed between the creation and the fall, but it is prefixed to both of them in antecedent fashion. Having this precedence, predestination ordains creation as the necessary context for the fall, and both creation and the fall are ordained as the occasion for executing the decree in order to demonstrate the justice of God in the punishment of sin, as well as divine mercy in its remission. To conclude otherwise leads to supposing the impossible, namely, the necessary result of creation was not actually intended by God. It

---

[85] Arminius is obviously quoting here, but he does not reveal his source. I have not located these precise words, but the teaching itself is thematically similar to opinions expressed by Gomarus.

[86] See p. 103–4 n. 46.

may well be the case that the necessity of the fall of Adam does not of logical necessity flow from these two theories, yet when the objections to the first theory on predestination are fully set out, with only slight modification, these objections apply as well to the latter two. This would be apparent if a conference were to be held for such a purpose.

Arminius' Fourfold Doctrine of Predestination

Up to this point I have set out the positions of others on the article of predestination as they are being taught in our churches and the University of Leiden—positions of which I disapprove. I have also set out several reasons why I disapprove these teachings. I now proceed to declare my personal opinions, teachings that I believe are most in harmony with the Word of God.

I. The first specific and absolute divine decree regarding the salvation of sinful humanity: God decreed to appoint his Son, Jesus Christ, as Mediator, Redeemer, Savior, Priest, and King in order that he might destroy sin by his own death, so that by his own obedience he might obtain the salvation lost through disobedience, and by his power communicate this salvation.

II. In the second precise and absolute decree, God decided graciously to accept those who repent and believe in Christ, and for Christ's sake and through him to effect the final salvation of penitents and believers who persevere to the end in their faith. Simultaneously, God decreed to leave in sin under divine wrath all impenitent persons and unbelievers, damning them as alienated from Christ.

III. The third divine decree: God decided to administer in a sufficient and efficacious manner the means necessary for repentance and faith—this being accomplished according to divine wisdom, by which God knows what is proper and becoming both to his mercy and his severity. And this all proceeds according to divine justice, by which God is prepared to adopt whatever his wisdom may prescribe and carry out.

IV. From these decrees the fourth proceeds, by which God decreed to save and to damn certain particular persons. This decree has its foundation in divine foreknowledge, through which God has known from all eternity those individuals who through the established means of his prevenient grace would come to faith and believe, and through his subsequent sustaining grace would persevere in the faith. Likewise, in divine foreknowledge, God knew those who would not believe and persevere.

This doctrine of predestination declares:

1. The foundation of all Christianity, both with regard to salvation and to the certainty of that salvation.
2. The essence of the Evangel. Indeed, it declares the Gospel itself, which must be believed for salvation (as far as the first two articles above are concerned).
3. Because predestination is a clear and explicit Scriptural teaching, it has never been examined by a general or particular Council of the Church, nor has it ever been contradicted by any orthodox divine.
4. Predestination has been consistently acknowledged and taught by all well-informed teachers.
5. Predestination is consistent with the harmony of all the confessions of faith made by the Protestant churches.
6. The Dutch Confession and [Heidelberg] Catechism are of one accord on this doctrine. This agreement is such that if in the sixteenth article of the Confession the two expressions "those persons who" and "others" be interpreted as "believers" and "unbelievers," my position on predestination will be comprehended in that article with the utmost clarity.[87] For this reason, when I held a

---

[87] This is a subtle but important suggestion by Arminius. With this suggested interpretation of the Heidelberg Catechism and Belgic Confession, he is shifting the focal point of predestination to believers, thereby taking out of play the concept of predestination as referencing individuals outside the context of the fall. He is setting up for his assertion that predestination must be seen in a straightforward fashion: those who believe will be saved and those who do not believe will be damned. This is not the same as the assertion: those whom God chooses for salvation will be saved, and those whom God does not choose will be damned. While it is not the case that Arminius disagrees with the latter sentence, he does want to interpret it in a manner different than his opponents. Note also that Arminius, using the same rubrics as earlier in his declaration, starts over here referencing the orthodoxy of his position, whereas he has previously asserted the heterodoxy (pp. 103-7) of the positions he is rejecting. The edition of the Belgic Confession and Heidelberg Catechism that Arminius referenced may have been his own copy, *Beleydenisse des Geloofs der Kercke Jesu Christi in de Nederlanden, na de suyverheyt der Evangely Ghiereformeert* (Dordrecht: 1583). The wording from the confession previously cited by Arminius (pp. 111-12)—*Verclaringhe* (1610), 17-18; and Hoenderdaal, 75-76—conforms to this edition of the confession; however, the exact phrase *eos quos* does not appear in the sixteenth article of the 1583 edition. According to Hoenderdaal, 107n27, it appears in an earlier version of the sixteenth article that was shortened at the Synod of Antwerp in 1566. Cf. J. J. van Toorenbergen, *De Symbolische schriften* (Utrecht, 1895), the reference to article sixteen. In the expanded version of article sixteen we read the phrase, ". . . that God has chosen to save some (Dutch: *sommige*)." Hoenderdaal goes on to say, "We may surmise that when Arminius is citing a long passage from the confession, he references a specific edition from his shelf, but if he is referring to a well-known passage, perhaps he is working from his memory of an older Latin version of the text." Cf. Hoenderdaal, 107 n. 27.

public disputation at the university, I required that the article of faith under consideration be composed in the exact words of the Confession. When compared, it is evident that there is complete harmony with the [Heidelberg] Catechism, specifically questions 20 and 54.[88]

7. Interpreted in this manner, predestination is in full harmony with the nature of God—his wisdom, goodness, and justice,[89] because it enshrines their primary content in the clearest possible witness to God's wisdom, goodness, and justice.
8. This predestination is in harmony with the nature of humanity at every level—in the primitive state of creation, in its fallen state, as well as in its restoration.
9. It is in complete accord with the act of creation. It affirms that creation is a genuine communication of goodness, both with regard to the intention of God as well as with regard to the actual creative act. Predestination has its origin in the goodness of God, so that whatever has reference to its being fully preserved and carried out proceeds from divine love. The act of creation is itself a perfect and appropriate divine act in which God is well pleased and through which humanity has received the requisite means to avoid falling into sin.
10. This predestination is in accord with the nature of eternal life and all the Scriptural nomenclature by which it is designated.
11. It also agrees with the nature of eternal death and all the names by which that death is described in Scripture.
12. This predestination underscores that sin is actual disobedience and therefore the meritorious cause of condemnation. For this reason predestination must be understood in the context of[90] the fall and sin.

---

[88] Question 20: "Are all men, then, saved by Christ as they have perished in Adam? No, only those who by true faith are ingrafted into Him and receive all his benefits." Question 54: "What do you believe concerning the 'Holy Catholic Church'? That out of the whole human race, from the beginning to the end of the world, the Son of God, by His Spirit and Word, gathers, defends, and preserves for Himself unto everlasting life a chosen communion in the unity of the true faith; and that I am, and forever shall remain a living member of this communion."

[89] The word *rechtveerdicheyt* (*rechtvaardigheid*) in sixteenth-century Dutch could be translated as either "justice" or "righteousness." Strictly speaking the word for "justice" was *gerechtigheyd* (Latin: *iustitia*). For Arminius, the heart of the matter is that God acts consistently and justly in all matters. One who does not act justly or acts inconsistently can hardly be said to be either righteous or just.

[90] Lit., "is consistent with."

13. It is in every way harmonious with the nature of grace, by ascribing to grace every rightful thing and by reconciling it entirely with the righteousness of God, as well as to the nature and liberty of the human will.
14. This predestination transparently declares the glory of God, his justice, and his mercy: God is the cause of all good as well as our salvation, and humanity is the cause of sin and therefore responsible for his own damnation.
15. It contributes to the honor of Jesus Christ by rendering him the foundation of predestination, as well as the meritorious and mediating cause of salvation.
16. This predestination promotes the salvation of humanity; indeed, it is the power and the veritable means to salvation. It awakens and creates within human consciousness a sorrow for sin, a deep concern for conversion and faith in Jesus Christ, as well as a diligence for good works and zeal in prayer—thereby causing human beings to work out their salvation with fear and trembling [Phil 2:12-13]. Likewise, it wards off despair, as far as such prevention is necessary.
17. It confirms and establishes the order in which the Gospel ought to be preached: First, by requiring repentance and faith, and then by promising the remission of sins, the grace of the Holy Spirit, and life eternal.
18. It strengthens the ministry of the gospel by making it profitable for preaching, the administration of the sacraments, and public prayers.
19. Indeed, it is the foundation of the Christian religion because in it the twofold love of God is united. God's love of justice[91] and his love of humanity are herein reconciled to each other with the greatest consistency.
20. And finally, this doctrine of predestination has always received the approval of the great majority of professing Christians, and even now, in these days, it enjoys the same extensive affirmation. It gives no one just cause for expressing objection, nor does it give any pretext for contention in the Christian church.

From the foregoing it would be desirable if people were to go no further in this matter, nor should we attempt to sort out the unsearchable judgments of God. At the very least, we should not proceed beyond what has been clearly

---

[91] Here Arminius employs *gerechtigheyt*.

revealed in Scripture. This, my Noble Lords, is all that I have to declare to you with respect to the doctrine of predestination—the doctrine that is currently causing such a great controversy in Christ's Church.

If it does not try the patience of your Lordships, there are some other points of the faith[92] that I would like to bring forward that are integral to a full declaration of my sentiments. Indeed, they are germane to the purpose for which I have been summoned into your powerful presence. These are articles of Christian doctrine that are in close affinity to the doctrine of Predestination, as they are in great measure dependent on it: the providence of God, the free will of humanity, the grace of God, the perseverance of saints, and the certainty of salvation. Briefly stated, these are my opinions on each of these points.

The Providence of God

I consider divine providence to be that earnest, ongoing, and universally present oversight and involvement of God by which a general care of the whole world is exercised, with special care and concern for every created being without exception, intentionally governing and preserving them in their own essence, qualities, action, and passions in a manner that is both worthy of God and suitable to the creature—all this to the praise of God's name and to the salvation of believers. By defining divine providence in this manner, I do not undermine any aspect of those dimensions that are properly in harmony with or belong to it; however, I declare that providence defined in this way preserves, regulates, governs, and directs all things—for nothing in the world happens fortuitously or merely by chance. Furthermore, I place both free will and even the actions of rational creatures in subjection to divine providence.[93] Nothing can be done without the will of God, not even those things that are done in opposition to it. Even as this is granted, we must observe a distinction between good actions and evil ones: God both wills and performs good acts, but God only freely permits actions that are evil. In addition, I readily concede that the entirety of God's actions that can be devised or invented as related to evil should be attributed to divine providence, but with this important caution: From this concession it must not be concluded that God is the cause of sin.

In my public disputations "On the Righteousness and Efficacy of the Providence of God concerning Evil,"[94] I have declared my position with sufficient clarity on two different formal occasions in Leiden over which I presided. In

---

[92] Lit., "points of religion."
[93] In the manuscript a line is drawn through the words "with appropriate distinctions."
[94] Public Disputations IX and X, in *Works*, 2:162–88. Regarding these public disputations, see also the letter from Arminius to Uytenbogaert (May 2, 1605), *Ep. Ecc.*, no. 76.

my public disputations, I attempted to ascribe to God whatever actions concerning sin that I could conceivably conclude from the Scriptures to belong to him. Indeed, it seemed to some that I had gone so far in this reasoning that I could appropriately be charged myself with making God the author of sin. Because of my reasoning on this issue, this same serious allegation has been levied against me numerous times from the pulpit in Amsterdam; however, the lack of warrant for this accusation (as I have previously stated) may be readily discerned from the contents of my written answers to the previously mentioned "Thirty-One Articles."[95]

Human Free Will

My position on human free will is as follows:[96] In its created original condition, humanity was endowed with sufficient knowledge, holiness, and power to understand, esteem, consider, will, and perform that which is truly good according to God's design; however, none of these actions could occur without the assistance of divine grace. In a lapsed and sinful state without divine assistance, humanity is not able to think, will, or do that which is truly good. The regeneration and renewal by God in Christ through the Holy Spirit of all human capacities, including the intellect, affections, and will, is required for humanity to understand, esteem, consider, will, and perform that which is truly good. When creatures receive this regeneration and renewal, humanity is delivered from sin and enabled to think, will, and do that which is good—and yet not without the continued assistance of God's grace.

The Grace of God

Regarding divine grace, I believe that it is an unearned divine favorable disposition in which God is kindly disposed towards poor miserable sinners,[97] so much so that he gives his Son in order that whoever believes in him might have eternal life [John 3:16]. Furthermore, God justifies the sinner in Christ Jesus for Christ's sake and adopts the justified into Sonship[98] and salvation. Second, the human understanding, the will, and the affections are infused with all those gifts of the Spirit that are the product of regeneration and renewal. These include faith, hope, and love, etc., for without these gracious gifts, humanity would be unable to think, will, or do anything that is good. Third, this grace entails a perpetual assistance and continued aid of the Holy

---

[95] "The Apology or Defence of James Arminius," in *Works*, 1:733–70.
[96] Cf. Public Disputation XI, "On the Free Will of Man and its Powers," in *Works*, 2:189–96; and Hoenderdaal, 32n45, on Public Disputations XI and XV.
[97] In the manuscript an illegible line has been marked through.
[98] Dutch, *kindtschap*, is lit.: "the condition of being a child."

Spirit, through which God acts upon and excites to good the creature who has already been renewed through the infusion of a holy disposition—a disposition inclined to good desires that lead to the actual performance of that which is good. God then wills and works together with the renewed creature to perform that which God wills.

I ascribe to grace the beginning, the continuance, and the consummation of all good.[99] I would go so far as to assert that the creature, although regenerated, can neither conceive, will, nor do any good at all, nor resist any evil temptation, apart from this preventing and awakening, this continuing and cooperating grace. Surely, despite my often being accused of such, it is clear that I do no injustice to grace by attributing too much to human freedom. This entire controversy can be reduced to answering this question, "Is the grace of God an irresistible force?" In other words, the controversy does not relate to those actions or operations that may properly be ascribed to grace, for I acknowledge and ascribe to grace as many of these actions or operations as any man has ever done. No, the controversy relates solely to the mode of operation, whether it be irresistible or not. I believe that Scripture teaches that many persons resist the Holy Spirit and reject the grace offered.[100]

The Perseverance of the Saints

Regarding the perseverance of the saints, I believe that all who have been grafted into Christ by true faith, having been made partakers of his life-giving Spirit, possess sufficient spiritual strength to fight against Satan, sin, the world, and their own flesh—and to gain the victory over these enemies—yet none of this at any time without the perpetual assistance of the grace of the same Holy Spirit. By his Spirit, Jesus Christ assists and supports them in all their temptations and keeps them from falling, provided they remain diligent, on guard, and implore his assistance. Given this, it is not possible for Satan by his cunning, craftiness, or power to seduce or drag them out of the hands of Christ. I believe it would be constructive and even necessary in our first gathering [synod] diligently to search the Scriptures to discern whether it is possible for some individuals through negligence to forfeit their existence in Christ—whether they might actually return to worldliness, turn away from the sound doctrine delivered to them, lose good conscience, and cause divine

---

[99] This perspective is taken up with specificity in the Remonstrance of 1610. Cf. Phillip Schaff, *The Creeds of Christendom* (Grand Rapids: Baker, 1996), 3:545–46.

[100] Arminius' notion of God's sovereignty is foundational to his concept of grace, as divine grace governs and steers human freedom in the right direction toward God without causally overriding the freedom to resist. This dialectic is fundamental to his concept of uncoerced freedom.

grace to become ineffectual.[101] Therefore, I firmly declare that I have never taught that a true believer either totally or finally falls away from the faith and perishes; but I do not deny that there are passages of Scripture that seem to indicate such.[102] Attempts to interpret these texts of which I am aware are not fully satisfying to me. On the other hand, other passages of Scripture may be produced to the opposite doctrine [asserting unconditional perseverance], and these too are worthy of serious consideration.

The Assurance of Salvation

With regard to the assurance of salvation, my opinion is that it is possible for one who believes in Jesus Christ to be persuaded with certainty.[103] If one's conscience is clear, he may be assured of being in the grace of Jesus Christ, a child of God. This certainty is wrought in the heart by the Holy Spirit and attested by the fruits of faith as well as from the believer's own conscience—the testimony of God's spirit co-witnessing with the conscience. I also believe that it is possible by the grace of God and his mercy in Christ for such a person to depart this life and appear before the throne of grace without anxious fear or terrifying dread of damnation. Nevertheless, this person should pray continually that God would not enter judgment against him.[104] Because "God is greater than our hearts and he knows everything" [1 John 3:20], and since an individual is not his own judge, even if unaware of guilt, this does not constitute justification before God; it is God who judges [1 Cor 4:3-4]. Even so, I

---

[101] This phrasing is used word for word in the fifth article of the Remonstrance (1610). Cf. Schaff, *Creeds of Christendom*, 3:545–46.

[102] My translation diverges here from both Conyers (*The Just Man's Defence; or, The Declaration of the Judgement of James Arminius* [London: Henry Eversden, 1657], 117); and Nichols (*Works*, 1:667). Conyers reads, "It was never taught by me that the true Believer *might* totally or finally fall away." Nichols reads, "I never taught that a true believer *can* either totally or finally fall away." The conditional words "might" and "can," while grammatically warranted by the contingent expression in the rest of the paragraph, are not explicitly repeated in the phrase that includes the verb for "depart" or "fall away." Assuming the contingency that governs the earlier parts of the paragraph brings Arminius in contradiction with himself: "I have indeed sometimes said . . . that the faithful *are able to* finally defect from faith and salvation; but I never said that the faithful *do* finally defect from faith and salvation" (*Works*, 1:741, emphasis added). Cf. discussion by Stanglin, 132–33, who concludes: "Therefore, Arminius affirms the possibility of apostasy; whether it actually happens he seems to leave open for discussion." To assert that they *could not* fall away would logically lead him back into absolute predestination.

[103] The expression "certainly persuaded" is a marginal addition in the manuscript, and the words about fear of damnation are also marginal annotations. Both annotations are included in the *Verclaringhe* (1610).

[104] Cf. Ps 143:2: "Do not enter into judgment with your servant, for no one living is righteous before you."

would not dare to place this assurance of salvation on a par with our certainty that there is a God and that Christ is the Savior of the world. Nevertheless, I do believe it would be appropriate for us to explore the boundaries of this assurance in our convocation.

The Perfection of Believers in This Life

In addition to the doctrines previously mentioned, there has also been much discussion about the perfection of believers (regenerate persons) in this life. It has been objected that I hold improper opinions nearly aligned with the Pelagian error on this issue—namely, that it is possible for the regenerate in this life perfectly to keep God's commandments. Even if this were my sentiment, it should not be concluded that I am therefore either partly or entirely a Pelagian. To every assertion regarding the possible perfection of believers, I have been careful to say that they could only keep the commandments by the grace of Christ and never without this grace. While I have never actually stated that a believer could perfectly keep the precepts of Christ in this life, I have not denied it either. This is a matter that I have always left open. I have been content with the opinions of St. Augustine on this subject, whose words I have frequently quoted in the university, typically saying that I had nothing to add.[105]

According to St. Augustine there are four questions that claim our attention. The first is whether there has ever been a sinless human, who from the beginning of life to death never committed a sin. Second, has there ever been, is there now or will there ever be, an individual who does not commit sin—or put another way, one who has attained such a state of perfection as not ever to commit a sin and to perfectly fulfill the law of God? The third question is whether it is possible for a human being to exist in this life without sin. Fourth, if it be possible for one to be without sin, why has this never occurred? Augustine's answer is that with the exception of Jesus Christ, no such person ever lived, nor will such ever be brought into existence. With regard to the second question, he asserts that no person attains perfection in this life. On the third point, Augustine holds the position that by the grace of Christ and the proper use of [grace-enabled] free will, it is possible for a human

---

[105] Arminius is here referring to Augustine, *De natura et gratia*, chaps. 59, 60, 63, and esp. 69. Arminius is summarizing based on his rather extensive referencing in his "Modest Examination of Dr. Perkins' Pamphlet," *Works*, 1:249–484; his appropriation of Augustine in his explications on Romans 7, *Works*, 2:471–683; as well as in his "Apology Against Thirty-One Articles," *Works*, 2:1–79. The expositions on Romans 7 contain "by far" the most references to Augustine. Cf. Aza Goudriaan, "'Augustine Asleep' or 'Augustine Awake'? Arminius's Reception of Augustine," in *Arminius, Arminianism, and Europe*, ed. Th. Marius van Leeuwen, Keith Stanglin, and Marijke Tolsma (Leiden: Brill, 2009), 51–72.

to be without sin. And fourth, we do not do that which is actually possible through the enabling grace of Christ because it escapes our attention that it is actually good, or because we do not deeply value it. It is apparent then that St. Augustine, one of the most adamant adversaries of Pelagian doctrine, held the opinion that it is possible by the grace of Christ for one to live without sin in this life. Indeed, Augustine asserts, "Let Pelagius admit that it is possible only by the grace of Christ for one to be without sin, and we will be at peace with each other." But Pelagius' opinion, according to Augustine, was that one could fulfill the law of God by his own strength, but that one could do this with even greater consistency and ease through the enabling grace of Christ. I have already made it clear that I distance myself completely from this opinion, and I would add that I consider Pelagius' opinion to be heretical, diametrically opposed to the words of Christ: "Apart from me you can do nothing" [John 15:5]. Furthermore, Pelagius' position is destructive and does serious harm to the glory of Christ.

I cannot imagine that there is anything in my declaration to this point that should lead to negative consequences or cause one to fear standing in the presence of God.[106] And yet, I am increasingly aware of reports that I harbor destructive sentiments and heresies. I cannot imagine what these charges are about, unless perhaps there is some concern about my teachings on the Divinity of the Son of God, or perhaps my opinions on the justification of humanity before God. It has recently come to my attention regarding my teaching on these points that there is considerable public rumor. This seems to be specifically related to the last hearing [at which Gomarus and I appeared, May 30, 1607] before the high council. In the light of this, it would seem wise for me to explain this in some detail.

The Divinity of the Son of God

At our university there have been some debates about the divinity of the Son of God and the expression αυτοθεος, and the nature of these has been such that I cannot imagine what the motivation can be on the part of some to render my character suspect. This is all the more amazing given the fact that these suspicions are totally unfounded and far from all reason and truth. The rumors against me that have been spread in connection with these disputes can only accurately be described as notorious slander. One afternoon, in the course of a university disputation on the announced topic of the Divinity of the Son of God, a student objected that the Son of God was αυτοθεος and that his essence was self-derived and not from the Father. I answered that

---

[106] This is perhaps a reference to Gomarus' public statements that he would not dare to appear in the presence of God holding the opinions of Arminius.

αὐτοθεος could be interpreted in two ways. It could signify "one who is truly God" or "one who is God of himself," the former rather than the latter meaning being most appropriately and correctly attributed to the Son of God. The student vehemently protested that the latter meaning is most applicable to the Son of God, and that the essence of the Father could not be said to be communicated to the Son and to the Holy Spirit in any other than an improper sense, as this essence is in perfect correctness and with strict propriety simultaneously common to the Father, Son, and Holy Spirit. He added that he was quite certain of the correctness of this position because he had the learned written authority of the younger Trelcatius' *Loci communibus* on his side.[107] I answered that this position was in harmony neither with the Word of God nor with the whole of the ancient church, both Greek and Latin, which had consistently taught that the Son has his deity from the Father by eternal generation. I added that his assertions necessarily led to two mutually conflicting errors: tritheism and Sabellianism. First, it logically follows that independently there would be three Gods with the same divine essence, and that as such the identity of any one of them could only be distinguished independently. Contrary to this, the only foundation that has ever been used for defending the unity of the divine essence in the trinity of persons is the proceeding of the origin of one person from another (*Processus originis unius personae ab alia*), that of the Son from the Father. Secondly, it also follows as a consequence [of the student's assumption], that the Son would himself essentially be also the Father, because he would differ from the Father in name only, which was the position of Sabellius.[108] If it be singularly the case that the Father derives his deity from himself, it would be accurate to say he derives it from no one; and if in this same sense the Son is called αὐτοθεος, "God of himself," it follows that he is the Father.

Accounts of this exchange were spread across the land, and it reached Amsterdam. One of the ministers there, who now rests in the Lord,[109] questioned me about what was actually said, so I related it accurately to him as I am now relating it to you. I requested that he contact Trelcatius (now deceased) and kindly suggest that he correct the inappropriate wording in his *Loci communibus*—a suggestion the minister halfway seemed to accept. In all the controversy surrounding this dispute, I am blameless, for I have defended the truth and the positions of the catholic, orthodox church. It seems to me

---

[107] For the senior Trelcatius (1542–1602), see *NNBW*, 10:1038; and for the younger Trelcatius (1573–1607), see *NNBW*, 10:1039.

[108] For a discussion of Trelcatius' teachings, see Hoenderdaal, 27.

[109] Helmichius died in 1608. Cf. Hoenderdaal, 13; and for biographical essays, *BLGNP*, 2:236–39; and *BWPGN*, 3:646–54.

that Trelcatius' approach to this doctrine detracts somewhat from accepted truth; however, when a disagreement occurs, either as a result of my own misfortune or due to the zeal of certain individuals, the blame always lands on me, as if I were conveying the truth less accurately than another. Actually, on this particular point I have Gomarus on my side.[110] Soon after Trelcatius published his *Loci*, a public disputation on the Trinity was announced at the University. In parts of his argued thesis, Gomarus diametrically opposed the position of Trelcatius on three specific points. When I pointed out the obvious differences between these two professors to the Amsterdam minister, he acknowledged as much. Nevertheless, no one has endeavored to protect me from accusation, while every effort has been exerted to make excuses for Trelcatius. This was typically done by offering qualifying interpretations of his opinions, even when it was quite impossible to reconcile them. Such are the results of partiality and zealous fervor.

A charitable reading of Trelcatius' interpretation is as follows: The Son of God may be styled αὐτοθεος, or may be said to have his deity from himself with reference to his *being* God, but he has his deity from the Father with regard to his being the Son. Expanding on this, it is asserted that God, or the Divine essence, may be viewed either absolutely or relatively. When viewed absolutely, the Son has his Divine essence from himself; when viewed relatively, he derives Divine essence from the Father. Not only are these novel assertions, they are inherently contradictory. The Son, both with regard to his being the Son as well as to his being God, derives his deity from the Father. When he is called God, this does not mean that he is God in any other sense than his Sonship brings with it. For the essence of God is not in the picture unless that Divine essence is communicated to the Son by the Father. Because the expressions would be irreconcilable and inherently contradictory, it cannot be asserted that the Divine essence is both communicated to him and not communicated to him. It follows also that if the Son has the Divine essence from himself in reference to its being absolutely considered, it cannot be communicated to him. If it be communicated to him in reference to its being relatively considered, he cannot have it from himself in reference to its being absolutely considered. If the Son has the Divine Essence from himself in reference to its being absolutely considered, it cannot be communicated to him. If it be communicated to him in reference to its being relatively considered, he cannot have it from himself in reference to its being absolutely considered.

If I am asked whether I acknowledge that to be the Son of God and to be God are two entirely distinct assertions, I respond affirmatively. Indeed they are. But when the interlocutor concludes that to be the Son of God signifies

---

[110] See discussion below, chap. 5 note 21.

that he derives his essence from the Father and his being God signifies nothing less than that he derives this essence from himself or no one else, I reject the conclusion. I assert that this is a great error, not only in sacred theology but likewise in natural philosophy. To be the Son of God and to be God are perfectly compatible assertions, but to assert that the Son derives his essence from the Father while at the same time deriving it from no one is an inherent contradiction. This fallacy is more apparent when it is viewed through three parallel propositions:

1. God is eternal and has for all eternity possessed the Divine essence.
2. The Father is derived from no one, nor is the Divine essence.
3. The Son is from the Father, his Divine essence being from the Father.

The Word "God" signifies that he has true Divine essence, but the word "Son" signifies that he has the Divine essence from the Father; therefore, the Son is correctly identified as both God and the Son of God. Since the Son cannot be the Father, he cannot possibly be said to have the Divine essence from himself or from no one. Much effort has been put forth on the part of some to diminish these distinctions by asserting that when reference is made to the Son being God, this means the Son has this Divine essence from himself, meaning simply that he has not derived that essence from anyone else. If this type of logic be allowed, almost any evil hypothesis can be asserted and made to appear good. Although God and Divine essence do not differ essentially, it does not follow that whatever may be predicated about God can be equally predicated of the Divine Essence. Our conceptual frameworks must be recognized for what they are—expressions through which we are enabled to perceive correctly. This becomes obvious when we assert with perfect correctness that [the Son of] God has died,[111] but we may not say that the Divine essence has died. We may say that the Divine essence is communicated, but we would not say that God is communicated. One who understands this distinction between the concrete and the abstract, a distinction that has given rise to frequent disputes between us and the Lutherans, readily perceives the consequences of allowing such teaching into God's church. It is not acceptable to assert, as some do, that the Son of God derives his essence from himself, nor can it be allowed that the essence of God is common intrinsically to the three persons. This is improper because the accepted teaching is that the Divine essence is communicated by one of them to the other. I would

---

[111] Nichols' translation (*Works*, 1:695) does not translate this phrase, leaving it as *Deum mortuum esse*. Conyers' translation (*Just Man's Defence*, 130) leaves out the entire reference to the "death of God."

underscore these comments because it is amazing how much we allow to be asserted by someone we do not suspect of heresy, while we blindly rush to conclusions about one who falls under suspicion. The foregoing is a notable example of this.

Justification before God

I am not aware that I have ever seriously considered or taught anything concerning the justification of humanity before God that is not both affirmed by the Reformed and Protestant Churches and in complete agreement with their positions. Recently there was a minor controversy on this subject between John Piscator at the University of Herborn in Nassau and the French Churches.[112] The debate centered on a difference of opinion regarding righteousness: Does the obedience and righteousness of Christ imputed to believers, which constitute their righteousness before God, consist only of the passive obedience of Christ in his submitting to suffering and death? This was the position of Piscator. Or as it is posed by the French: "Does the believer's righteousness consist not only of Christ's passive righteousness but also his active righteousness as well—that holiness in which he was born as well as his obedience to the law of God in the whole course of his life?" I took care never to get involved in or attempt to resolve this dispute, for I deem it quite possible for those who confess the faith to differ on this point without any breach of Christian peace or unity. This reconciling perspective seems to have been amenable to the parties of that dispute, for they exercised a friendly toleration of each other and did not use their differences as an excuse to renounce one another. In our land, some people did not agree with this mutual toleration.

A question has been raised regarding the words of the Apostle Paul in Romans 4 on faith being reckoned for righteousness. ["Abraham believed God, and it was reckoned to him as righteousness" (Rom 4:3b).] The issue is whether such expressions may properly be interpreted to mean that faith itself, as an act performed according to the command of the Gospel, is graciously imputed by God for or unto righteousness. Since it is not the righteousness of the law, should such expressions be figuratively[113] understood to mean that the righteousness of Christ, being apprehended by the believer through faith, is imputed for righteousness? Or finally, as some believe, faith works instrumentally to account righteousness for and to the believer? When I delivered my university oration "On Justification," I held generally to the first interpretation—though not setting it out in detailed precision—having previously

---

[112] See Hoenderdaal, 28. Piscator, originally Lutheran but then later Reformed, had left Strasbourg and Heidelberg successively, going finally to Herborn.

[113] Lit., "figuratively and even improperly."

done so in a particular letter.[114] For this reason, some have a negative opinion regarding my teaching on the justification of humanity before God. Just how unfounded this is can be sorted out in convocation at the appropriate time. For now, let me simply say: "I believe that sinners are accounted righteous solely by the obedience of Christ, and that the obedience and righteousness of Christ constitute the only meritorious cause through which God pardons the sins of believers and accounts them as righteous, as if they had perfectly fulfilled the law. However, since God imputes the righteousness of Christ to no one except believers, I conclude that it may be accurately and properly asserted: To one who believes, faith is imputed for righteousness by grace. For God sent his Son, Jesus Christ, to be a propitiation (a throne of grace / a mercy seat) through faith in his blood." Whatever one might say about this, no one among us accuses Calvin or considers him heterodox on this point, and my position is not so different from his as to prevent my signing my name to the positions he takes in Book III of his *Institutes*.[115] To these opinions, I am prepared to state my full approval at any time.

Most Noble Lords, in your august presence and in obedience to your commands, these are the principal points of my opinions that I deem necessary to clarify.

SECTION THREE

The Call for a National Synod

In addition, I have a few annotations on the Confession of the Dutch Churches and the Heidelberg Catechism, but these are more appropriately handled in a synod, which we hope will convene soon with your noble consent, if not

---

[114] Public Disputation XIX, "On the Justification of Man before God," in *Works*, 2:253–58. See also point V ("On Justification") in Arminius' "Letter to Hippolytus," in *Works*, 2:701ff.

[115] The high esteem in which Arminius holds Calvin is apparent in his letter to Sebastiaan Egberts, May 3, 1607. Cf. *Ep. Ecc.*, no. 101; Brandt, *Historie*, 2:89: "Next to the Holy Scriptures, which I ardently inculcate and to which I turn more than anyone else (as may be attested by witness of the entire Academy and the conscience of my colleagues), I urge my students to read Calvin's teachings. Indeed, I esteem these higher than Helmichius ever has, as he himself acknowledged to me. I say that with regard to the interpretation of Holy Scripture, Calvin's *Commentaries* are incomparable and that they should be held in higher esteem than anything the Fathers have left us in their library of thought. Next to these, for a more comprehensive interpretation, I encourage reading our Catechism; however, I admonish, as is the case with all human compositions, that we should consult these discerningly." Arminius includes Calvin's *Institutes* among these "human compositions." Arminius would have in mind sections of the *Institutes* where Calvin engages in "Legal Theology." On this, see chap. 5 below.

by your actual call. However, I pray that I may be permitted to comment a little on a certain clause in the official act by which your Honors, the States General, consent that a national synod be held in this province, expressly for the revision of the Confession and the Catechism of the Dutch Churches, which clause displeases many people who think that it is not only unnecessary to revise the Confession and the Catechism, but also that it is improper.[116] They also assume that I and a certain very influential person were the persons who prevailed on the States General to have this call for revisions inserted in the minutes.[117] It is certainly not the case that the revision of the Confession and Catechism is unnecessary or unfit, and furthermore, we were not the source of your Noble Lords' involvement in this affair. We had no involvement at all in the origin of this clause in the minutes, as it arose eleven or twelve years ago through a pressing request from the states of South Holland and West Friesland. At the behest of many of their churches, they called for a national synod, and, in the process of making that formal decision, they concluded that it was appropriate to include a provision that such a synod would include reviewing the Confession of the Dutch Church. We did not make any attempt, by either advice or influence, to encourage this measure. Even if we had made such an attempt, we would not have been doing anything that was not included in our official duties.

For the following reasons it is clearly reasonable and equitable, even necessary in the present state of affairs, to adopt such a measure. First, so that all the world may see us affirming that only the Word of God is privileged above and beyond all dispute, worthy of total acceptance. Secondly, these writings [Belgic Confession and Heidelberg Catechism] are human productions that may contain some degree of error. It is therefore proper to initiate a formal inquiry, as would be the case with a national synod, whether there be anything in these formulations that requires amendment:

---

[116] Arminius is referring to the minutes of a gathering of the States General that took place on March 15, 1606, in which the following words are recorded: "The purpose of the National Synod would be the revision of the Confession and the Catechism of the subscribing churches." Cited by Uytenbogaert, *Historie*, 329.

[117] That important person would be Johannes Uytenbogaert. The reason people assumed that Arminius and Uytenbogaert were responsible for the insertion of the call for a national synod is that the formal source was the provinces of Holland and Utrecht. Note in what follows, however, that Arminius is careful to make the point that the issue of revision had been on the table for at least eleven years, dating from a resolution before the States of Holland in 1597. Cf. Uytenbogaert, *Historie*, 329. In his *Geschiedenissen*, 359–60, 368, Triglandius notes the objections to the call for revision, and records his own detailed refutation of the need for such.

1. Whether these human writings are in accord with the Word of God in every part—with regard to the wording itself and the manner of expression, as well as the meaning conveyed.
2. Whether they comprehended everything necessary to be believed for salvation, so that by this rule [of faith] salvation is not ascribed to the undeserving.
3. Whether they do not incorporate too much, including things unnecessary for faith, whereby salvation might be denied to whom salvation is due.
4. Whether certain expressions contained therein lead to disputes because they are capable of being understood in several different ways. Thus, for example, in the Fourteenth Article of the Confession, we read: "Nothing is done without God appointing it." If by this word it is signified that God appoints things of any and every kind, it would be erroneous. It follows that God is the cause of sin.[118] If this signifies that whatever God does, it has been ordained to a good end, that formulation would be correct.[119]
5. Whether there be items that are actually in conflict with each other. For instance, a highly respected person in the church sent a letter to Johannes Piscator, Professor of Divinity at the University of Herborn in Nassau. In this letter he admonished Piscator to be consistent with the Heidelberg Catechism in the doctrine of justification. He cited three related passages from the Catechism that he considered to be at variance with Piscator's opinions. Piscator replied that he stood firm on his interpretation of the Catechism, and he proceeded to cite ten or eleven passages from the Catechism as proofs. I simply do not see how these passages can be reconciled.[120]
6. Whether everything contained in these writings is worded in ways that the Scriptures require.
7. Whether these writings are formulated in ways that promote peace and unity with all Reformed churches.

Third, a national synod is held for the purpose of discovering whether the Church is in a state of overall good health. One of the primary responsibilities

---

[118] This last phrase about "cause of sin" is a marginal addition.

[119] The word *ordonnantie* does not actually appear in article fourteen, but rather in article thirteen: "that in this world nothing happens without His *ordonnantie*; however, God is not the author of sin, nor is God responsible for sin that occurs."

[120] Arminius wrote a long letter about this to Uytenbogaert. Cf. *Ep. Ecc.*, Letter to Uytenbogaert (August 3, 1604), no. 70, pp. 128–35.

of such a gathering is the examination of doctrine, whether it be unanimously agreed upon, or representative only of particular teachers.

Fourth, a review along these lines would procure for these formulations a greater degree of authority. Through the process of a rigorous and thorough[121] examination, they would be found to agree with the Word of God, or they could be brought into greater conformity to it. Such a process would also encourage a wider heartfelt appreciation for the clergy, when it is perceived that these ministers hold in highest esteem the truth of God that is revealed in Scripture, and that their dedication to this is so great that it leads them to make every effort to bring their own doctrines into conformity with that revealed truth.

Fifth, this is especially necessary at the present time: (1) There are several individuals among our ministerial ranks who quietly and secretly hold some reservations about certain points in the church's formulations, because they hope that these will become topics of discussion in a national synod. (2) Based on the promise that this might occur, they have been convinced not to reveal their views. (3) Because this would be the intention of a national synod, the Noble Lords of the States General may be pleased to establish an ecclesial ordering by which every clergyman in God's Church would be required to comply. For the Noble Lords to make such a decision with a clear conscience, it is necessary that you be convinced in your own minds that the doctrine in the formula of union be agreeable to the Word of God. This is reason enough to request an examination of our Confession in your presence, Esteemed Lords, to demonstrate that it is in accord with the Word of God or to bring it into conformity.

The rationale of the sixth reason is drawn from the example set by those churches united under the Augsburg Confession, as well as the Swiss and French Churches, that after two or three years of review saw fit to enrich their Confession with an entirely new article. Our Dutch Confession has not been reviewed comprehensively since its initial formulation, even though a few things have been added, others taken out, and the rest having undergone slight editorial changes.[122]

Numerous other reasons might be produced, but I omit them because I consider those already mentioned to be quite sufficient to demonstrate that the clause providing for revision was quite properly inserted in the instrument of consent mentioned previously. I am well aware that reasons to the contrary have been produced. One in particular has received the most attention and

---

[121] Lit., "mature."

[122] This entire sixth rationale is written in the margin of the manuscript, and it is included in the *Verclaringhe* (1610), 48; and Hoenderdaal, 130.

is the most substantial. It deserves brief attention. Such an examination is deemed neither appropriate nor necessary by some, because it would call into question the church's doctrine. This is asserted to be the case because, first, this doctrine has received the approval and support of many respected and learned men who have defended it against all opposition, and secondly, because it has been sealed with the martyrs' blood of thousands. And finally, because it is feared that such an examination would lead within the church to offense, confusion, scandal, and the weakening of conscience. And outside the church, the result would be ridicule, slander, and accusation.

In response to these I offer the following: It would be better to avoid derogatory and other similar expressions raising doubt about a human composition that might contain some degree of error. On what basis can any writing rightfully be called into question or doubted when it was never intrinsically unquestionable, or ever should have been considered beyond doubt? Second, the approval of learned men, the defense of a composition against its opponents, and its sealing with the blood of martyrs do not render any doctrine authentic or place it beyond the limits of doubt. It is quite possible for both divines and martyrs to err—the possibility of which we must allow in this context. Third, distinctions should be made among the different contents of the Confession. While some parts touch the very foundation of salvation and are fundamental to the Christian Religion, others are added atop the foundational structure[123] and are not absolutely necessary to salvation. The doctrines contained in the former category are supported unanimously by all the Reformed, and as such are successfully defended against all opposition. But those of the latter classification have become topics of controversy among differing parties, and with some semblance of truth or justification are attacked by enemies. Among the many things sealed by the blood of martyrs, these are not among them. Here careful distinctions must be made with regard to reasons why recent martyrs have suffered and shed blood.

If we do this, we will discover that no one has ever been questioned about, much less sealed with their blood, the subject that I honestly believe should be made prominent in the deliberations of a synod. For example, when a question was raised about interpreting the seventh chapter of the Epistle to the Romans, it was asserted by one that the passage was quoted in the margin of the Confession exactly in the same sense that he proposed, and that the martyrs had sealed it with their own blood. To this assertion it was answered

---

[123] Lit., "carpentered on." My decision to translate this rather freely is based on Arminius' contention in several places that there are textual additions to the originally formulated Belgic Confession that are not fundamental to its essential teachings. In addition to this section, pp. 150–53, see also pp. 49ff., and 57, 60, 62.

that a comprehensive search of the great book of the martyrs, published by the French,[124] would not turn up a single example of a martyr having been examined on that passage, much less having shed any blood for it. In summary, the blood of the martyrs tends to confirm the truth that they professed their faith with a sincere conscience, but this is not conclusive proof that their confession is irrefutable on every point, or that they were led by Christ into all truth in such a manner as to avoid any chance of error.[125]

Fourth, if the Church[126] is properly instructed to distinguish between that which really does and always should belong to the Word of God, as well as that which belongs to human writings, and if the Church be properly instructed concerning the liberty that the Church and all Christians possess and will always enjoy as long as human compositions are measured by the standard of God's Word, she will never find herself in turmoil or distress. As long as human compositions are brought to the touchstone of God's Word, the Church may rejoice that God has provided pastors and teachers who carefully and with precision examine their own doctrines thoroughly. They do so according to the standard of God's Word to be certain that they are in harmony, even on the smallest points.

Fifth, the doctrine received should be subject to ongoing examination, even if it be feared that turmoil would follow when evil-minded persons made such revisions the subject of ridicule, accusation, or slander; or even when they misrepresent the proposal for revision in such a way as to suggest that those who suggested the review are themselves inadequately versed in their faith. God's Word commands us, "Test the spirits to see whether they are from God" [1 John 4:1]. If Luther, Zwingli, and others had been hindered by such thoughts, they would never have examined and tested the teachings of the Papists. Nor would those who adhere to the Augsburg Confession have seen fit to submit that formulation of the faith to examination and to alter it on specific points—an act applauded by us all. Indeed, towards the end of his life, Luther was encouraged by Philip Melanchthon (as reported by some) to take steps toward resolving the controversy on the sacrament of the Lord's Supper. Luther refused to take the step and put it off on Melanchthon under the guise, or so he said, that by such a move the entire doctrine would be undermined.

---

[124] Jean Crespin (1520–1572), *Histoire des martyrs, persecutez et mis a mort pour la verité de l'Euangile*. The book can be found also under the Latin title, *Acta martyrum*. The first edition for which I find a record is 1554. It was published at least five times during Crespin's life and was translated into many languages.

[125] This last sentence is written in the margin of the manuscript taken up fully in the *Verclaringhe* (1610), 49; and Hoenderdaal, 133.

[126] In this section, Arminius capitalizes "Church" because he has the Church universal in view.

Following this kind of reasoning, the Papists have every right to resist any doctrine being doubted or subjected to examination, for their positions have been received for many centuries. It has also been suggested that if the teachings of the church were examined every time a national synod was convened, the church would never have any permanent, foundational documents on which to depend. One might say of such a church that it is left with no more than an annual faith, being tossed to and fro and carried about by every wind of doctrine [Eph 4:14].

My first response is that the church has always had Moses, the prophets, the Evangelists and the Apostles—in other words, the entirety of the Old and New Testaments. These contain with complete clarity everything necessary for salvation, and the Church will build her faith and establish herself on this sure foundation. Even though we have catechisms and confessions, in the final analysis every decision on matters of faith and religion must obtain its final resolution in the Scriptures. Secondly, there are foundational doctrines in the Confession that are certain and not open to question, and no one but a heretic would dare call them into question. There are, however, other parts that are of such a nature as to admit frequent deliberation and discussion among learned and godly leaders in order that these may be brought as nearly as possible into harmony with foundational unquestioned teachings. And finally, the goal is that the Confession should contain as few articles as possible, and these should be stated concisely using only Scriptural language as far as possible. All detailed explanations, proofs, digressions, exaggerations, amplifications, and exclamations should be eliminated. Only those truths necessary for salvation should be allowed to stand. In its brevity, the Confession will be less liable to error, less open to discredit, and less subject to examination. Let us follow the example of the ancient church, using so few words as practically possible to define those things required for belief.

Some among us distinguish different levels between the [Belgic] Confession and the [Heidelberg] Catechism regarding the need for revision. Since the Confession is intended for a relatively small population, specifically for the Dutch churches, they conclude that it may be examined and revised in a synod. But since the Catechism belongs not only to us but to a much broader population, principally to all the churches in the Palatinate, they feel its examination to be especially risky. I would respond that as long as we desire the Heidelberg Catechism to be a unifying document among the church's divines, and if they be required to subscribe to it, then it ought to be examined. No document of the church should be held in such high esteem that we be required to receive its formulations without the freedom of submitting them to careful examination. It is for this reason that churches in different regions, although in complete agreement on foundational Christian doctrine, have composed for themselves their own confessions of faith. If the Heidelberg Catechism is not viewed in this light, and adequate latitude is granted to discern its meaning, then revision is not necessary. In that case, however, the requirement for subscribing to it should be removed, and a degree of latitude should be allowed in its interpretation.

Conclusion

This, Noble Lords, is all that I propose to you, my wise and prudent masters. I accept that next to God I am responsible to this noble and powerful assembly for all my actions, and I humbly and gratefully acknowledge that you have granted me a courteous and patient hearing. I solemnly declare that I am prepared to participate in an amicable and fraternal conference with my respected colleagues to discuss these and any other issues at whatever time, place or occasion this esteemed assembly may deem appropriate. Furthermore, I pledge in every gathering to conduct myself with moderation and reason, ready to be instructed as much as to offer instruction. With regard to all issues that might come before such a gathering, two things should be preserved on all points: whether the point embodies truth and whether it must be believed for salvation—both of which must be decided on the basis of Holy Writ. Regardless of the cogency of well-constructed arguments I might offer demonstrating any article's conformity to the Word of God, I will not force it as an article of belief on my fellow ministers who might differ with me unless I have clearly demonstrated its veracity from the Word of God and established it as necessary for every Christian to believe in order to receive salvation. If my colleagues are willing to proceed along the same lines, I cannot imagine that any schism or controversy will easily arise among us. Furthermore, to remove all concern about issues that might arise at my initiative (realizing that this esteemed assembly is fully engaged with weighty matters of the highest import related entirely to the stability of our country and the Reformed Church), I would add: Only in connection with differences over numerous and truly significant issues shall my patience with fellow ministers be tested. I do not wish to have dominion over the faith of others, only to minister to believers with a design to promote in them an increase of knowledge, truth, godliness, peace, and joy in Jesus Christ our Lord. If, for one reason or another, my colleagues cannot find a way to tolerate me or to allow me a place among them, I would still hope that my actions would not lead to schism. May God forbid such a catastrophe, because far too many schisms have arisen and spread already in Christianity, and it is incumbent on us all to strive to diminish their number and influence. Even amid the eventuality [that I might be dismissed by my colleagues], I will guard my soul with patience. Even if it becomes necessary for me to resign my office, I will serve our common Christian faith as long as it may please God to extend my days[127]—never forgetting: *SAT ECCLESIAE, SAT PATRIAE DATUM* ["I have fulfilled my duty to the Church and to my native land"].

---

[127] The sentiment about God extending days and prolonging life is in parentheses in the margin of the manuscript and included in its entirety in the *Verclaringhe* (1610), 52; and Hoenderdaal, 138.

PART III
A THEOLOGICAL POSTSCRIPT

5

THE EVANGELICAL, PRACTICAL THEOLOGY OF JACOB ARMINIUS

Arminius was in almost every way a product of his theological era, especially in method—long, drawn out close reasoning characterized by syllogistic logic. Attempts by earlier Arminian defenders to cast him as a "biblical theologian" in an attempt to rescue Dutch theology from the clutches of an anti-biblical scholasticism are off target. Certainly Arminius meant to be biblical, but that is not to say that his opponents were not also so inclined. On this point they were all theologians of the Reformation with deep commitments to *sola scriptura*. At the same time, Arminius was of the opinion that undue commitments to "man-made formulae" endangered this Reformation principle. Throughout his entire corpus of writings, we can discern a theological intentionality that works with a dialectic holding these two emphases—biblical faith and historic Christianity—in constructive tension. His is a theological intentionality that was formed in the crucible of fifteen years as an Amsterdam pastor. If we read Arminius anticipating that his goal is first and foremost to win a syllogistic argument, then we are not reading him accurately. We have not listened long enough to what he himself said in places other than the most recent theological debate into which he was forced by his ministerial or university colleagues. Regardless of the topic, I would submit, there is a proximate as well as an ultimate goal in all his theological debates. The proximate goal is to make a theological point (and win that particular dispute), but this must be understood as part and parcel of a larger vision—to discern the salvific disposition of God. His intention is to render the gospel of Jesus Christ as Savior more intelligibly, in order that it may be appropriated and lived out by Christian believers so that they will worship the one true God.

Arminius' theology is always both evangelical and practical; however, those words meant something quite different to Arminius than they do to most modern readers, especially those who have been influenced by "evangelical" or "practical" theology in the last hundred years. In this more recent context, the word "evangelical," especially in North America, connotes to a large extent forms of creedal propositionalism that Arminius spent all his pastoral and professorial life polemicizing against. The expression "practical theology" is even further from finding a place in the theological world inhabited by Arminius. The "how to" connotation of getting things done in the routine life of the church would have been a complete conundrum to pastors in Arminius' time. For Arminius the most practical thing that any pastor could do was lead parishioners in authentic praise and worship of God, and the best way to do this was by formulating a theology that would prove to be foundational to such worship. The formulation of theology that encouraged people to believe and participate in authentic praise and worship was in itself evangelical theology. Any theology that caused confusion about who God is or what God's salvific intentions are for humanity was, by definition, not an evangelical theology. This was the grounding intention of Arminius' entire theological agenda, and this is evident from his first inaugural lectures at Leiden; it was also the agenda of his theological compositions in Amsterdam.

It is well known that Arminius produced long expositions on Romans and an examination of Perkins on predestination during this period. If we can take Arminius at his word, we now know that he began as a pastor to develop his "systematic theology" as formal propositions. Based on Arminius' correspondence with Uytenbogaert, Clarke makes the case that previous scholars were wrong when they assumed that the "Private Disputations" were begun during his Leiden years, perhaps even as late as 1607.[1] This issue is potentially much

---

[1] Cf. Carl Bangs, "Introduction," *Works*, 1:xviii, where he argues that the private disputations were written for university students and notes that the private disputations were interrupted by illness and death. Granting that several of the private disputations "came late" does not mean that they were begun late. Muller seems to follow Bangs in this assumption (25, 50, 111). It seems to me that Clarke and Bangs may both be correct: Arminius began setting out the parameters of his formal theology in Amsterdam, but he prepared his "Private Disputations" after going to Leiden. The implication of this is that the contours of Arminius' theology were well formed (and written out) when he went to Leiden, and these formulations were essential to the preparation of all his disputations, public and private.

more than simply a matter of correcting chronologies. In 1599 Arminius wrote to the trusted Uytenbogaert:

> I am engaged in constructing an order for a Synopsis of Common Places in Divinity; I have determined to re-read all the ancient and modern divines which are at hand and which can be obtained. . . . I am making a beginning with the Doctrine of God, who is first in order and dignity in theology. In this I shall consider both nature and persons.[2]

He notes shortly thereafter in a letter to Uytenbogaert, dated June 10, that he is including a brief overview of his *Synopsis*. This early dating of the theological formulations foundational to the "Private Disputations" means at the very least that Arminius the pastor was composing formal, systematic theological compositions for several years prior to his arrival as a professor at Leiden. The content of his inaugural orations were not composed *de novo* in the months immediately prior to his ascending the lectern in the *Academiegebouw* on the Rapenburg as a new professor.

As both pastor and theologian, Arminius believed the ultimate goal of theology to be "the union of God with man."[3] As scholastic as Arminius was in his methods of argumentation, he was, in the final analysis, disposed against scholastic assumptions that led to theology being purely intellectualist, even if there is a strong intellectualist strand in his thinking.[4] God does not reveal himself to us in order that we might simply know *about* him, but rather that we might worship him:

> The object [God] is not laid before our theology merely to be known, but, when known, to be worshipped. For the theology which belongs to this world is PRACTICAL *and through faith*; THEORETICAL THEOLOGY belongs to the other world, and consists of pure and unclouded vision, according to the expression of the Apostle, "We walk by faith, and not by sight." (2 Cor. 5:7) [and] . . . For this reason, we must clothe the object of our theology in such a manner as may enable it to incline us to worship God, and fully to persuade and win us over to that practice.[5]

---

[2] Letter to Uytenbogaert (February 15, 1599), *Epp. Ecc.*, no. 44, p. 85.
[3] "The Author and the End of Theology," *Works*, 1:362.
[4] See pp. 165–66, below.
[5] "The Object of Theology," *Works*, 1:328 (emphasis in original).

Similar to the motive and motif in his "Private Disputations," Arminius announces in his inaugural address that he intends to do none other than he has done as a pastor in Amsterdam: theologize in such a way as to facilitate the saving knowledge of God by envisioning a compelling vision of God characterized by love and justice. As we have seen, Arminius' opponents accused him of desiring to undermine the authority of the Belgic Confession and the Heidelberg Catechism, no matter how often he protested otherwise. That is not what, in Arminius' mind, lay at the heart of their differences. These represented differences along the way to a much broader vision. He was pushing for a theological frame of reference that would allow Scripture to have the final authority in matters of faith (a genuine Reformed perspective!), and he believed that if such a move could be made, then the narrow interpretations of the confession and creed could give way to a slightly different perspective, both with regard to what the Scriptures teach as well as how the creedal formulae were interpreted. In retrospect, we can look at Arminius' theological agenda with a level of clarity (in his inaugural orations and beyond) that his contemporaries might not have seen.

Arminius makes distinctions between Legal Theology and Evangelical Theology, and Muller has argued for a "logical priority of legal over evangelical theology." He sees this assumption as parallel to the "logical priority of God as primary over Christ as a secondary object of theology"—pointing toward a "logical priority of the foundational, non-soteriological topics in Arminius's system over soteriological topics."[6] I believe that Arminius' first response to this would be, "There are precious few topics in my theological compositions that are in their motive and motif non-soteriological." Arminius would recognize logical precedence, but not the logical *priority* of "foundational, non-soteriological" topics.[7] As Muller himself acknowledges, Arminius is careful to assert that because the Father and the Son together are the authors of salvation, "Evangelical Theology far surpasses Legal Theology."[8] Clarke muses whether Muller would have read Arminius differently if

---

[6] Muller, 74.

[7] It is quite possible that Muller and I are in agreement—his asserting "logical priority" meaning prior in the literal chronological sense, not logical priority in the sense of logical or substantive importance.

[8] Muller, 76; *Works*, 1:359.

he had known that a significant number of Arminius' "Private Disputations" were foundational to the Leiden phase of Arminius' thought.[9] I doubt it. My own interpretation would be that Arminius' dialectic of holding the Legal and Evangelical in tension is at work: "The wisdom, goodness and power of God shown in creation (Legal Theology) are great, but the wisdom, goodness and power shown in the incarnation and new creation are greater, and constitute the claims by which Evangelical Theology asserts it precedence."[10]

Muller treats God's intentions regarding both "Creation" and "Providence" as "non-christological and non-soteriological," and asserts that it is not clear to him that Arminius' theological system as a whole should be regarded as Evangelical Theology. I believe this would come as a surprise to Arminius. Arminius is intent to demonstrate that the nature of God and his actions in creation and providence underlie both legal and evangelical theology. These remain essentially unchanged and unaffected by the fall of humanity into sin, even though the ways in which providence operates adapts to the situation of fallen humanity. If we go back and read Arminius' foundational work that led to his "Private Disputations" as chronologically prior to and laying the foundation for his Leiden theology, then we can perhaps discern more readily the soteriological line that flows through his thought. Even as he allows and argues the logical and chronological components of Legal Theology, he is moving inexorably toward the soteriological *telos* of his Evangelical Theology.

This reading of Arminius does not fundamentally contradict Muller's reading of Arminius as intellectualist, but it does underscore the "synthesis of the practical with the intellectualist model"—an emphasis that complements "the alliance of revelation and reason" in Arminius.[11] Muller asserts, "Arminius' argument for the priority of intellect in the final vision of God *perfectly reproduces* the classic intellectualist thesis of Thomas Aquinas."[12] Following Muller's logic, Arminius' theology represents a significant departure from the major medieval paradigms characterized by a particular type of eclectic. In this scholasticism, theological practice (*praxis*) is typically associated with love

---

[9] Clarke, 41, 61–63.
[10] Clarke, 62.
[11] Muller, 79.
[12] Muller, 78 (emphasis added). Muller cites Thomas Aquinas, *Summa Theologica*, Ia, q. 82, art. 3.

and will; contemplation (*speculation* or *contemplation*) are associated with intellect. In that Arminius is inclined toward a *praxis* advocated by "the more Ramist of the Reformed," he connects his notions of *praxis* to an "intellectualism quite unparalleled among his Reformed contemporaries."[13] This helps to explain why he differed with a number of his Dutch contemporaries, but it does not make such a move "wrongheaded." Arminius assumes that practical theology can also be intellectualist because, with regard to the question of human salvation, "the intellect leads the will."[14] Muller's axiomatic conclusion is that for Arminius, "Reason can play a greater role in the construction of [a] theological system than it could on the assumption of a soteriological priority of will,"[15] the tendency of the more nominalist voluntarism characteristic of many theologians of his era. This intellectualist vision has implications for discerning the mind of God. It helps to explain why Arminius asserts, for example, that there are some things related to soteriology that God "cannot do." It is not reasonable to assert that God can do something simply because God "wills" to do it. The intellectualist vision allows the theologian to press with regard to motive as to "why" God would choose to act irrespective of all rationality.

As we have already been indicating, we can discern an interplay in Arminius' theology among motive, motif, and method. William den Boer makes the case that Arminius' theology is not purely intellectualist; it is characterized by an "ethical-pastoral" motive.[16] This is consonant with the line of interpretation I am following. Den Boer, however,

---

[13] Muller, 79.

[14] Muller (79) references Public Disputation XI, "On the Free Will of Man and its Power," points i, v, viii, ix, x. Cf. *Works*, 2:189–95.

[15] Muller, 79.

[16] William den Boer, "Defense or Deviation? A Re-examination of Arminius's Motives to Deviate from the 'Mainstream' Reformed Theology," in *Revisiting the Synod of Dort (1618–1619)*, ed. Aza Goudriaan and Fred van Lieburg (Leiden: Brill, 2011), 26–28 . Den Boer sets off the word "Mainstream" in his title with single quotations, but he fails to note the anachronism of the usage. What one might consider to be mainstream after Dort was not broadly accepted to be so twenty years before when Arminius was a pastor in Amsterdam, or even when he was professor at Leiden. Cf. Jeremy Dupertuis Bangs, *Strangers and Pilgrims, Travellers and Sojourners: Leiden and the Foundations of Plymouth Plantation* (Plymouth, Mass.: General Society of Mayflower Descendants, 2009), 472–73, on the use of "orthodox," and the expanded discussion in his chap. 13, pp. 509ff.

does not seem to recognize that he moves from motive and leitmotif to formal method when he shifts the emphasis of his essay on this topic to God's justice. He is moving toward his own goal of describing the *duplex amor Dei* as foundational for Arminius. Well and good, but den Boer needs to be more consequential in making this move. In Arminius' *Declaration*, as well as in other essays, the dialectic of love and justice constitutes his foundational theological method. This method is the path along which Arminius validates the practical-ethical motive that drives his theological intentions.

Arminius' theological motive is comprehensively soteriological. He is intent to develop a vision of God as one whose disposition is to save and is therefore worthy of our worship. God is inclined to save, and God is disposed to make every provision that makes salvation available to every creature. This practical, pastoral concern may be said to be the controlling motif for Arminius. In Arminius' vision, the disposition of God is always leaning positively into the salvific provisions. While Arminius would not dispute the reality that not all will be saved, his vision of God does not include God's actually deciding the destiny of the damned. His is a provision that all may come to faith. This salvific motif flows consistently from God's saving disposition. When we press the soteriological disposition issue with regard to God's essential nature, we encounter the dialectic of love for justice and love for the creature. When we enter this more formal theological domain, however, we misconstrue Arminius if we interpret the dialectic of twofold love in isolation from his practical and pastoral concerns. Indeed, it is the formal foundation on which these soteriological concerns are built.

Even when he appears before the States of Holland, it is clear that there are pastoral and ethical issues at stake. In this oration we encounter Arminius the rhetorician, Arminius the historian of doctrine, and Arminius the systematic theologian. In many ways the *Declaration* is Arminius' most "mature" theological essay, at least in the sense that he has his entire theological oeuvre as a pastor and professor to work with. His prior essays and disputations cover the theological *encyclopedie* of his era, but progressively he has been forced by his colleagues in Leiden (*all* supralapsarians) to defend himself on an increasingly narrow set of issues—invariably coming back to predestination. His *Declaration* in The Hague, set out in three divisions, is his final attempt to defend himself. The second part is the longest of the three, and it is theologically the most substantial.[17]

In part one of his *Declaration*, Arminius is expressing his "sentiments" in the sense that he is giving a personal response to the implicit and explicit charges that have been leveled against him over the years. He reports the events, and he is not hesitant to reveal the depth of his feelings about the accusations. He does not go all the way back to the discussions within the Amsterdam consistory, as that would have been outside the purview of the States General to whom he is speaking. He does make clear, however, that there is considerable continuity here, because the tension and assumed differences are present from the very beginning, even from the time of his proposed appointment to the Leiden post. Indeed, the Reformed clergy (Plancius, Helmichius, and Hommius) are constantly in the shadows, if not in full view.

In part two, Arminius begins by setting out in nine points what he feels are the primary supralapsarian assumptions of his opponents. The crux of the concern about their concept of election is that even prior to the fall, God had already decided precisely who would be saved and who would be damned. He ascribes this teaching specifically to Gomarus, his primary public opponent in Leiden (although all the Leiden theologians were intended). Arminius recognizes that there is both a milder form of election (infralapsarianism) as well as the more extreme form (supralapsarianism), but he contends that the practical result of each is the same. Both "happen" in the mind of God prior to the act of creation, the softer view simply having the fall and subsequent need for salvation in God's all-knowing view. Even though the milder view of election would seem to save God from being responsible for the origin of sin and evil in the world, according to Arminius that supposed rescue is at most an abstract gain. In order for the fall to occur, God must have withheld or suspended his gracious assistance to the first humans, or else they could have by gracious assistance remained obedient. The practical result is the same: God either planned the fall in order to carry out the prior decisions to save and damn, or God withdrew or withheld the grace needed for obedience, and humanity fell—thereby necessitating God's saving plan.

---

[17] Be reminded that the physical division of the *Declaration* into three sections is imposed by the translator/editor. Clarke, 148–64, provides a section-by-section overview of the *Declaration*'s entire contents.

This point about necessary actions or events returns often in Arminius' thought—that which must happen of necessity is a fundamental violation of freedom, both divine and human.

Arminius describes his essential doctrine of election in four main headings, with twenty short sub-points.[18] Arminius speaks of a practical dialectic in his election soteriology, as he tries to hold a constructive tension between scriptural teachings in passages like Ephesians 2:8-9 ("For by grace you have been saved through faith; and this is not your own doing, it is the gift of God—not because of works lest any man should boast"), and Philippians 2:12 ("Therefore, my beloved, as you have always obeyed, so now, not only in my presence but now much more in my absence, work out your own salvation with fear and trembling"). Arminius cites Augustine favorably against Pelagius to assert that he is not Pelagian, a point that he makes abundantly clear in the *Declaration*: grace is the beginning, the continuation, and the completion of everything that is salutary.

Arminius then proceeds to summarize several items that had already led to conflict, as well as some that might be conceived to be suspicious or to produce friction: foreknowledge, free will, divine grace, perseverance of the saints, assurance of salvation, and the perfection of believers. Here Arminius again favorably cites Augustine against Pelagius, and finally, he touches on the divine nature of Christ. The accusations against Arminius of heresy regarding Christology may be counted among the most painful emotionally.[19] Arminius asserts that

---

[18] This is an essential recapitulation of what Arminius had set out in Public Disputation XV, "On Divine Predestination," *Works*, 2:226: "Predestination therefore, as it regards the thing itself, is the Decree of the good pleasure of God in Christ, by which He resolved within himself from all eternity, to justify, adopt, and endow with everlasting life, to the praise of his own glorious grace, believers on whom He had decreed to bestow faith." Almost the exact same wording can be found in Private Disputation XL, *Works*, 2:392; as well as in Private Disputation XL. Cf. Calvin, *Institutes of the Christian Religion*, trans. Henry Beveridge (Grand Rapids: Eerdmans, 1975), 3:21, esp. 3.21.5, in which we find the same definitions for what Arminius calls "predestination in itself." See also Letter to Hippolytus (April 5, 1608), *Ep. Ecc.*, no. 114, p. 207; in comparison with Calvin, *Institutes*, 3.21.5. Those who assert that predestination is not integral to Arminius' theology simply do not understand Arminius. This crux issue is how God works this predestination out in the lives of believers.

[19] Cf. Letter to Hippolytus (April 5, 1608), *Ep. Ecc.*, no. 114, pp. 204–9, one of his longer letters; as well as his complaint to Sebastiaan Egberts (September 24, 1608), *Ep. Ecc.*, no. 118, pp. 212–13.

he and Gomarus hold the same doctrinal position on Christ's divinity.[20] There does not seem to be any explicit reason in their respective writings for Arminius to think otherwise, and on this point Gomarus did not inveigh publicly against him. When Lubbertus circulated the rumors abroad against Arminius in early 1608, he may have been aware that Gomarus was privately contradicting Arminius' assertion that they agreed on the christological point.[21] Feeling that he is on solid ground, Arminius presses his case.

In his *Declaration*, Arminius makes prominent use of the *duplex amor Dei* motif. It is a debated issue whether this is the decisively formative factor in his theology as a whole, and it has of late also been asserted that assurance of eternal destiny plays a key role.[22] I would suggest that there does not need to be a winner and a loser in the debate about the key to interpreting Arminius. Both motifs are important, and both play key roles. *Duplex amor Dei* plays a formal role ontologically. This defines who God *is*, and this is foundational to what God does outwardly to rescue humanity. In this outward salvific move, God's love is revealed in ways that render his love accessible and discernible, even as the depths of divine justice remain mysterious. The discernible dimensions, the "knowability" of God's salvific intentionality, are experienced by faithful, believing converts through the witness of the Holy Spirit as assurance of salvation. In this way, proleptic hope for salvation becomes a present reality in the hearts and minds of the faithful. Arminius' opponents feared that his allowing that believers might fall away and lose their salvation entailed the loss of certainty of salvation.[23] Here again, we see Arminius holding to a dialectic in his *Declaration*. He does not assert that true believers *will* fall away, only that it is *possible* to be lost through unbelief and rejecting the wooing and leading of God's Spirit, which is in effect "blaspheming" the Holy Spirit.

Mention has already been made regarding Arminius' emphasis on grace-enabled cooperation on the part of believers, and we have also

---

[20] See *Declaration*, p. 146.

[21] Cf. G. P. van Itterzon, *Franciscus Gomarus* (The Hague: M. Nijhoff, 1930), 395: Letter to S. Lubbertus (October 23, 1607), in which Gomarus lists Arminius' erroneous teachings, the first among them to the effect that Arminius was indeed guilty of Sabellianism.

[22] Cf. dissertations by William den Boer, *Duplex amor Dei*; and Stanglin, *Arminius on the Assurance of Salvation*, for this debated issue.

[23] Cf. Stanglin, esp. 36–41.

made an anticipatory comment about a practical dialectic in Arminius' theology of election. What either or both of these mean can best be understood by a closer examination of how *duplex amor Dei* functions. William den Boer has done this in his dissertation, but we can also do it in a much more focused way by reviewing the *Declaration of Sentiments*. Amid Arminius' descriptions of his sentiments in the personal sense, we encounter the formal argument in which the twofold love of God is axiomatic—justice and love in a constructive dialectic.

The word "justice" for Arminius refers to an internal divine logic rather than an external retributive system. To be sure, Arminius is in agreement with Aristotle and later theologians who follow the ancient philosopher in asserting "render to each his due" (*suum cuique tribuere*); however, in Arminius this is always theologically connected with divine covenant, freedom, reward/punishment, order, and harmony—all within the logic of non-contradiction. Justice always seeks to do what is "fitting" for the recipient, thereby guaranteeing a harmonious relationship between the one on the giving side and the one on the receiving end of the justice. The result is reconciliation. Arminius is consequential in his theological reasoning with regard to divine consistency. There are some things that God will not and cannot do.[24] So it is more accurate to say that God *is* justice rather than God *has* justice. Because this is the way God *is*, this is what God "naturally" *does*. God, in his justice, can only do that which is completely right in relation to the recipient of divine justice, and the result is a graciously wrought sustained harmony. God cannot act in such a way as to contradict his essential justice.[25] This essential justice always operates in a constructive dialectic with divine love. In God's salvific initiative toward creation, this love requires respect for human dignity and freedom. For Arminius, freedom is real only when it excludes any and every form of necessity—with regard to God's freedom as well as human freedom. Dekker has called this the "two dimensions [Dutch: *graden*] of freedom."[26] The mutuality regarding freedom that Arminius puts

---

[24] Den Boer says: "Remarkable about Arminius' writings is how often he states that God cannot do something because it does not befit one of his attributes, or else God has to or may not do something because He is who He is, because something does not fit his nature or revelation" (35).

[25] Cf. *Duplex amor Dei*, 40ff.

[26] Cf. *Rijker dan Midas*, 59, 135–36, 237.

forward fundamentally contradicts the one assumed by his opponents. In their definition, freedom has been adequately defined and preserved when "spontaneity" or "absence of coercion" has been preserved. For Arminius, these must be part of the formal definition of freedom, but absence of coercion as well as the lack of necessity (non-necessity) must be present for an adequate definition of freedom.[27]

It is perhaps not an exaggeration to say that these insights into Arminius' definitions of love, justice, and freedom are absolutely essential to understanding his public and private theological disputations as well as his *Declaration*. These insights must also be kept in view when reading the Leiden inaugural orations that set out the contours of his evangelical, practical theology. He knows that many theologians of his day are preoccupied with what he calls "Legal Theology"—an abstract theology conceived in the mind of God prior to creation and before the fall.[28] We can almost hear him say, "Well and good, but that is not Christian Theology. When you add the actual saving work of Jesus Christ to the theological amalgam, you have Christian Theology. Otherwise, all you have is Legal Theology!" His expression is "Evangelical Theology." When you add Christ as Savior to the picture, you have Evangelical Theology, and this is the only kind of theology that makes any difference in the life of the church. Christians at worship do not pray to a god in which Christ is only conceptually, in the mind of God, a part of the picture. So extensive preoccupation with Legal Theology is not a constructive exercise because it is not conducive to worship. Actually, Arminius is arguing, the Legal Theology being put forward by his opponents is counterproductive to worship. It is pure abstraction devoid of incarnational content. It is pure thought in the mind of God. Theology is intended to facilitate worship, and in order to do this, theology must at some level be amenable to human understanding—which is not to say that God must be reduced comprehensively to human understanding. Den Boer gets it right about Arminius when he says that the object of theology, which is God, must be clothed descriptively by the theologian in such a way as to "incline" (*suadere*) people to worship God and to "persuade" (*persuadere*) them to do it.[29] This requires that God's justice remain in constructive tension with divine love.

[27] *Duplex amor Dei*, 44–48.
[28] *Works*, 3:170.
[29] Den Boer, 36.

In his inaugural orations, Arminius sets out the foundational knowledge essential to attaining theology's practical goal: Christian worship. This is rooted in (1) God's nature; (2) God's acts; and (3) God's will. These are "necessary and sufficient" to attain the ultimate theological goal.[30] Any theology adequate to the task begins with God's nature, and the best theology describes the nature of God in such a way as to be *worthy* of worship. This can only be accomplished if God is characterized by justice. Divine wisdom flows from this essential justice, even as God in his wisdom has chosen to make himself known. It is this divine self-disclosure that is visible in God's creative and providential saving acts. If one theologizes in a strictly "legal" manner, then God's right to determine how humanity ought to worship could be done in ways that remain absolutely mysterious to the creature; however, in wisdom and providence flowing from the *duplex amor*, God brings this to pass in a "holy, just and wise" manner,[31] through a "covenant" that God enters with humanity.[32] But the notion of covenant is more than a mere legal agreement, as it is characterized foundationally by worship as well as extravagant gift. God "wills" to enter this covenant in which humanity's fundamental attitude must be one of "worship," and in return, God promises to "abundantly compensate" humanity in such a generous manner that it will lead to the "consummation of his felicity."[33]

Arminius is not blind to the possibility that all this could be worked out "in the mind of God" in an a priori fashion, but he is not content to leave theology in the "legal" state. If one proceeds solely along these legal lines, then Arminius fears that the theologian will be required to assume that God also provided for sin and evil along the way as a means to accomplish the end. This would impinge on God's freedom

---

[30] "The Object of Theology," *Works*, 1:329.

[31] "The Object of Theology," *Works*, 1:329.

[32] Cf. B. Loonstra, *Verkiezing-Verzoening-Verbond: Beschrijving en Beoordeling van de leer van het* pactum salutis *in de gereformeerde theologie* ('s Gravenhage: Boekencentrum BV, 1990), 21–22. Loonstra makes the sweeping assertion that in his inaugural orations, especially "The Priesthood of Christ," in July, 1603. Arminius connects the covenant between God and Christ concerning the salvation of humanity "for the first time in Reformed Theology." The eternal covenant between Father and Son is then foundational for the salvific covenant between God and humanity through Christ the mediator.

[33] "The Object of Theology," *Works*, 1:329.

as well as humanity's, for freedom in both those dimensions must be characterized by lack of coercion as well as absence of necessity. Obviously, no one stands above God to "coerce," but neither must the reality of sin be conceived in such a way that it was "necessary" in order for God's salvific design to be accomplished. The fall happened and sin is real, but not in ways that can be theologically construed as either necessary or coerced. Den Boer notes, "Through the fall into sin, the Legal Theology is no longer sufficient to attain the goal [of salvation]"[34]—either in the sense of Legal Theology in the mind of God prior to the fall, or Legal Theology in the sense of salvation being attained through keeping the law of Moses.[35] Arminius proposes that only an Evangelical Theology is adequate to the situation, and he has a specific way in which this is to be formulated. An adequate Evangelical Theology is a Trinitarian one in which both Father and Son are worshipped in Spirit and in truth. This is impossible without faith, and faith is impossible without God's revelatory self-disclosure. This evangelical or Christian theology has three inseparable "objects"—God the Father, God the Son, and God the Holy Spirit—even as in their unity the second person of the Trinity is "subordinate" to the first, made manifest through the Holy Spirit.[36]

Den Boer offers a critically important insight on this point: "Christ, the God-man and Mediator, is subordinate to God; however, that does not take away from the fact that He as Second Person, together with the Father and Holy Spirit, is the electing God.[37] Arminius insists that

---

[34] Den Boer, 38.

[35] "The Object of Theology," *Works*, 1:333–35.

[36] "The Object of Theology," *Works*, 1:335–36. This and "absolute Trinity" are *the* areas of Arminius' theology that are least consequentially developed and perhaps most out of step with historic orthodoxy. Clarke comments: "Certainly there are faults in Arminius' . . . doctrine of the Persons of Christ and of his Holy Spirit, and, therefore also in his doctrine of the Trinity. It is strange that one who insisted so strongly that Christ was the primary and ultimate cause of human salvation, and not subject to any secret counsel or hidden purpose of a predestinating God, should also be so anxious to stress Christ's subordination, and that of the Holy Spirit, to God the Father in all respects. . . . Crudely stated, Arminius believed [wrongly] that Christ had to be subordinate to his Father for salvation to work at all" (174). See also, R. Muller, "The Christological Problem in the Thought of Jacobus Arminius," in *NAKG* 68 (1988): 145–63.

[37] See chap. 5, n. 32. Loonstra's point about the *pactum salutis* is important here.

Christ's subordination (however it is understood and defined) must be seen in the background of his view that God, before He can proceed to election out of grace, must have a basis for that election in the atonement provided by Christ's Mediatorship."[38] In other words, the "subordination" of Christ is an internal logic of the Godhead. Every saving act of God toward humanity, as well as the responding worship of humanity toward God, occurs through the mediation of Christ, "because God created all things, including humankind, through his Word and Spirit. There is no *communicatio* with humanity except through the intervention of the Son and the Spirit. And this divine movement outward from God is 'indivisible' because it reflects with precision the inward divine procession."[39] Had Christ not been provided as mediator (had the Father not entered into covenant with the Son to provide Christ as savior), God's "strict/unshakeable justice" would have prohibited fellowship with humanity because of sin and corruption; however, in divine wisdom and mercy, God has provided a way in Christ for those who believe, while those who do not believe remain outside this mercy.[40] Lest this emphasis on divine "unshakeable justice" remain an abstraction, Arminius grounds it in God's twofold love, because Arminius contends that the *duplex amor* constitutes the "foundation" of Christian religion. Not only do we encounter this in his inaugural orations, but as early as 1599, we encounter the special emphasis on justice in a ten-page letter to Uytenbogaert. There he complains to his closest friend that where divine justice is not functioning properly, the very foundations of religion are already in process of decay—"perit funditis religio."[41]

The methodological heart of Arminius' *Declaration* is argument number nineteen, his exposition on twofold love (pp. 124–28), the

---

[38] Den Boer, 38–39, 39n36. Den Boer pushes back explicitly against the interpretation of Richard Muller, "The Christological Problem in the Thought of Jacobus Arminius," *NAKG* 68 (1988): 145–63, esp. 158–59: "Arminius' views clearly belong to the category of . . . [Johannes] Piscator [Reformed professor at Herborn]: he not only attributes no soteriological purpose to Christ's active obedience, he [Piscator] also restricts the purpose of the nominally passive aspects of Christ's obedience in life and ministry to a preparatory testing of the Mediatorship."

[39] "The Author and the End of Theology," *Works*, 1:354

[40] "The Object of Theology," *Works*, 1:339–42. See also, Private Disputations XXXII and XXXIII, *Works*, 2:376–79; and Private Disputation XL, *Works*, 2:392–93.

[41] Letter to Uytenbogaert (undated), *Ep. Ecc.*, no. 45, p. 95. Also *Works*, 2:749.

longest of his twenty points. Arminius is convinced that this theological dialectic can help heal religion's decaying foundations, and in point seven he has already anticipated his extended explication on God's nature. He argues in point seven that supralapsarian predestination "changes the twofold wisdom of God as it is displayed in Scriptures by reversing their order." In decree-centered fashion their supralapsarian doctrine places God's merciful decision to save prior to the actual circumstance of Christ's death (pp. 115–17). This reversal is "repugnant to the justice of God with regard to that attribute by which God loves righteousness and hates iniquity, and also with regard to God's consistent and constant desire to render to everyone that which is due to them . . . [decreeing to save them] with no regard for righteousness or obedience." This reversal also means, "God robs himself of that which rightfully belongs to him [justice] and then imparts to the creature that which does not rightfully belong to him [damnation]," since in this scheme the creature has not yet even been created, much less committed sinful acts that would deserve punishment (p. 115).

Point nineteen is a tightly woven sustained argument exhibiting a fine example of Arminius' scholastic inclinations. He starts where his opponents start, with Legal Theology in the pre-fall situation, logically irrespective of Christ's saving work. God is characterized by justice, which produces a hatred for sin, and God is characterized by his "love for humanity" as creatures endowed with reason (p. 124). At this juncture he invokes Hebrews 11:6, because in Arminius' theological dialectic, election is God's free decision to save those who by grace come seeking and believing: "For whoever would draw near to God must believe that he exists and that he rewards those who seek him." Regardless of where one encounters the doctrine of election in Arminius, one finds also the dimensions of uncoerced, non-necessitated freedom. It is important to keep this in mind, even as we see how Arminius weaves his notion of the *duplex amor Dei*:

> A mutuality exists between these two kinds of love. The love that God extends to humanity cannot come into play unless it is permitted by God's love of justice. This implies that God's love for justice is the more excellent of the two; however, love for the creature abounds, except where the love of justice would prohibit its expression. The consequence of this is demonstrated by God's condemning humanity on account of sin. God clearly demonstrates this love relationship in the original created order; however, this does not imply that God's love for the creature supersedes

his love for justice. Had this been the case, God would have manifested a stronger aversion to the eternal misery of the creature than to the creature's disobedience. The abundant place for divine love is clear because God condemns no person for any reason other than sin, and God saves the multitudes of humanity who are converted from sin. In the divine dispensation, this salvation would not be possible unless it was God's will to allow an abundant scope for his love toward the creature under God's judgment, to the extent this is permitted by his justice. (p. 124)

Then Arminius revisits the point he has made previously about how the supralapsarians reverse the *duplex amor*, a reversal that involves God in an internal contradiction, for he chooses to love the creature more than his own justice. In the final analysis this move detracts from God's love for humanity. It violates not only God's love for justice and righteousness, but it undermines human dignity as well:

> The proposed doctrine inverts this order and mutual relationship in two ways: (1) This happens first when it is stated that God wills to save specific individuals without any reference to the creature's obedience. It places God's love for humanity prior his love for justice, and as such reflects that God loves humanity more than justice. It thereby manifests a stronger aversion to human misery than to their sin and disobedience. (2) The other way in which this doctrine violates the order and mutuality [of justice and love] is the assertion that God wills to damn certain particular people without manifesting in his decree any consideration of disobedience. This detracts from God's manifest love for humanity, a love the creature is rightfully due. This doctrine implies that God hates the creature, but this hatred is not caused by or rooted in either his love of justice, nor in his hatred of iniquity. But is it not the case that sin is the primary object and the only meritorious cause of God's hate? (pp. 124–25)

Then, on the basis of the formal argument, Arminius returns to the practical goal of theology. He tells a parable in order to demonstrate that the goal of worship must be connected to obedience. Arminius rejects the "carelessness" or false security of the disobedient son (who presumes that his father will make him his heir even if he fails to respect him in obedience) in favor of affirming the obedient son who worships in spirit and in truth. This reflects the essence of Arminius' Evangelical Theology, for he cannot abide a notion of election that logically opens the door to spiritual "carelessness":

God's love of justice is manifested daily in the preaching of the Gospel truth that it is God's will to grant a communication of Christ and his saving work to humanity, but only to those who convert from sin and believe in Christ. (2) The second point of the twofold love, on which the Christian faith is founded, is God's love for miserable sinners, that love by which he gave his Son for them and constituted Christ as Savior of those who are obedient to him. This love for sinners and the required obedience does not rest on the rigor and severity to which God is supremely entitled, but according to his grace and mercy. To this is added the promise of forgiveness for sin, provided the fallen sinner earnestly repents. (pp. 125–26)

For Arminius, these are not simply finely sharpened polemical points to win a theological debate. These matters are important for the minister's caring for faithful parishioners who are seeking the face of God to know his saving intentions. So Arminius returns to Hebrews 11:6 and places the text in conversation with his theological narrative:

In order that we may understand more clearly the nature of this twofold order of love as the foundation of all religion, especially the manner in which mutuality exists between the two orders, it is profitable for us to pay close attention to these words of the Apostle to the Hebrews: "[And without faith it is impossible to please God, for] whoever would approach him must believe that he exists and that he rewards those who seek him" [Heb 11:6]. Herein are two foundational assumptions of religion in opposition to the two fiery darts of Satan that are most pernicious, each of which by itself is able to overturn and destroy true religion. One is carelessness [*securitas*] and the other is despair [*desperatio*]. Carelessness is operative when one is persuaded that regardless of how inattentive he may be to the worship of God, he will not be damned and is certain to obtain salvation. Despair reigns when a person is persuaded that no amount of reverence toward God will lead to a positive reception from God. When either of these deadly dispositions is operative, it is impossible for true and proper worship of God to follow. Both of these, however, are overturned by the apostolic teaching that when one firmly believes that God will bestow eternal life on those who seek him, but that he will inflict eternal death on those who do not, one cannot on any account indulge himself in [the false security that leads to] carelessness. Likewise, when one believes that God is indeed the rewarder of those who diligently seek him, by applying himself to the search, he will not be in danger of falling into despair. The foundation of the former kind of faith, by which one firmly believes that God will bestow eternal life on all who seek Him, is that God loves justice more than he loves humanity. This prioritizing of justice is the only adequate protection against carelessness. At the same time, the foundation for the latter kind of faith, one that dares to believe that God will undoubtedly reward those who diligently seek Him, is that great love for humanity which neither can nor will prevent God from effecting salvation for the sinner—unless God be hindered by his greater love for justice. . . . God's twofold love, and the mutuality that each part bears toward the other, serve together to form the foundation of religion, without which no true religion can possibly exist. Any doctrine, therefore, that is in open hostility to this twofold love and to the relationship that mutually exists between them, subverts the foundation of all religion. (pp. 126–28)

In Arminius' Evangelical Theology, even when he uses words like election and predestination, we read him wrongly if we think he is referring to those topics discretely. He is constantly weaving a theological coat of many colors and threads. He is writing theology in which twofold love, covenant, decree, election, predestination, divine will, and multi-dimensional freedom come together in such a way that if any single one of them should be isolated from the other, we would no longer be talking about the gospel. All of these together constitute the foundation of the Christian religion, for together they narrate the sum of the gospel. So, when we read his fourfold decrees of election/predestination in the *Declaration*, we must read them through the multi-dimensional lens of his Evangelical Theology, lest we caricature Arminius' theological intentions—the typical mistake of many previous attempts to interpret Arminius.[42] God has entered into a salvific covenant relationship with humanity that is grounded in twofold love, characterized by a reciprocal uncoerced, non-necessitated freedom. Within this frame, Arminius sets out his Christocentric fourfold structure of predestination:

---

[42] A notable exception to this is pointed out by den Boer, 47n59, where he references C. Graafland, *Van Calvijn tot Comrie* (Zoetemeer: Boekencentrum, 1996), 195. Graafland (not a great admirer of Arminianism) helps provide a corrective when he remarks that even though Arminius continually spoke about election, what he wrote about it coincided in content with what he wrote about covenant. Cf. *Duplex amor Dei*, 80, 108–10, 164.

I. The first specific and absolute divine decree regarding the salvation of sinful humanity: God decreed to appoint his Son, Jesus Christ, as Mediator, Redeemer, Savior, Priest, and King in order that he might destroy sin by his own death, so that by his own obedience he might obtain the salvation lost through disobedience, and by his power communicate this salvation.

II. In the second precise and absolute decree, God decided graciously to accept those who repent and believe in Christ, and for Christ's sake and through him to effect the final salvation of penitents and believers who persevere to the end in their faith. Simultaneously, God decreed to leave in sin under divine wrath all impenitent persons and unbelievers, damning them as alienated from Christ.

III. The third divine decree: God decided to administer in a sufficient and efficacious manner the means necessary for repentance and faith—this being accomplished according to divine wisdom, by which God knows what is proper and becoming both to his mercy and his severity. And this all proceeds according to divine justice, by which God is prepared to adopt whatever his wisdom may prescribe and carry out.

IV. From these decrees the fourth proceeds, by which God decreed to save and to damn certain particular persons. This decree has its foundation in divine foreknowledge, through which God has known from all eternity those individuals who through the established means of his prevenient grace would come to faith and believe, and through his subsequent sustaining grace would persevere in the faith. Likewise, in divine foreknowledge, God knew those who would not believe and persevere. (p. 135)

There it is! For twenty years Arminius' ministerial and theological colleagues have been pressing him to set out his theology of election and predestination, and here he does it in four brief sets of declarative statements. We note that Arminius' decree structure uses "absolute" language, but the absoluteness of God's salvific provision is first and foremost christologically centered. It does not begin with a decree regarding the identity of those receiving the salvific provision. Also, the path to this absolute intentionality to save is through the destruction of sin, so that through the obedience of Christ this destruction of sin can become the saving reality communicated to every person who repents and believes. Perhaps he does not go so far, but it is almost as if Arminius is saying that Christ is the predestined one. He is, to be sure, the only way of salvation. This too is absolute. Everyone that repents and believes becomes co-heirs with Christ in God's initiative. The obverse is also absolutely true. Those who do not repent and believe are without exception certainly damned. The recipients of this extravagant, undeserved gift of salvation are sinners—and as such, they are incapable of making even the slightest move toward receiving this gift. Comprehensive provision for this is also provided by God. Arminius is arguing for a gracious twofold election: election to faith and election to salvation. Divine grace not only awakens the sinner to the need for salvation by grace through faith, divine gracious assistance also works the ability in the awakened to repent and believe. I kept anticipating that Arminius, in a sharp rhetorical move, might assert that he is in agreement with Calvin "properly understood":

> There is nothing in that reasoning of Calvin that I cannot heartily approve, if all things (in it) are rightly understood. For I confess that the grace by which the Holy Spirit is given, is not common to all men; I also confess that the origin [*fontem*: source, principal cause] of faith can be said to be the gratuitous election of God, but it is election to bestow faith, not to communicate salvation. For a believer is elected to participate in salvation, a sinner is elected to faith.[43]

One could wish that Arminius had stopped with three dimensions to his absolute decrees. These three ascribe to God all the initiative and all the glory for salvation—a pure theology of salvation by grace through faith. This is, to be sure, his Evangelical Theology, but he also digresses, as it were, into Legal Theology in point four. He knows that his opponents will not let it rest if he stops after his third decree. To a certain extent he has already tried to let such a position suffice. Supralapsarian predestination is specific about individuals, so Arminius is compelled himself to be specific: "God decreed to save and to damn certain particular persons." Well yes, but is it not enough to say that those persons saved are "all who believe"? The answer to this in his context is: "No, who specifically are those persons?" This is truly the barbed wire over which every theologian has had to climb when

---

[43] *Works*, 1:747. These lines from his *Apology* in response to the Thirty-One Articles were not published until after his death, so his apologetic did not play a public role in events leading to 1608.

they took this path in connection with the issue of predestination. Like so many before him, Arminius resorts to a reliance on *scientia media*, middle knowledge. This move lands Arminius squarely in the middle of another debate that has a long and venerable history. It does not seem to me that Arminius works out a consequential and thoroughgoing epistemology of middle knowledge, but it is not necessary in the present discussion to sort this out in detail.[44] We do find in Arminius a soteriologically oriented concept of middle knowledge that allows him to assert those things he finds crucial to his purposes in connection with divine knowledge and human freedom—while avoiding what he feels are the "dead ends" of his opponents. Arminius' construction of *scientia media* preserves two important points: (1) God's knowledge is comprehensive and certain; and (2) God is not responsible for sin. Once again, the implications of this reflect a dialectic in Arminius' theology. Den Boer's summary of Arminius' soteriological concerns is both concise and accurate:

> The theory of middle knowledge offered Arminius a strong theoretical basis for maintaining God's omniscience, predestination and grace, as well as human freedom, all at one and the same time. Through it, Arminius could maintain creaturely contingency, and yet [hold] that this did not come at the cost of God's omniscience. . . . Arminius uses middle knowledge to illustrate that God remains able, in spite of human freedom, to govern all things as He wills: God knows what result will follow from certain "administrations" [*beleydinghe*] of means and circumstances in combination with creaturely contingency. However, he does not have this knowledge because He can "determine" human freedom through the means and circumstances, but purely because of his all-encompassing foreknowledge through which each moment is for God an eternal "today" or "now."[45]

---

[44] There is a significant body of literature on Arminius and middle knowledge. An entrance into this conversation may be gained by consulting Richard Muller, *God, Creation, and Providence*, 154–66; E. Dekker, *Rijker dan Midas*, 76–103; and W. G. Witt, "Creation, Redemption and Grace in the Theology of Jacob Arminius" (PhD diss., University of Notre Dame, 1993), 1:336–70. With regard to the disputed issue whether Arminius strictly follows Luis de Molina, see E. Dekker, "Was Arminius a Molinist?" in *Sixteenth Century Journal* 27, no. 2 (1996): 337–52. Clarke, 76, asserts that Dekker's connecting Arminius to Molina is not judicious; similarities in emphasis do not constitute dependence.

[45] *Duplex amor Dei*, 147. See especially den Boer's footnotes 315 and 316 with regard to Beza and related points.

Arminius' logic is this. God foreknows the specific identity of every believer (as well as unbeliever), but God's knowing this does not necessitate in an a priori fashion that it will and must be so. At every juncture and with regard to every inclination, the logic of un-coerced and non-necessitated action prevails. God knows which sinners will repent and convert, but they do so with un-coerced freedom, even as each is graciously aided in that free and responsible decision. This is the nature of the saving covenant into which God has entered with humanity. So, when forced by his opponents to re-engage more abstract forms of Legal Theology, Arminius still insists on doing it on his own terms. The disposition of God is to save, but not in a way that does violence to human dignity. This is who God essentially (ontologically) is, a God who enters into saving covenant with his people. So this is who God reveals himself to be. This self-disclosure reveals that God designs to offer this salvation to the entirety of humanity—so extravagant is this gift. For Arminius this must be the case, not only in the realm of mysterious Legal Theology, but in his disclosed Evangelical Theology as well.

Arminius' concern for human dignity is rooted in some specific anthropological assumptions about human freedom and ability, but his theological heirs did not strictly follow his teachings. Of course, we cannot hold Arminius responsible for the actions of his theological children, even if their actions have discolored posterity's perspective on his theology. A case can be made that the Synod of Dort entered judgment against Remonstrant anthropological assumptions that were slanted soteriologically in different directions than Arminius' own assertions.[46] Aza Goudriaan has pointed out that in 1618, Festus Hommius (erstwhile opponent of Arminius), published *Specimen controversarium Beligarium*, a book that "significantly influenced opinions" at Dort. Hommius' central assertion was that with regard to human freedom, Arminius' anthropology was highly optimistic—"not a slave of sin,

---

[46] This has previously been noted by G. J. Hoenderdaal in various essays, esp. "Arminius and Episcopius," *NAKG* 60 (1980): 203–35. Richard Muller, "The Federal Motif in Seventeenth Century Arminian Theology," *NAKG* 62 (1982): 102–22, is specific in his assertions that Episcopius (and later Limborch) depart from Arminius: "The fall of man does not appear as an element either structural or doctrinal in Episcopius.... Man has a natural inclination toward God, and the right reason (*ratio recta*) with which he is endowed enables his mind to apprehend the good and the just.... This *recta ratio*, moreover, prescribes the love and worship of God" (110).

but free to will good and evil."⁴⁷ Goudriaan is of the opinion that this is significant for the judgment entered against Arminius as well as the Remonstrants: "Those who came to the Synod of Dordrecht [Dort] with Hommius's book in hand were confronted by what could be called an 'optimistic' view of the abilities of the human being." He proceeds to point out that these opinions do not "fit especially well into the text of Articles three and four of the Remonstrance of 1610, which insists that the human being cannot 'think, will or do anything that is good' [salvific] except when he is given grace by God"⁴⁸—these words being taken directly from Arminius (p. 141). Even if the Remonstrants after him were not consequent in this assertion, in Arminius we actually find what might be called a "pessimistic" anthropology apart from divine grace. Without grace, nothing salvific is possible for humanity, but grace begun is grace continued for Arminius. Awakening prevenient grace becomes enabling saving grace, which is an ongoing sanctifying grace. In Arminius we encounter consistently a pessimism regarding human ability without grace, but an optimism about the possibilities of grace for those who believe.

By describing the divine disposition to save in this manner, Arminius is clothing his theology in ways that make believing and trusting in God for salvation amenable to finite humanity. He was convinced that the "supralapsarian God" was so mysterious, and his divine ways so far past finding out, that God was at best unbelievable (since assurance of salvation could not possibly be discerned as a present reality, albeit a well-founded hope) and at worst reprehensible—guilty of devising evil and planning sin so that the eternal divine plan of damnation could be carried out. Arminius the pastor-theologian simply could not bring himself to fall in line with this way of theologizing. Even to those who insisted on theologizing along these lines, he insisted that such theology is deficient on two counts: it does not do justice to God, and it carries out an injustice against those who wish to repent, believe, and worship. His conclusion is that such a theology is not practical. Expressed in the vernacular, "It won't preach." To the very end, Arminius insisted that theology—our attempts to discern and describe God—must be both evangelical and practical. The disposition of God in Christ is to save, and all who by grace believe will be saved.

---

⁴⁷ Aza Goudriaan, "The Synod of Dort on Arminian Anthropology," in *Revisiting the Synod of Dort*, 82.

⁴⁸ Goudriaan, "Synod of Dort," 83–84.

CONCLUSION

There lived in Holland a man whom they who did not know could not sufficiently esteem, whom they who did not esteem had never sufficiently known. So, let us presume that we do not know the identity of this unusual person as we review what we have learned. We have a description of his life, career, and teachings—and a rather detailed one at that. He was born into a violent world characterized by war, devastation, and resulting poverty for its victims. His father had died before he was born, and one of the consequences of war was the destruction of his hometown and the murder of his mother and family. Orphaned as a teenager, he was taken in by a former Roman Catholic priest sympathetic to the Protestant cause. When the priest died only a few years later, the boy was more or less adopted by a Christian intellectual who introduced him to the great Protestant centers of learning in Europe. Because the lad was precocious, doors began to open for him to become a student in these great universities, and perhaps partly due to the formation of the religious people who had become for him *in loco parentis*, he decided to study theology.

The wealthy merchants in the largest and most powerful city in his country learned of this young man, and after proper deliberation decided to fund his entire theological education—including travel and all living expenses. Clearly he made a great first impression on them, and he continued to impress. They rescued him from the penury of his student years, and with periodic reviews to assess his progress, they funded his studies in Switzerland for more than six additional years, after which he returned home to become one of their pastors. Their great city was situated in the northern part of Europe where the Protestant Reformation was a bit late in taking permanent hold, having been secured only during his youth. When this budding theologian arrived on the scene, the reformation of their city was reasonably assured. The man who later became his father-in-law had played an important role in this religious transition. A kind of truce was in place between the warring countries, and leaders were making room at local and regional levels to sort out social, political, and religious differences. This was a very complicated process with many starts and stops, and at times a step forward was followed by a step to the side, or perhaps even a half step backward. This was especially the case when it came to the decision-making processes in the church, for at that time the local magistrates actually had final say, even in the appointment of pastors to local congregations. Theological emphases were part and parcel of these negotiations, and after the first synod of Dutch Protestant churches (held in neighboring Emden, Germany), there was a strong interest expressed by some influential clergymen to lead the church in tolerant and non-judgmental ways, even as it was also being asserted that the decision-making capacity of local consistories should be strengthened. Interestingly enough, this recent theology graduate was the first one from the magistrates' and merchants' own area to be ordained to the ministry in that great city, almost exclusively as the result of power vested in them. They had used this same power to appoint their other ministers. All the other ordained ministers among them were "imports," but now they had taken the steps to install one of their own. The city fathers were proud.

They soon learned that this man, though young, possessed considerable wisdom. Sorting out religious and political differences was a messy affair, and when the young pastor was asked to mediate between two sharp factions over a doctrinal matter, he reflected his commitment to *sola scriptura* by taking a few years to exegete and to preach from the texts related to this difference of opinion. He was unwilling to accept the authority of secondary sources; like every good Protestant, he went *ad fontes*. Furthermore, from his student years in Switzerland, he knew that the presenting issues were both complicated and potentially explosive. Before too long, some of his senior colleagues became a bit impatient. They knew what they believed without having to study the Scriptures for months and years on end. To make matters worse, the sermons from their junior colleague seemed in subtle but persistent ways to challenge their pet assumptions about the doctrines in question. So, they brought complaints to the church board. Actually, taking a different approach each time, they complained officially on several different occasions to the consistory. Each time that the complaints were formally heard and responded to, the answer was the same: no real problems here—nothing of substance to be concerned about. Looking back, we can see that there was a real struggle going on with regard to who had the power. Was it the clergy or was it the laity? It is also interesting to note that by the definitions of their day and time, the clergy were the more conservative and the lay leaders in this great city were the more open-minded and liberal. And while these struggles over power in the church board were taking place, a remarkable thing was happening: the congregation was thriving and the influence of the younger clergyman was growing by leaps and bounds. He mediated every challenge and grew to such national prominence that, after fifteen years of ministry in the most influential city in the nation, he was nominated to be a professor of theology in that nation's first university. His sound preaching and fifteen years of effective pastoral leadership placed him on the national stage at the age of forty-four. Despite the concerns that a few had raised from time to time, his responses to every question had been so thorough that official letters of commendation were offered from every quarter in support of his university nomination. In the minds of the lay magistrates, their pastor was just the right kind of person to be forming future ministers. He reflected the openness that was needed in a land where so many issues were still in the process of being settled. He was certainly Reformed, even if he was not to be counted among the most "strictly Reformed." After all, with their help he had been educated at the feet of the most esteemed Reformed theologian of his era in the great academy at Geneva, and he often espoused his regard for the magisterial Calvin himself. The cherished doctrine of predestination was at the heart of his theology, and he even expounded it in ways that the laity could appreciate and understand. Only the Amsterdam pastor himself seems to have been surprised at the lofty appointment being offered to him, for he fully expected to serve out his entire ministry as a pastor. (On the quiet, one of his opponents is reported to have said, "Not good. At least in Amsterdam he could only poison a single congregation; here he can poison many.")

Even those who were at times not on his side were forced to concede that his representation of the historic Christian faith was acceptable, even if not exactly to their liking on a few points. Truth be told, however, had it come to a purely democratic vote among all the clergy and lay members of their churches across the land in that decade, the new professor likely would have enjoyed a majority. He represented the tolerant perspective that many in church leadership were voicing—the official position expressed formally at the Pacification of Ghent as well as the Union of Utrecht, both of which underscored the necessity for latitude of theological perspective so long as the historic faith and scriptural authority were in no real danger of being lost. This pastor was not merely one among the many any longer; he was recognized as a leader among the Reformed of his day. Those who knew him well esteemed him so highly that they placed him in a position of highest public visibility for all Europe to see—for Leiden was among the most highly esteemed Protestant universities at the turn of the seventeenth century. There was no apparent concern in the minds of those responsible for the weighty decision that some of his "strict Calvinist" ministerial colleagues felt he did not reflect their particular perspective. The newly minted professor had demonstrated time and again that the Scriptures themselves constituted his guide to interpreting the church's confessional documents. One could hardly be more Protestant and faithful to the emerging Reformed identity that was so integral to the unity and harmony of the rather recently constituted United Netherlands.

By the time of his appointment to Leiden, calls were being heard to convene a national synod to sort out various theological and church-state issues. He was not the only clergyman to join the magistrates and other church laity in seeing the need for such a formal gathering—even if his reasons to call the synod were different from those of others. A few of his former accusers from Amsterdam were still finding ways—through clergymen in Leiden as well as at least one university colleague initially—to question his orthodoxy. But each time that push came to shove over such issues, the result was the same as in Amsterdam previously: no real problems here. As a matter of fact, when the differences of theological perspective threatened to become a public nuisance in the churches, all the Leiden theologians signed a formal statement affirming that as far as the Reformed Christian faith was concerned, their differences were minimal—"not striking at the foundations of the faith." Still the calls for a national synod were being heard, so the national leaders decided to assemble a preparatory committee for such a convocation. So great was the magistrates' confidence in the Amsterdam pastor-become-professor that they appointed him to the planning committee. Even as he worked to this end, his accusing interlocutors persisted in placing his integrity in doubt—one even going so far as to circulate theological gossip about him in diplomatic channels abroad. Even though this was almost *pure* gossip and innuendo, easily deflected in a point-by-point rebuttal, damage to his public image was done at home and abroad.

In private correspondence the professor corrected his accuser and elicited a mild apology. In public he issued formal declarations affirming his commitments, not only to Scripture but also to the Belgic Confession and to the Heidelberg Catechism. For the peace of the Dutch church, he even offered to resign his post. He was finishing his term as university provost, and there was no inclination from any official quarter to see him step down. So he declared, as he had done on many previous occasions, that when the national synod convened, he stood ready to answer (again!) all questions about his teachings. He had set out the design and purpose of his theology at his inaugural lectures in 1603, and in every public and private disputation at the university, he had done his best to clothe his theology in ways that he believed would persuade his hearers and readers to worship and praise God. With regard to the Reformed doctrine of predestination, he affirmed continually his belief therein—with one caveat. He did not believe nor did he teach that God has predetermined with individual specificity persons to be damned for eternity, as he saw no way to affirm God's purposefully condemning the greater majority of humanity to damnation through a decision in eternity before all time without simultaneously making God the author of evil and sin. To clothe the God of his theology with such a dark image would not incline the hearer or persuade the reader to worship, which for him was the primary purpose of theology. Certainly God is a predestining God, but however he chooses to predestine, it must be done in such a way that both divine love and divine justice are maintained. God's decisions in this domain must be consistently uncoerced and non-necessitated; otherwise, one cannot speak of real freedom—either on the side of God or on the side of humanity. Only such a vision reflects the dignity of divinity, and only such a vision can incline and persuade one to worship this one true God.

The moment he used words like "freedom" for humanity, charges of Pelagian heresy were floated; however, he made it clear time and again that the sinfulness of humanity is so complete that only by grace, and by grace alone, is human freedom even a possibility.

He cited favorably not only Calvin but also the great Augustine to show that he understood and affirmed the Reformed faith. Finally, after a series of formal confrontations and convocations, the pastor-theologian appeared before the highest council of the land (since no national ecclesial synod was yet in the offing). In a verbal presentation accompanied by a written position paper turned in immediately thereafter, he declared his sentiments. The doctrine of predestination was front and center, and furthermore, God's decrees of predestination, he declared, are "absolute!"

In four sets of declarative sentences, he stated the essence of his teachings on election and predestination. God's first decree is absolutely to elect Christ as the only way by which humanity may be saved. This first absolute decree is not simply first chronologically; it is the foundational assumption for every dimension of election and predestination. The other decrees flow from this christological center, and to read or review the others separately is to misread him as well as them. His second decree speaks with specificity about the scope of this first precise and absolute Christ-centered decree. Salvation is obtained for sinners by Christ, and he is the only one who mediates this salvation. It is mediated to those who with God's gracious assistance repent and believe. Those who repent and believe are saved, and those who continually live into this gracious salvific assistance (persevere in the faith) will finally be saved. His third decree flows from the first two both logically and theologically. Herein is described how this salvation is sufficiently and efficiently administered. So, in summary, Christ is the elect one. All are elect who are in Christ, and no one is in Christ except by faith. Election in its primary sense refers to Christ, and the predestining extension of this is that it includes all who believe.

It was when he tried to answer how this soteriology related to God's comprehensive knowledge of all things that he found himself dealing as much with philosophy (speculative epistemology) as with theology. He probably should have left well enough alone with his first three statements, but it was the issue of God's knowing and planning soteriology with specific reference to individuals that had been at the nub of the first questions he was supposed to answer as a young pastor in Amsterdam. It simply was not possible to ignore the question, even though it was clearly an exercise in speculative thought—characterized more by what he termed Legal Theology than by the Evangelical Theology he preferred. He asserted that God knows and has known all things from eternity, but he specifies assumptions about this divine foreknowledge. Those whom God has foreknown, he has foreknown in Christ and not apart from him. Therefore, even from eternity, God regarded the sinner affectionately through Christ. If our professor was going to be forced into speculative theology, then he insisted on doing it within a comprehensively Christocentric frame.

He knew what he was doing when he formulated his theology this way, but he felt it was Reformed even as it undercut his colleagues' supralapsarian assumptions. This predestination did not determine the specific individuals who would believe, but rather that those who do believe are elect in Christ. To those who assert that the freedom by which one repents and believes is an exercise in "free will" that makes the salvation contingent on the individual decision, he would say, "Not so." Salvation, being in Christ, is not dependent on the graciously assisted decision, even as that freed will is exercised in repentance and belief. Not only has God made provision for election in Christ, but this sovereign God also leads and enables the faithful in that repentance and belief. The actions of the saved make no contribution, either to the salvation offered or to the salvation received. The salvation of all believers is secure in Christ, and the believer can receive assurance of this reality by remaining obedient and faithful. Assurance of salvation is a well-founded hope in God's electing grace for all who believe and trust in Christ.

The assembly of the States General in The Hague was satisfied. The theologian's views were comfortably within the parameters of acceptable Reformed theology. Within a year tuberculosis claimed his life, and he died in the good graces of his beloved Reformed Church. The national synod for which he and others had called was held, but not before a full decade had passed. By that time, not only the ecclesial but the political landscape of the country had changed radically. A pamphlet war broke out, and theological positions on every side were caricatured almost beyond recognition. The United Provinces were in serious danger of fracture. In the pulpits and the taverns, on the streets, in high places and low, were heard violent discussions in which no bitter term was spared. The quarrel threatened the existence of the young nation. The academic discussion between two university professors had become a bone of contention that divided the United Provinces into two hostile camps. In a series of calculated steps rooted in political expediency designed to hold the republic together, Prince

Maurits had removed all the Leiden-inclined magistrates throughout the land, replacing them with strict Calvinist "precisionists." In the complicated political landscape of the period, Maurits also had his grand pensionary (attorney general) convicted on trumped-up charges of treason and beheaded. Even the eminent Hugo Grotius was imprisoned.[1] When the great synod convened in 1618–1619, those clergy who sympathized with the theological inclinations of the Amsterdam pastor-theologian were not formally seated as delegates, but rather placed as "the accused" at a table in the center of the room.[2] His theological heirs were condemned for holding heretical positions, as was he, *post mortem*. The sentiments for toleration that had characterized the early decades of the republic, formally expressed at the

---

[1] While these are factual events, the period is highly complicated. Cf. Works, 3:642. With uncharacteristic vitriol, Arminius had written in his examination of Gomarus' Thesis XXX: "This treatise on God's predestination is an inversion of the whole divine decree . . . wherefore, it must be exploded and ejected from the Church of Christ." The Arminian magistrates in league with Grand Pensionary Oldenbarnevelt and with Court Chaplain Uytenbogaert, Arminius' close friend, seem unwisely to have taken Arminius' suggestion to heart. They were not guiltless in this tumultuous decade. A pro-Arminian "Resolution for Peace" was pushed through the States of Holland by Oldenbarnevelt. Strict Calvinist pastors (Contra-Remonstrants) were systematically removed and replaced by Arminians (Remonstrants). Cf. Michael Abram Hakkenberg, "The Predestinarian Controversy in The Netherlands, 1600–1620" (PhD diss., University of California, Berkeley, 1989), esp. "Introduction."

[2] In a recent essay, Donald Sinnema still views Dort as an ecclesial convocation at which the real problem procedurally was that the Remonstrants "refused to cooperate." See his "The Canons of the Synod of Dort: From Judgment on Arminianism to Confessional Standard," in *Revisiting the Synod of Dort (1618–1619)*, ed. Aza Goudriaan and Fred van Lieburg (Leiden: Brill, 2011), esp. 314, 317. The *Acta*, written from the perspective of those who possessed the power at Dort, can certainly be read that way. The *Minutes* can also be read another way. The Arminians objected that they appeared as ministers accused of heresy, as it was clear that the intention of the synod was to pass judgment on them. In that process they were consistently unwilling to be compliant. Since it was the stated intention of the synod to pass judgment on theological positions, the Arminians made the point that they would prefer to start the theological judgments on the topic of eternal reprobation, by which the "strict Reformed" taught that God had condemned the greater majority of humanity to hell before they were even born. Early in the proceedings, they tried several times to get this onto the agenda. Of course, on procedural grounds, Chairman Bogerman refused to allow the accused to dictate procedure. From this perspective, the refusal to be cooperative cut both ways. Cf. W. Stephen Gunter and Johannes van den Berg, *John Wesley and The Netherlands* (Nashville: Kingswood, 2002), 30–35.

Pacification of Ghent (1576) and in the Union of Utrecht (1579), were swept away by the vindictiveness the pamphlet warfare. One of his perennial opponents caricatured his teachings in a book widely read during the years immediately prior to the Synod of Dort. There could now only be winners and losers. Unfortunately, for the Leiden professor as well as for Reformed Christianity in general, this is how he has been remembered—as a loser, a heretic.

It is interesting to note in retrospect that the great synod which condemned his teachings was careful to safeguard their predestinarian theology against several of the extremes to which this Amsterdam pastor-theologian had continually and strenuously objected: First, the synod recognized that however predestinarian doctrine was theologically clothed, it must never appear to reflect that God is the author of evil and sin in the world. About this the national synod was explicit. Secondly, the synod implicitly rejected the supralapsarian doctrine in favor of an infralapsarian definition, a move our theologian would have certainly affirmed as a move in the right direction, even if they did not go as far as he would have preferred. Finally, the great synod also took care to make the Christocentricity of the cherished Reformed doctrine more central. All of this together constituted a move to dull the sharp edges of the rigid double predestination of the supralapsarians—a move the Leiden theologian would have affirmed.

One might wonder whether his worries over the implications of supralapsarianism had anything at all to do with those theological moves by the synod—emphases that he had himself built into his own doctrines of election and predestination! So while we are wondering about such things, we might also wonder about the trajectory of his influence among those who count him as a theological mentor. He would not likely have been an enthusiastic participant in Cartesian rationalism and the race toward an Enlightenment understanding that defined free will and human autonomy apart from divine grace—especially as these characterized his immediate successors in the church they founded after being expelled from the Netherlands. He would have worried greatly over the loss of soteriological focus in the theology of many of his theological children. Have they forgotten him completely? For four hundred years the only English translation of his most important theological declaration was from a second-hand text he had not composed. Besides being a poor translation in many ways, it was simply inaccurate on a few important points. Even for those who chose to study his thought, these inaccuracies have led to confusion about his soteriology. Adding insult to injury, the special edition of a magazine commemorating the four-hundredth anniversary of his death has the front cover headline: "Champion of Free Will"—this soteriological inaccuracy coming from his direct denominational descendants. And what about those for whom soteriological concerns have not been altogether lost, his Wesleyan children? At a theological symposium in 1975, Hendrikus Berkhof opined that the evangelical Wesleyans had the best chance of wearing his "true ring."[3] They had named their first periodical after him, and for two hundred years a hyphenated form of his name was the defining adjective for their theology. Regarding them, the Leiden professor would simply shake his head in dismay at the thoroughgoing Pelagian ways in which being "in Christ" has been reduced to a "free will" decision. And to the holiness folk who did not seem to realize that he had some theological points to make about sanctification by grace, a gaping gaze of incredulity might be the only physical response he could muster to those among them who reduced scriptural holiness to a reified experience to be grasped. Much more could be said here, but, as interesting as those speculations might be to a modern reader, they take us beyond our desire to define the identity of this man. One thing is certain: if these "descendants" of his assembled a parade under their respective banners, he would not join their march.

What might we conclude about the theological identity of this pastor-theologian from Amsterdam? Of course, he was a Protestant; however, he was not a Lutheran, and he was not a Mennonite. He was too Calvinistic to be Lutheran, and he was too Erastian to be a Mennonite. Predestination was foundational to his theology, and he spoke about this doctrine using expressions like divine decree and absolute decree. His essential message was that God is eternally disposed to save, and all who by grace believe will be saved. God has predestined this. Clearly, both from his teachings as well as from his ecclesial and university standing and reputation, he lived and died a Reformed theologian. His name is Jacob Arminius. *If he were better known, he would be more sufficiently esteemed.*

---

[3] Hendrikus Berkhof, "De Ware Ring van Arminius," in *In Het Spoor van Arminius*, ed. H. J. Adriaanse (Nieuwkoop: Uitgeverij Heuff, 1975), 151–58.

SELECTED BIBLIOGRAPHY

PRIMARY SOURCES

Acta et Scripta Synodalia Dordracena ministrorum Remonstrantium in Foederato Belgio. Herderwiici: Ex Officina Typographi Synodalis, 1620.

Alberti, G. W. *Briefe betreffende den allerneuesten Zustand der Religion und der Wissenschaften in Gross-Brittanien*, vol. 1. Hannover: J. C. Richter, 1752.

Arminius, Jacobus. *Jacobi Arminii opera theologica*. Leiden: G. Basson, 1629.

———. *The Just Man's Defence; or, The Declaration of the Judgement of James Arminius before the States of Holland . . . to the Regulators of the University of Leyden with Their Solution*. Translated by Tobias Conyers. London: Henry Eversden, 1657.

———. *The Works of James Arminius: The London Edition*. Translated by J. Nichols and W. Nichols. Introduction by Carl Bangs. 3 vols. Kansas City: Beacon Hill, 1986. First published in London, 1825–1875.

Arminius, J., and F. Gomarus. *Twee disputatiën vande goddeliicke predestinatie*. Leiden: Jan Paets Jacobszoon, 1609.

Augustine, Saint. *On Christian Doctrine*. Translated by R. P. H. Green. New York: Oxford University Press, 1997.

Beza, Theodore. *A Briefe Declaration of the Chiefe Poyntes of the Christian Religion: set foorth in a table.* London: Dauid Moptid & Iohn Mather, 1575.

———. *A Briefe and Pithie Summe of the Christian Faith.* Translated by R[obert] F[yll]. London: Roger Ward, 1589.

———. *A Booke of Christian Questions and Answers*. Translated by Arthur Golding. London: William How, 1574.

———. *A Little Book of Christian Questions and Responses*. Translated by

Kirk Summers. Allison Park, Penn.: Pickwick Publications, 1986.

———. *The Treasure of Trueth*. Translated by John Stockwood. London, 1576.

Calvin, John. *Institutes of the Christian Religion*. Translated by Henry Beveridge. 2 vols. Grand Rapids: Eerdmans, 1975.

Coornhert, D. V. *Op zoek naar het hoogste goed*. Edited by H. Bonger. Baarn: Ambo, 1987.

Crespin, Jean. *Histoire des martyrs, persecutez et mis a mort pour la verité de l'Euangile*. N.p., 1554.

Donteklok, Reynier, and A. Cornelisz. *Responsio ad argumenta quadam Bezae et Calvini ex Tractatu de Praedestinatione, in caput IX ad Romanus*. N.p, 1589.

[Episcopius, Simon]. *Apologia pro Confessione sive Declaratione Sententiae eorum, Qui in Foederato Belgio vocantur Remonstrantes, super praecipuis Articulis Religionis Christianae*. N.p., 1629.

———. *Confessio sive Declaratio, Sententiae Pastorum, qui in Foederato Belgio Remonstrantes vocantur, Super praecipuis articulis Religionis Christianae*. Herderwiici: Apud Theodorum Danielis, 1622.

Erastus, Thomas. *Explicatio gravissimae questionis utrum excommunicatio*. N.p., 1589. Translated by Robert Lee as *The Theses of Erastus Touching Excommunication* (Edinburgh: Myles McPhail, 1844).

Gomarus, Franciscus. *Bedencken over de Lyck-oratie Petri Bertii*. Leiden, 1609.

Groenewegen, H. Y. *De Remonstrantie op haren 300sten gedenkdag in den oorspronkelijken vorm uitgegeven*. Leiden, 1910.

Grotius, Hugo. *Ordinum hollandiae ac westfrisiae pietas*. N.p., 1613. Critical Edition with English translation and Commentary by Edwin Rabbie (Leiden: Brill, 1995).

———. *Resolutie tot den Vrede der Kerken*. 's Gravenhage: Hillebrant Jacobsz., 1614.

Hessels, J. H., ed. *Archives of the London Dutch Church: Register of the Attestations; or, Certificates of Membership*. London: Nutt & Muller, 1892.

Melanchthon, Philip. "No. 5040, C. Peucero," in *Epistolae, Praefationes, Consilia, Iudicia, Schedae Academicae*. Vol. 7 of *Opera Quae Supersunt Omnia*, edited by Carolus Gottlieb Bretschneider. Saxony: Schwetschke & Sons, 1840.

Molhuysen, P. C. *Bronnen tot de Geschiedenis der Leidsche Universiteit*. 7 vols. The Hague: M. Nijhof, 1913–1924.

Pearson, J., ed. *Golden Remains of the Ever Memorable Mr. John Hales.* London: Robert Pawlet, 1659.
Reformed Confessions of the 16th Century. Edited with historical introductions by A. C. Cochrane. Philadelphia: Westminster, 1966.
Rogge, H. C. *Brieven en onuitgegeven stukken van Johannes Uytenbogaert, 1584–1618.* 2 vols. Utrecht: Kemink, 1872.
Triglandius, Jacobus. *Kerckelycke Geschiedenissen.* Leiden: Adriaen Wyngaerten, 1651.
Unie, Eeuyvich Verbond ende Eendracht: Tusschen die Landen, Provincien, Steden ende Leden Utrecht. Utrecht: Contaet Henricksz., 1579. [Pamphlet, University Library of Utrecht: RARIORA.br.oct.75.]
Veluanus, Ioannes. *Kort bericht in allen principalen punten des Christen geloves . . . und in des halven genant der leken wechwyser* [1554]. In *Bibliotheca Reformatoria Neerlandica: Geschriften uit den tijd der hervorming in de Nederlanden*, edited by S. Cramer and F. Pijper, vol. 4, 123–76. The Hague: M. Nijhoff, 1906.

SECONDARY SOURCES

Aelst, A. C. van. *Schets der Maatschappenlijken Toestand der Staatkundige en Kerkelijke Geschiedenis en van den Stad Oudewater.* Gouda: Edauw & Johannissen, 1893.
Album Studiosorum Academiae Lugundo Batavae. The Hague: M. Nijhof, 1875.
Baird, H. M. *Theodore Beza: The Counsellor of the French Reformation.* New York: G. P. Putnam, 1899.
Bakhuizen van den Brink, J. N. *De Nederlandsche Belijdenisgeschriften.* Amsterdam: Uitgeversmaatschappij Holland, 1940.
———. "Arminius te Leiden." *Nederlands Theologisch Tijdschrift* 15 (1960): 2.
Bangs, Carl. *Arminius: A Study in the Dutch Reformation.* Nashville: Abingdon Press, 1971.
———. "Arminius and the Reformation." *Church History* 30, no. 2 (1961): 155–70.
———. "Arminius as a Reformed Theologian." In *The Heritage of John Calvin*, ed. John H. Bratt. Grand Rapids: Eerdmans, 1973.
Bangs, Jeremy Dupertuis. *Strangers and Pilgrims, Travellers and Sojourners: Leiden and the Foundations of Plymouth Plantation.* Plymouth, Mass.: General Society of Mayflower Descendants, 2009.

———. "Dutch Contributions to Religious Toleration." *Church History* 9, no. 3 (2010): 585–613.

Barger, H. H. *Een predikant uit den patriottentijd*. Rotterdam: Bredée, 1906.

Becker, B. "Coornhert, de zestiende-eeuwse apostel der volmaaktbaarheid." *NAKG* 19 (1926): 59–84.

Berkhof, Hendrikus. "De Ware Ring van Arminius." In *In Het Spoor van Arminius*, edited by H. J. Adriaanse, 151–58. Nieuwkoop: Uitgeverij Heuff, 1975.

Bertius, Petrus (the younger). *Petri Bertii oratio in obitum revenendi & clarissimi viri d. Iacobi Arminii*. Leiden, 1609.

———. *Petri Bertii Lück Oratie over de Dood vanden Heere Iacobus Arminius*. Leiden, 1609.

Bie, J. P. de, and J. Loosjes, eds. *Biograpisch Woordenboek van Protestantische Godgeleerden in Nederland*. 6 vols. The Hague: M. Nijhof, 1911–.

Biografisch Lexicon voor de Geschiedenis van het Nederlandse-Prostestantisme. 6 vols. Kampen: Kok, 1978–2006.

Biographisch Woordenboek van Protestantsche Godgeleerden in Nederland. 's Gravenhage: Martinus Nijhoff, [ca. 1925]–1949.

Blok, Petrus Johannes. *History of the People of the Netherlands*. New York: G. P. Putnam, 1907.

Boer, A. W. den, and Johan Schouten. *Oud-Oudewater*. Oudewater: Stichting Waagebouw, [1966].

Boer, William den. "Defense or Deviation? A Re-examination of Arminius's Motives to Deviate from the 'Mainstream' Reformed Theology." In Goudriaan and van Lieburg, *Revisiting the Synod of Dort*, 23–48.

———. *Duplex amor Dei: Contextuele karakteristiek van de theologie van Jacobus Arminius (1559–1660)*. Apeldoorn: Instituut voor Reformatieonderzoek, 2008. Translated by Albert Gootjes as *God's Two-Fold Love* (Göttingen: Vandenhoek & Ruprecht, 2010).

———. "Jacobus Arminius: Theologian of God's Twofold Love." In Leeuwen, Stanglin, and Tolsma, *Arminius, Arminianism and Europe*, 25–59.

Bonger, H. *Leven en Werk van D. V. Coornhert*. Amsterdam: G. A. van Oorschot, 1978.

Brandt, Caspar. *The Life of Arminius, D.D.* Translated by John Guthrie with introduction by T. O. Summers. Nashville: E. Stevenson and F. A. Owen, 1857.

Brandt, Gerard. *The History of the Reformation and Other Ecclesiastical*

Traditions in and about the Low Countries. London: T. Wood, 1720–1723. Originally published as *Historie der Reformatie en andre Kerkelyke Geschiedenissen, in en omtrent de Nederlanden*, 4 vols. (Amsterdam: Jan Rieuwertsz., Hendrik en Dirk Boom, 1671–1704).

Clarke, F. Stuart. *The Ground of Election: Jacobus Arminius' Doctrine of The Work and Person of Christ*. Milton Keynes, UK: Paternoster, 2006.

Coornhert, D. V. *Op zoek naar het hoogste goed*. Edited by H. Bonger. Baarn: Ambo, 1997.

Dekker, E. *Rijker dan Midas: Vrijheid, genade en predestinatie in de theologie van Jacobus Arminius (1559–1609)*. Zoetermeer: Boekencentrum, 1993.

———. "Was Arminius a Molinist?" *Sixteenth Century Journal* 27, no. 2 (1996): 337–52.

Dillen, J. G. van. *Bronnen tot de Geschiedenis van het Bedrijfsleven en het Gildewezen van Amsterdam 1512–1611*. The Hague: M. Nijhoff, 1929.

Duke, Alastair. "The Ambivalent Face of Calvinism in the Netherlands, 1516–1618." In *International Calvinism, 1541–1715*, edited by Menna Prestwich, 109–34. Oxford: Clarendon, 1985.

Edwards, W. F. "The Logic of Jacopo Zabarello (1533–1589)." PhD diss., Columbia University, 1960.

Ekker, A. *Berigt omtrent de Latijnsche Scholen te Utrecht*. Utrecht: n.p., 1864.

Evenhuis, R. D. *Ook dat was Amsterdam*. 2 vols. Amsterdam: W. ten Have, 1965–1967.

Geisendorf, P. F. *Theodore de Bèze*. Geneva: Julien, 1967.

Glasius, V. B., ed. *Godgeleerd Nederland: Biographisch Woordenboek van Nederlandsche Godgeleerden*. 3 vols. 's Hertogenbosch: 1852–1856.

Gootjes, Nicolaas H. *The Belgic Confession: Its History and Sources*. Grand Rapids: Baker, 2007.

Goudriaan, Aza, and Fred van Lieburg, eds. *Revisiting the Synod of Dort (1618–1619)*. Leiden: Brill, 2011.

———. "The Synod of Dort on Arminian Anthropology." In Goudriaan and van Lieburg, *Revisiting the Synod of Dort*, 81–106.

Graafland, C. *Van Calvijn tot Barth: Oorsprong en ontwikkeling van de leer der verkiezing in het Gereformeerd Protestantisme*. 's Gravenhage: Boekencentrum, 1987.

———. *Van Calvijn tot Comrie: Oorsprong en ontwikkeling van de leer van het

verbond in het Gereformeerd Protestantisme. 3 vols. Zoetermeer: Boekencentrum, 1992–1996.
Graves, F. P. *Peter Ramus and the Educational Reform of the Sixteenth Century*. New York: Macmillan, 1912.
Groenveld, Simon. *Unie, Bestand, Vrede: Drie Fundamentele Wetten van de Republiek der Verenigde Nederlanden*. Hilversum: Verloren, 2009.
Gunter, W. Stephen, and Johannes van den Berg. *John Wesley and The Netherlands*. Nashville: Kingswood Books, 2002.
Haentjens, Anton Hendrik. *Simon Episcopius als Apologeet van het Remonstrantisme, in zijn leven en werken geschetst*. Leiden: A. H. Adriani, 1899.
Hakkenberg, Michael Abram. "The Predestinarian Controversy in The Netherlands, 1600–1620." PhD diss., University of California, Berkeley, 1989.
Hoenderdaal, G. J. "Arminius en Episcopius." *NAKG* 60 (1980): 203–35.
———. "De Theologisch Betekenis van Arminius." *Nederlands Theologisch Tijdschrift* 15 (1960): 90–98.
———. "The Debate about Arminius outside the Netherlands." In Scheurleer and Meyjes, *Leiden University in the Seventeenth Century*, 137–59.
———. "Uytenbogaert in Utrecht." *Nederlands Theologisch Tijdschrift* 22, no. 1 (1967): 3–12.
———. *Verklaring van Jacobus Arminius van 1608*. Lochem: De Tijdstroom, 1960.
Hohrop, P. C. *The Bolsec Controversy on Predestination from 1551–1555: The Statements of Jerome Bolsec, and the Responses of John Calvin, Theodore Beza and Other Reformed Theologians*. Lewiston, N.Y.: Edwin Mellen, 1993.
Hovius, J. "Zijn de Dordtse Leerregels van 1619 in Friesland aangenomen en ingevoerd?" In *Uw knecht hoort*, edited by Johannes Kruis, 11–44. Amsterdam: Bolland, 1979.
Israel, Jonathan. *The Dutch Republic: Its Rise, Greatness and Fall, 1477–1806*. Oxford: Clarendon, 1995.
Itterzon, G. P. *Franciscus Gomarus*. The Hague: M. Nijhoff, 1930.
Kaajan, H. *De Groote Synode van Dordrecht in 1618–1619*. Amsterdam: De Standaard, 1918.
Keuning, J. *Petrus Plancius: Theoloog en Geograaf*. Amsterdam: van Kopen & Zoon, 1946.

Kingdon, R. M., and J. F. Bergier, eds. *Registres de la Compagnie des Pasteurs de Genève au Temps De Calvin*. Geneva: Droz, 1962. Translated by Wallace McDonald as *Registers of the Consistory of Geneva in the Time of Calvin* (Grand Rapids: Eerdmans, 2000).

Kooi, Christine. *Liberty and Religion: Church and State in Leiden's Reformation, 1572–1620*. Leiden: Brill, 2000.

Kootte, T. G., ed. *Rekkelijk of Precies: Remonstranten en contraremonstranten ten tijde van Maurits en Oldenbarnevelt*. Utrecht: Rijksmuseum Het Catharijnenconvent, 1994.

Leclerc, Joseph. *Toleration and the Reformation*. 2 vols. New York: Association Press, 1960.

Leeuwen, Th. Marius van, Keith Stanglin, and Marijke Tolsma. *Arminius, Arminianism and Europe: Jacobus Arminius (1559/60–1609)*. Leiden: Brill, 2009.

Limborch, Philip van, and Christian Hartsoeker, eds. *Praestantium ac eruditorum virorum epistolae ecclesiasticae et theologicae*. 3rd edn. Amsterdam: Franciscus Halma, 1704.

Lindeboom, J. "Erasmus Bedeutung für die Entwicklung des Geistiges Leben in den Niederlanden." *Archiv für Reformationsgeschichte* 43 (1952): 1–12.

Los, F. J. *Grepen uit de Gesciendenis van Hervormd Amsterdam*. Amsterdam: J. H. Vrolijk, 1929.

Mallinson, Jeffrey. *Faith, Reason, and Revelation in Theodore Beza, 1519–1605*. Oxford: Oxford University Press, 2003.

Maronier, Jan Hendrik. *Jacobus Arminius: Een Biographie*. Amsterdam: Y. Rogge, 1905.

Meursius, Johannes. *Athenae Batavae*. Leiden: n.p., 1625.

Molhuysen, P. C. *Bronnen tot de Geschiedenis der Leidsche Universiteit*. 7 vols. The Hague: M. Nijhof, 1913–1924.

Molhuysen, P. C., P. J. Blok, and K. H. Kossman, eds. *Nieuw Nederlandsch Biographisch Woordenboek*. 10 vols. Leiden: Sijthoff, 1911–1937.

Motley, John L. *Het leven en sterven van Johan van Oldenbarnevelt, met een blik op de eerste aanleiding en ontwikkeling van den dertigjarigen oorlog*. 's Gravenhage: W. P. van Stockum, 1874.

Muller, Richard. "The Christological Problem in the Thought of Jacobus Arminius." *NAKG* 68 (1988): 145–63.

———. "The Federal Motif in Seventeenth Century Arminian Theology." *NAKG* 62 (1982): 102–22.

———. *God, Creation and Providence in the Thought of Jacob Arminius*. Grand Rapids: Eerdmans, 1991.

———. "Grace, Election and Contingent Choice: Arminius's Gambit and the Reformed Response." In *The Grace of God and the Bondage of the Will*, edited by Thomas Schreiner and Bruce Ware, 2:251–78. Grand Rapids: Eerdmans, 1995.

Nauta, D. *Opera Minora: kerkhistorische verhandelingen over Calvijn en de geschiedenis van de kerk in Nederland*. Kampen: Kok, 1961.

Oberman, Heiko. "Calvin and Farel." In *John Calvin and the Reformation of the Refugees*, 195–222. Geneva: Droz, 2009.

———. *The Harvest of Medieval Theology*. Grand Rapids: Eerdmans, 1963.

Olson, Roger E. *Against Calvinism*. Grand Rapids: Zondervan, 2011.

———. *Arminian Theology: Myths and Realities*. Downers Grove: IVP Academic, 2006.

———. *The Story of Christian Theology: Twenty Centuries of Tradition and Reform*. Downers Grove: IVP Academic, 1999.

Otterspeer, Willem. *Groepsportret met Dame*. Vol. 1, *Het bolwerk van de vrijheid: De Leidse Universiteit, 1575–1672*. Amsterdam: Bert Bakker, 2000.

Raitt, J. "Theodore Beza, 1519–1605." In *Shapers of Religious Traditions in Germany, Switzerland and Poland, 1560–1600*, edited by J. Raitt, 89–104. New Haven: Yale University Press, 1981.

Reitsma, J., and S. D. van Veen, eds. *Acta der Provinciale en Particuliere Synoden*. 8 vols. Groningen: J. B. Walters, 1892–1899.

Rogge, H. C. *Caspar Janszoon Coolhaes, de Voorlooper van Arminius en de Remonstranten*. 2 vols. Amsterdam: Y. Rogge, 1865.

———. *Johannes Wtenbogaert en Zijn Tijd*. 3 vols. Amsterdam: Y. Rogge, 1874–1876.

Rutgers, Frederick L., ed. *Acta van de Nederlandsche synoden der Zestiende Eeuw*. 's Gravenhage: M. Nijhoff, 1899. Reprint, Dordrecht: J. P. Van den Tol, 1980.

Schaff, Philip. *History of the Christian Church*. 3rd edn. 8 vols. New York: Charles Scribner's Sons, 1907–1910. (Reprint, Grand Rapids: Eerdmans, 1949–1950.)

Scheurleer, Th. H. Lunsingh, and G. H. M. Posthumus Meyjes, eds. *Leiden University in the Seventeenth Century: An Exchange of Learning*. Leiden: University Press/Brill, 1975.

Sepp, C. *Het Godgeleerd Onderwijs in Nederland Gedurende de 16ᵉ en 17ᵉ Eeuw.* 2 vols. in 1. Leiden: de Breuk van Smits, 1873–1874.

———. *Johannes Stinstra en zijn tijd: een bijdrage tot de geschiedenis der kerk.* Amsterdam: Sepp, 1866.

Sinnema, Donald. "The Canons of Dort: From Judgment on Arminianism to Confessional Standard." In Goudriaan and van Lieburg, *Revisiting the Synod of Dort*, 313–34.

Soermans, Martinus. *Kerkelijke Register van de Plaatsen en Namen der Predikanten . . . van Zuyd-Holland.* Haarlem: Wilhelmus van Kessel, 1702. (Bound with Soermans, *Academisch Register.*)

———. *Academisch Register . . . der Universiteyt tot Leiden.* Leiden: Hendrik Teering, 1704. (Bound with Soermans, *Kerkelijke Register.*)

Spijker, W. van 't, C. C. de Bruin, H. Florijn, A. Moerken, and H. Natzijl. *De Synode van Dordrecht in 1618 en 1619.* Houten: den Hertog, 1987.

Stanglin, Keith. *Arminius on the Assurance of Salvation: The Context, Roots and Shape of the Leiden Debate, 1603–1609.* Leiden: Brill, 2007.

Tex, Jan den. *Oldenbarnevelt.* 5 vols. Haarlem: Tjeenk Willink, 1960–1972.

Thomas, G. Michael. "Constructing and Clarifying the Doctrine of Predestination: Theodore Beza's Letters During and in the Wake of the Bolsec Controversy (1551–1555)." *Reformation and Review* 4 (2000): 7–28.

Tideman, Johannes. *De Remonstrantsche Broederschap: Biographische Naamlijst van hare Professoren, Predikanten en Proponenten.* Amsterdam: Y. Rogge, 1905.

Tracy, James D. *Erasmus of the Low Countries.* Berkeley: University of California Press, 1966.

Uytenbogaert, Johannes. *De Kerckelicke Historie.* 2nd edn. Rotterdam: Bastian Wagens, 1647. (Bound with Uytenbogaert, *Leven, Kerckelijcke bedieninghe ende Zedige Verantwoordinghe.*)

———. *Tractaet van't ampt ende authoriteyt eener hoogher christelicken Overheydt in kerckelicke saecken.* 's Gravenhage: Hillebrant Jacobsz., 1610.

———. *Leven, Kerckelijcke bedieninghe ende Zedige Verantwoordinghe.* Rotterdam: Bastian Wagens, 1647. (Bound with Uytenbogaert, *De Kerckelicke Historie*, 2nd edn.)

Venema, C. P. "Heinrich Bullinger's Correspondence on Calvin's Doctrine of Predestination." *Sixteenth Century Journal* 17, no. 4 (1986): 435–50.

Verboom, W. *De belijdenis van een gebroken kerk*. Zoetemeer: Boekencentrum, 2005.
Vries [de Heekelingen], Herman de. *Genève: Pépinière au Temps de Théodore de Bèze*. Vol. 2, *Correspondence des Elèves de Théodore de Bèze après leur Départ de Genève*. The Hague: M. Nijhoff, 1924.
Vries, Marthe F. de. "'Wij waren er eerder dan gij.' De historische legitimatie van de Remonstranten Zoals door Johannes Uytenbogaert gegeven in zijn *Kerckeliike Historie*." Doctorandus Scriptie, Leiden, 1988.
Waddington, Charles. *Ramus, sa Vie, ses Ecrits et ses Opinions*. Paris: Librairie de Ch. Meyruels, 1855.
Walvis, J. *Beschrijving van Gouda*. Gouda: n.p., n.d.
Wijnman, H. F. *Historische Gids van Amsterdam*. Amsterdam: Allert de Lange, 1971.
Witkam, H. J. "Een Lijst van Lidmaten der Leidse Universiteit op 22 November, 1577." *Jaarboekje voor Geschiedenis van Oudheidkunde van Leiden en Omstreken* 61 (1970): 101–5.

SCRIPTURE INDEX

Genesis		3:9	123
2:17	115	4:3-4	142
17:7	105	2 Corinthians	
Exodus		2:14-16	123
12:35-36	131n81	6:1	119
Psalms		7:10	121
143:2	142n104	Ephesians	
Matthew		2:8-9	169
3:9	125	4:14	155
5:12	117	Philippians	
23:37	119	2:12	169
26:24	116	2:12-13	138
Mark		2 Thessalonians	
1:15	122	1:8-9	118
16:16	108, 122	1 Timothy	
Luke		2:3-4	123
7:30	119	2 Timothy	
11:1-13	121	4:7-8	117
John		Titus	
1:12	117	3:7	117
3:16	122, 140	3:14	121
3:36	122	Philemon	
15:5	144	2:12	121
Acts		2:12-13	138
7:51	119	Hebrews	
Romans		6:10	117
1:16, 17	108	10:27	118
4:3b	148	11:6	124, 126, 176, 178
6:23	118	12:15	119
7	54–55, 57, 143n105	1 John	
9	59–62	3:20	142
9:18	60	4:1	154
10:5	115	Revelation	
1 Corinthians		2:5	121
1:21	113	2:10	117

AUTHOR INDEX

Aelst, A. C. van, 13n12, 16n23, 17n26, 197
Augustine, Saint, 36-37n55, 39, 107n48, 110-11, 143-44, 169, 190, 195

Baird, H. M., 31n42, 197
Bangs, Carl, 2n4-5, 3n8, 4, 5n13, 7, 11n1, 4, 12n6-7, 10, 14n13, 15n16, 16n22, 18n29, 21n3, 24n9, 25n11, 13, 26n15, 27n24, 30, 28n32, 29n34-35, 37n57, 38n58-59, 61, 42n76, 43, 44n1-2, 45n5, 47n13, 48n18, 49n21, 50n29, 51n30, 32, 54n39, 56n48, 58n51, 59n4, 60n57, 63n63, 65n1, 66n5, 71n25, 75n32, 76n36, 77n40, 79n45, 82n52, 84n59, 92n13, 95n20, 162n1, 197
Bangs, Jeremy Dupertuis, 1, 3, 23n7, 29n37, 31n41, 45n7, 47n11, 90n5, 162n1, 166n16, 195, 197
Becker, B., 55n44, 198
Berg, Johannes van den, 192n2
Bergier, J. F., 31n44, 32n46, 200
Berkhof, Hendrikus, 194, 198
Bertius, Petrus (the younger), 11, 12n8, 14-16, 17n24, 18-19, 41n72, 51-53, 70, 198
Boer, William den, 6-7, 17, 166-67, 170n22, 171-72, 174, 175n38, 179n42, 182, 198
Bonger, H., 51n33, 55n44, 196, 198, 199
Brandt, Caspar, 12n6, 12n8, 17n24, 51n32, 55n43, 55n43, 55n45, 56, 57n49, 58n52, 60n57, 61n58-59, 62n61, 69n19, 72n27, 73n28, 74n30-31, 77n39, 84n55, 85, 198
Brandt, Gerard, 27, 28n30, 40n66-67, 67n10, 68, 84n55, 93n16, 149n115, 198

Calvin, John, 19n30, 28-37, 52n34, 57, 63, 70, 82-83, 149, 169n18, 181, 187, 190, 196
Conyers, Tobias, 142n102, 147n111, 195

Coornhert, D. V., 51-52, 54, 55n44, 61, 82, 196, 199
Cornelisz, A., 52, 196

Dekker, E., 6, 21n2, 28n30, 38n58, 71, 79n45, 80, 171, 182n44, 199
Dillen, J. G. van., 29, 199
Donteklok, Reynier, 52, 196
Duke, Alastair, 12n4, 15n18, 47n14, 53n38, 199

Edwards, W. F., 41n73, 199
Ekker, A., 15n17, 199
Evenhuis, R. D., 199

Geisendorf, P. F., 31n42, 199
Gomarus, Franciscus, 65-70, 71n22, 73-75, 77, 83, 85, 90-91, 93, 107n49, 108n52, 109, 130n79, 134n85, 144n106, 146, 168, 170, 192n1, 195, 196, 200
Gootjes, Nicolaas H., 45n6, 102n42, 198-99
Goudriaan, Aza, 143n105, 166n16, 183-84, 192n2, 198-99, 203
Graafland, C., 192n42, 199
Graves, F. P., 38n59, 200
Groenewegen, H. Y., 104n46, 196
Groenveld, Simon, 47, 200
Grotius, Hugo, 77n39, 192, 196
Gunter, W. Stephen, 192n2, 200

Hakkenberg, Michael Abram, 192n1, 200
Hoenderdaal, G. J., 1-2, 3n5, 5, 12n6, 18n29, 67n10, 89n3, 92n12, 97n24, 99n31, 100n35, 103-4n46, 115n67, 116n68, 118n69, 123n72, 130n79, 136-37n87, 140n96, 145n108-9, 148n112, 152n122, 154n125, 157n127, 183n46, 200
Hohrop, P. C., 31n44, 34n48-49, 35n51-52, 200

Israel, Jonathan, I., 11n4, 12, 200
Itterzon, G. P. van, 65n1, 170n21, 200

Keuning, J., 45n5, 50n23, 58n53, 77n40, 200
Kingdon, R. M., 31n44, 32n46, 200
Kooi, Christine, 25n11, 201
Kootte, T. G., 46n8, 201

Leclerc, Joseph, 47, 201
Leeuwen, Th. Marius van, 3n7, 143n105, 198, 201
Lieburg, Fred van, 166n16, 192n2, 198, 199, 203
Lindeboom, J., 47n14, 201
Los, F. J., 41–42, 44n2, 48, 49n19–20, 61n59, 201

Mallinson, Jeffrey, 30, 201
Maronier, Jan Hendrik, 12n6, 49n22, 51n32, 55n43, 57n50, 60n57, 61n60, 62n61, 63n62, 63n64, 201
McDonald, Wallace, 31n44, 201
Melanchthon, Phillip, 15n18, 18, 47, 53, 128, 129n76, 154, 196
Meursius, Johannes, 17n24, 201
Meyjes, G. H. M. Posthumus, 22n3, 200, 202
Molhuysen, P. C., 26n17, 66n4, 196
Motley, John L., 48n15, 201
Muller, Richard, 3, 6, 70, 71n23, 162n1, 164–66, 174n36, 175n38, 182n44, 183n46, 201

Oberman, Heiko, 30, 39n62, 202
Olson, Roger E., 3, 4n11–12, 202

Raitt, J., 31n42, 202
Rogge, H. C., 16n19–20, 21n2, 22n4, 23, 28, 54n41, 197, 202

Schaff, Philip., 32, 41n99, 142n101, 202
Scheurleer, Th. H. Lunsingh, 22n3, 200, 202
Sepp, Christian, 27n25, 28n31, 49n22, 202
Sinnema, Donald, 35n50, 192, 203
Soermans, Martinus, 14n14, 25n14, 203
Stanglin, Keith, 3, 6–7, 39n65, 65, 66n5, 67, 70–71, 78, 97n26, 127n74, 142n102, 143n105, 170n22–23, 198, 201, 203

Tex, Jan den, 48n15, 203
Thomas, G. Michael, 31n43, 32, 34n48–49, 35n51–52, 203
Tideman, Johannes, 73n29, 203
Tolsma, Marijke, 3n7, 143n105, 198, 201
Tracy, James D., 39n63, 203
Triglandius, Jacobus, 54n42, 55n43, 56n46, 67n10, 150n117, 197

Uytenbogaert, Johannes, 15–16, 27n29, 40, 41n70, 42n9, 51n32, 54, 63, 67–69, 72, 74n31, 76, 79–80, 83–85, 90n7, 91n9–10, 92n14, 94n17, 95n20, 95n22, 96n23, 102n42, 139n94, 150n116–17, 151n120, 162–63, 175, 192, 203

Veluanus, Ioannes Anastasius, 47, 197
Venema, C. P., 32n46, 203
Verboom, W., 3n9, 69n18, 204
Vries [de Heekelingen], Herman de, 29n34–35, 42, 204
Vries, Marthe F. de, 46n9, 204

Waddington, Charles, 38n60, 204
Walvis, J., 17n26, 204
Witkam, H. J., 25n12, 204

INDEX OF SUBJECTS AND NAMES

a priori, 37, 83, 116, 173, 183
ad fontes (return to the textual sources), 15, 186
absolute decree, 117, 121, 135, 180, 181, 190, 194
absolute trinity, 6, 174n36
academiegebouw, 22, 163
academy, 22, 28–31, 52, 149n115, 187
actual sin, 35, 114n64
Adam, 33, 36, 96, 107, 112, 126, 131–35, 137n88
adoptive parents, 53; see also *in loco parentis*
Aemilius, Theodorus, 14–17
Ambrosius, Johannes, 50, 57
Anabaptists, 61, 95, 128–29
angels, 61–62, 118, 126
anti-catholic, 24
apostles/apostolic teaching, 109, 127, 129, 155, 178
Aquinas, Thomas, 165
Arbitral Accord, 25n11
Aristotelian, -ism, 16–17, 37–38
Aristotle, 15, 38, 171
Arius, 109
Arminians, 45n5, 46, 48, 192n1–2; Arminianism, 42, 54n42, 59, 63, 179n42, 192n2; see also Remonstrants
assurance of salvation, 6, 39n65, 142–43, 169–70, 184, 191
Augsburg Confession, 111, 152, 154
Augustine, Saint, 36n55, 39, 107n48, 110–11, 143–44, 169, 190
author of sin (God as), 69, 180, 119, 133–34, 140, 151n119; see also cause of sin; origin of sin
αὐτοθεος, 144–46

Belgic Confession, 43, 45, 48–50, 55, 57, 60, 62, 73, 82–85, 92–93, 96n23, 99n31, 101n39, 102n42, 111–12, 136n87, 150, 153n123, 155, 164, 189
Bertius, Petrus, 11, 14–19, 51–53, 70

Beza, Theodore, 28, 30–37, 40, 42, 44, 52–54, 57, 61–62, 66, 69–71, 82, 108n52, 182n45; Bezan predestination, 54, 70
biblical piety, 12n4, 15
Bogardus, Johannes, 75, 92
Bolsec, Jerome Hermes, 31–32, 34–35
Borrius, Adriaan, 76
Brethren of the Common Life, 15, 24, 39
Bullinger, Heinrich, 15n18, 31–32, 34–35, 47, 71
burgomasters, 24, 26, 44–45, 48, 51, 55–58

Calvin, John, 19n30, 24, 29–32, 34–37, 57, 63, 70, 82–83, 149, 169, 181, 187, 190; Calvinism/Calvinist, 4, 8, 11–12, 15, 24, 27–28, 30, 36, 41–42, 47, 50, 52, 62, 70, 74, 77, 82, 188, 192, 194
carelessness, 126, 127n74, 128, 177–79
Cartesian rationalism 193
catechism, 56, 59, 83, 85, 155; see also Heidelberg Catechism
Catholic Church, 24, 26, 112, 137n88
cause of sin, 104, 138–39, 151, 151n18, 175; see also author of sin; origin of sin
certainty of salvation, 139, 170
character of God, 39, 164, 173, 176; see also Nature of God
Christ/Jesus Christ, 8, 33, 36, 55, 62, 67, 79, 104–6, 108–113, 116–18, 120, 122, 125–26, 129, 131, 135, 137n88, 138, 140–44, 148–49, 154, 156, 161, 164, 169–70, 172, 173n32, 174, 175–76, 178, 180–81, 184, 190–91, 194
Christology, -ical, 6, 77, 165, 169–70, 174n36, 180, 190
classis, 43–44, 46, 49, 55–57, 58n53, 63, 72, 75, 78, 85, 92
communicatio, 175
condemnation, 61, 102, 104, 107, 116–17, 122–23, 132, 137

confession, 46, 49–50, 56, 59, 70–71, 73, 82, 83, 111, 136, 154–56, 164 ; *see also* Belgic Confession; Helvetic Confession
conscience, 83, 91, 97, 100, 106, 141–42, 149n115, 152–54
consistory/church council/church court, 25, 43–49, 51–52, 54–63, 72, 76–77, 94, 168, 186
conversion, 7, 33–34, 122, 138
Coolhaes (Koolhaes), Caspar Jansz., 21–26, 28, 37, 51–52, 99
Coornhert, Dirck Volckertsz., 51–52, 54, 55n44, 61, 82
Corneliszoon, Pieter, 25
councils (of the Church), 107n48, 109–10, 136
covenant, 105, 123, 171, 173, 175, 179, 183
creation/act of creation, 33–36, 52n34, 69, 104, 114, 116–17, 123, 133–34, 137, 165, 168, 171–72
Cuchlinus, Johannes, 50, 57, 60–61, 74
curators, 22, 26, 67n10, 75, 77–79, 93n15, 94, 98n30

damnation, 32–34, 36–37, 69, 103, 113–14, 116, 118–19, 122, 131–34, 138, 142, 176, 184, 189; *see also* reprobation
Danaeus, Lambertus, 19, 26, 28
De doctrina Christiana, 39
despair, 122, 126–28, 138, 178
desperatio, 126, 178
destiny, 118, 167, 170
determinism, 4, 69
dignity: (divine), 35, 39, 163, 189; (human), 171, 177, 183
disputation: private, 71, 162–65, 169; public, 7, 40, 66, 68–69, 73–76, 97, 109, 136, 139–40, 146
divine decree/eternal decree, 33, 36–37, 62, 69, 73, 103–9, 112–22, 125, 127, 130–35, 169n18, 176–77, 179–81, 190, 192, 194
doctrina (doctrine), 39, 129n76
Dolegius, Daniel, 92
Dort (Synod of), 3, 5, 12n4, 23, 31n41, 35n50, 45n5, 52n34, 59, 76n37, 77, 79n43, 83n54, 84n56, 91n8, 102n42, 105n47, 130n79–80, 166n16, 183–84, 192n2, 193
double predestination, 32, 36, 40, 130n79, 193
duplex amor Dei (Twofold Love of God), 167, 170, 176; *see also* twofold divine love
Dutch Confession, 136, 149–50, 152, 155,
Dutch Protestant Church, 23, 186
Dutch Reformers, 28

early church/ancient church/earliest church, 55, 81, 109n54, 128, 145, 155
Egbertszoon, Sebastiaan, 59, 83–84
elect, 34, 36, 62, 80, 104–7, 121–22, 129, 130n79, 132, 191
election/eternal election/decree of election, 5–6, 32–35, 62, 69, 78, 80, 103–4, 106, 108n51, 112, 120, 130n79, 131–33, 168–69, 171, 175–77, 179–81, 190–91, 193
Erasmus of Rotterdam, 39, 57n50
Erastian, -ism, 22, 24–25, 28, 51n33, 52, 55, 58n53, 81–82, 90n4, 93n15, 194
eternal death, 34, 80, 104–5, 118, 122, 128, 131, 137, 178
eternal life, 34, 36, 104, 113, 115–18, 122–24, 127–28, 137, 140, 178–79
Evangelical Theology, 162, 164–65, 172, 174, 177, 179, 181, 183, 190
explorationis poena induratio, 132

fall/fall of Adam/fall of humanity, 35–37, 52n34, 80, 96, 104, 114n64, 130n79, 133–35, 136n87, 137, 165, 168, 172, 174, 176, 183n46
Fathers/Doctors of the Church, 55, 83, 111, 129, 130, 149n115
fides, 80
fiducia, 80
foreknowledge, 37, 66, 69, 80, 120, 126, 130n79, 132, 135, 169, 180, 182, 191; see also *praescientia*
foundation of Christianity/religion, 136
foundational doctrine, 78, 82, 155

fourfold doctrine of predestination, 135
Fraxinus, Libertus, 75, 91
free will/freedom of the will, 36, 75–76, 95n20, 96, 107, 115, 118, 120, 139–40, 143, 169, 191, 193–94
"friendly" conversation/conference, 57, 67, 75, 92–93

Geneva, 16, 19n30, 21, 24–26, 28–32, 35, 37–38, 40–42, 45, 47, 54, 71, 108n52, 111, 128, 187
gift (divine), 35, 80, 105–6, 114, 119, 131–32, 140, 169, 173, 181
glory of God, 113, 119, 138
Gomarus, Franciscus, 65–71, 73–75, 77, 83, 85, 90–91, 93, 107n49, 108n52, 109, 130n79, 134n85, 144, 146, 168, 170, 192n1
good works/acts, 61–62, 105, 121, 138–39
goodness of God, 114, 137
gospel, 33, 49–50, 76, 80, 90, 106, 108–9, 117–18, 122–23, 125–26, 136, 138, 148, 161, 178–79
grace, 33–36, 40, 50n44, 76, 79–80, 104–7, 109–11, 118–19, 121–23, 126, 129–35, 138–44, 149, 168–70, 175–76, 178, 180–82, 184, 189, 191, 193–94
Grand Pensionary, 192; see also *landsadvocaat*
gratia sufficiens (sufficient grace), 80
Grotius, Hugo, 77n39, 192
Grynaeus, J. J., 40–41, 44

habitus, 39
Habsburg Regime, 11
Hallius, Johannes, 49–50, 60
Halsbergius, Johannes, 42, 55, 60
hardening (of the heart), 60n56, 106, 132
Heidelberg Catechism, 43, 55, 57, 73, 82–85, 99n31, 102n42, 111–12, 136–37, 149–51, 155–56, 164, 189
Helmichius, Wernerus, 42, 83, 90n7, 95n22, 97n24, 145n109, 149n115, 168
Herberts, Hermano/Hermannus, 85, 99, 129
heresy, 85, 110, 148, 169, 189, 192n2

Hoenderdaal, G. J., 1–2, 5, 12n6, 18n29, 67n10, 89, 92n12, 97n24, 99n31, 100n35, 103–4n46, 115n67, 116n68, 118n69, 123n72, 130n79, 136–37n87, 140n96, 145n108–9, 148n112, 152n122, 154n125, 157n127, 183n46
Holy Spirit, 72, 76, 104–5, 109, 138, 140–42, 145, 170, 174, 181
Hommius, Festus, 67, 71–72, 94–95, 168, 183–84
honor of God, 101, 120
human freedom, 23, 141, 171, 182–83, 189
humanism/humanist, 15, 26, 61
human nature/nature of humanity, 115, 118, 131, 137

immutable decree, 103–4, 130
imputed righteousness, 133, 148–49
in loco parentis, 15–16, 185; *see also* adoptive parents
infants and children (salvation of), 61–62, 96, 105, 123
infralapsarianism, 35, 52, 130n79, 168
Institutes of the Christian Religion, 36n54, 169n18
integrity: of God, 60n56; of humanity, 131–32
intention of God, 106, 120–21, 123, 137
irresistible action/force/power/grace, 119–23, 125, 141
iusta desertio (just desertion), 132

Junius, Adrian, 41–42
justice (divine), 7, 33, 36–37, 103–4, 107, 113–14, 119, 124–26, 128, 131–32, 134–35, 137–38, 141, 164, 167, 170–73, 175–80, 184, 189
justification, 33, 40, 55n44, 105, 114, 131, 142, 144, 148–49, 151, 153

landsadvocaat, 46; *see also* Grand Pensionary
Lansbergius, Francis, 75, 91–92, 94
Latitudinarians, 26; see also *rekkelijk*
Lauerman, 16
Legal Theology, 149n115, 164–65, 172, 174, 176, 181, 183, 190

Leiden, 3, 12, 17–18, 21–22, 24–25, 27–28, 51, 68, 72, 76–77, 82, 84, 91, 93–97, 99, 129, 139, 188, 192; *see also* University of Leiden
Lieve-Vrouwenkerk, 24
Loci/Loci communibus, 145–46
love of/for humanity, 7, 124–25, 128, 138, 176–77, 179
love of justice, 7, 124–26, 138, 176–78
Luther, Martin, 18, 128, 154; Lutherans, 24, 61, 128–29, 147, 194
Lydius, Martinus, 52, 54

magistrates, 22, 24–25, 43–44, 46, 51, 57–60, 70, 72, 74, 77n39, 81, 90n4, 99, 104n43, 186–88, 192
Marburg, 17–18, 53; Colloquy, 18
Martinists, 61; *see also* Lutherans
martyrs, 153–54
Maurits (Maurice), Prince, 45–47, 192
Melanchthon, Philip, 15n18, 18, 47, 53, 128, 129n76, 154
Mennonites, 24, 61
mercy (divine), 36–37, 60, 104, 107, 110n56, 113, 119, 126, 132, 134–35, 138, 142, 149, 175, 178, 180
meritorious cause, 118, 120, 125, 134, 137, 149, 177
middle knowledge, 66, 68, 182; see also *scientia media*
mind of God, 35, 39, 52n34, 166, 168, 172–74
"moderate" Calvinists, 42, 50
Moses, 129, 155, 174

Narsius, Joannes, 72–73, 92n14
national synod, 45, 47, 56, 78, 81–83, 84n56, 93–95, 96n23, 98, 102n40, 149–52, 155, 188–89, 191, 193
nature of God, 66, 113, 137, 165, 167, 169, 173, 176; *see also* character of God
new/neo-Calvinism, 4
new determinism, 4

Oberman, Heiko, 30, 39n62
Oldenbarnevelt, Johan van, 45–48, 84, 192n1

omnipotence of God, 69, 73, 116
ordination, 48–50
ordo salutis (order of salvation), 4–5, 7
origin of sin, 73, 168; *see also* author of sin; cause of sin
original righteousness, 104, 107
original sin, 61–62, 96
Oudewater, 12–14, 16–18, 25

Pacification of Ghent (1576), 47, 188, 193
pactum salutis, 173n32, 174n37
Padua, Italy, 21, 41
Paul (Apostle), 40, 123, 148
Pelagius, 107n48, 110–11, 144, 169
Pelagian, -ism, 55, 61, 107, 110, 143–44, 169, 189, 194
perfection/perfectibility, 55, 143, 169
perit funditis religio, 175
Perkins, William, 71, 143n105, 162
Perrot, Charles, 40
perseverance of believers/the Saints/faith, 105, 131, 139, 141–42
Philip of Hesse, 18
Piscator, John/Johannes, 102n42, 148, 151, 175n38
Plancius, Petrus, 45n5, 49–50, 54–56, 58–59, 61–63, 67–68, 70, 72, 75, 77, 95n22, 168
praescientia, 130n79; *see also* foreknowledge
prayer, 25, 48, 67, 71–72, 121, 123, 138
processus originis unius personae ab alia, 145
preciezen/precisionists, 26, 46, 48, 50, 82, 192
predestination, 4–6, 18, 23, 26, 30–36, 39–40, 44, 51–55, 61–63, 68–71, 74, 76–78, 80, 89, 95n20, 96, 103, 106–23, 126–28, 130–39, 142, 162, 167, 169n18, 176, 179–82, 187, 189–94
predetermination (divine), 37n55, 116, 131
prescience (divine), 69, 131
prevenient/preventing grace, 135, 141, 180, 184
primus inter pares, 18, 21
privata collatio/private conversation, 62, 99–100
professor of theology, 28, 89, 187

promise, 67, 91, 95, 105, 109, 122–23, 126, 152, 173, 178
proponent/candidate (for ministry), 45, 48–49, 75, 92n14
Protocollen, 49, 60n57, 62n61
providence of God, 72–73, 134, 139, 165, 173, 189

Ramus, Petrus (Pierre de la Ramée), 17, 37–38; Ramism, 17, 40
Reael, Laurens Jacobsz., 56, 58n51
Reformation, 30–31, 39, 128–29, 161, 185
Reformed, 15, 21, 24–25, 27, 32–33, 35, 37, 43, 49n19, 53, 57, 59–61, 70, 75–76, 79, 89n3, 111–12, 148, 151, 153, 156, 164, 166, 168, 173n32, 175n38, 187–94; Orthodoxy, 27, 37, 76
regeneration/regenerate, 35, 55n44, 57, 76, 80, 95n20, 121, 140–41, 143
regula fidei, 49
rekkelijk, -en, 26, 45–47, 49, 56, 84n56; *see also* Latitudinarians
Remonstants, 21n2, 45n5, 59, 73, 84n56, 130n79, 184, 192n1–2; *see also* Arminians
repent, -ance, 67, 109, 121–22, 126, 132, 135, 138, 178, 180–81, 183–84, 190–91
reprobation, 32, 34–35, 103–6, 116–17, 131–33, 192; *see also* damnation
righteousness, 103–4, 106–7, 114–15, 117, 122, 137n89, 138–39, 148–49, 176–77
Rolandus, Jacobus, 75, 92
Roman Catholic/Roman Church, 11–14, 25–27, 31, 41, 47, 53, 128, 185

Sabellianism, 145, 170
salvation of infants and children, 61–62, 96, 105, 123
sapida scientia ("savory knowledge"), 38–39
sat ecclesiae, sat patriae datum, 157
Satan/devil, 106, 112, 115, 118, 126, 132, 141, 178
scientia, 39; *scientia media*, 66, 182; *see also* middle knowledge

Scripture, 2n3, 5, 12n4, 27, 36, 39, 49n22, 52, 56, 59, 82–83, 85, 113, 117–19, 137, 139–42, 149n115, 151–52, 155, 164, 176, 186, 188–89; *see also* Word of God
Second Helvetic Confession, 32
securitas, 126, 127n74, 178
sine qua non, 53
single predestination, 130n79
Snellius, Rudolphus van Roijen (Rudolf Snel), 16–17, 53
sola scriptura, 161, 186
soteriology, 39n65, 63, 77, 166, 169, 190, 194
Spain, 11, 43
Statenvertaling, 105n47
Stoics, 128–29
strength (human), 107, 117, 131–32, 141, 144
Subordinationist Christology, 6
Supralapsarianism, 32, 36, 52–53, 63, 70–71, 130n80, 168, 193
suum cuique tribuere, 171
Swieten, Adriaen van, 17
Sybrants, Tako, 99, 129
Synod: of Antwerp (1566), 136n87; of Dort (1618–1619), 3, 5, 12n4, 23, 31n41, 35n50, 45n5, 52n34, 59, 76n37, 77, 83n54, 91n8, 102n42, 105n47, 130n79–80, 183, 193; of Emden (1571), 24, 44–45; of The Hague (1586), 44

Trelcatius, 75, 93, 145–46
Trinity/Trinitarian, 6, 37n56, 145–46, 174
twofold divine love/love of God, 7, 124–26, 128, 138, 167, 171, 175, 178–79; see also *duplex amor Dei*
twofold nature of Reprobation, 133
twofold Wisdom of God, 113, 176

Union of Utrecht (1579), 46, 83, 188, 193
University of Leiden, 2–3, 17–18, 21, 22n5, 23, 25–29, 37, 54n42, 59, 62–63, 66, 70–72, 74–75, 77–78, 89, 94, 101n37, 103, 135, 162–63, 165, 166n16, 167–68, 172, 188, 193–94

Uytenbogaert, Johannes, 15–16, 40, 42, 46n9, 54, 63, 67–69, 72, 76, 79–80, 83–85, 90n7, 95n20, 95n22, 96n23, 102n42, 139n94, 150n117, 151n120, 162–63, 175, 192

Verklaring, 2–3
Vlietius, Abraham, 73–74

Wesleyan, 5, 194
Wiggerts, Cornelius, 129
William I, the Prince of Orange, 18, 46

William of Orange (William the Silent/ Willem de Zwijger), 22, 27, 45
wisdom of God, 33, 36, 104, 113, 116, 135, 137, 165, 173, 175–76, 180
Word of God, 81, 83, 93, 97n28, 101, 135, 145, 150–52, 154, 156; *see also* Scripture
worship of God, 126–27, 162, 178, 183
wrath, 13, 36–37, 82, 114, 135, 180

Zwingli, 31–32, 154

www.ingramcontent.com/pod-product-compliance
Lightning Source LLC
Chambersburg PA
CBHW030343240426
43661CB00052B/1722